Advances in Universal Web Design and Evaluation:
Research, Trends and Opportunities

Sri Kurniawan
University of Manchester, UK

Panayiotis Zaphiris
Centre for HCI Design, City University, UK

T0321959

IDEA GROUP PUBLISHING
Hershey • London • Melbourne • Singapore

Acquisitions Editor: Kristin Klinger
Development Editor: Kristin Roth
Senior Managing Editor: Jennifer Neidig
Managing Editor: Sara Reed
Assistant Managing Editor: Sharon Berger
Copy Editor: Angela Thor
Typesetter: Diane Huskinson
Cover Design: Lisa Tosheff
Printed at: Integrated Book Technology

Published in the United States of America by
        Idea Group Publishing (an imprint of Idea Group Inc.)
        701 E. Chocolate Avenue
        Hershey PA 17033
        Tel: 717-533-8845
        Fax: 717-533-8661
        E-mail: cust@idea-group.com
        Web site: http://www.idea-group.com

and in the United Kingdom by
        Idea Group Publishing (an imprint of Idea Group Inc.)
        3 Henrietta Street
        Covent Garden
        London WC2E 8LU
        Tel: 44 20 7240 0856
        Fax: 44 20 7379 0609
        Web site: http://www.eurospanonline.com

Library of Congress Cataloging-in-Publication Data

Advances in universal web design and evaluation: research, trends and
    opportunities / Sri Kurniawan and Panayiotis Zaphiris, editors.
      p. cm.
    Summary: "This book deals with a significant but often overlooked
issue of Web design: universality. As the internet has become more
pervasive, information disseminated through the Web grows in an
exponential rate; there is a call for more universal design so that more
people from different backgrounds are able to access this information"
--Provided by publisher.
    Includes bibliographical references and index.
    ISBN 1-59904-096-4 (hardcover) -- ISBN 1-59904-097-2 (softcover)
-- ISBN 1-59904-098-0 (ebook)
    1. Web sites--Design. 2. Computers and people with disabilities.
3. Assistive computer technology.   I. Kurniawan, Sri, 1970-   .
II. Zaphiris, Panayiotis.
TK5105.888.A38 2006
006.701'9--dc22
                                        2006027708
British Cataloguing in Publication Data
A Cataloguing in Publication record for this book is available from the British Library.

Advances in Universal Web Design and Evaluation:
Research, Trends and Opportunities

Table of Contents

Section V: Accommodating Disabilities

Preface

Overview and Motivation

The Web has rapidly become more and more pervasive in almost everybody's lives. There are many daily activities that can be performed much more comfortably online. There are also daily activities that cannot be performed without using the Web. Much of the power of the Web comes from the fact that it presents information in a variety of formats and, therefore, is theoretically accessible by users using a variety of technologies, devices, and computer applications. The Web also becomes a medium to disseminate information in more places and times, and to more people of varying characteristics than any other media can ever achieve.

To create resources that can be used by the widest spectrum of potential visitors rather than an idealized "average," there is a need to consider universality of Web delivery. As director of the W3C, Tim Berners-Lee, puts it: "The power of the Web is in its universality. Access by everyone regardless of disability is an essential aspect."

This requires consideration of the needs and requirements of individuals with disabilities, older persons and children, people for whom English is a second language, people whose cultures and backgrounds are dissimilar to those of Web developers, and those using outdated hardware and software. This list is not an exhaustive list, and this book only scratches the surface of the need to think about nontraditional Web users in the Web design process.

For that reason, the key objective of this book is to look at the topic of universal Web design and evaluation in a new direction by focusing on the user aspect of universal Web design and interaction, and to present the wide range of advanced technology that can help disadvantaged users get access to Web information. The book discusses the basis of a broad framework for the development and evaluation of Web sites for people with various special needs, enriched with contributions from domains as diverse as education, information systems, library and information studies, computer science, business, clinical health, and many others.

The book puts the emphasis on the users, and proposes methodologies, strategies, and approaches for designing and evaluating interfaces that facilitate effective interaction of users with special needs.

The book's objective is to provide information on the state-of-the-arts research in the area of universal Web design to university educators and educators in general; university administrators; researchers; librarians; accessibility and usability consultants; Web-based system managers, designers, technicians, and evaluators.

Description of Chapters

Universal Web design is an approach to the design of Web-based systems, services, and environments to be as usable as possible by as many people as possible regardless of age, ability, background, or situation. For that reason, our book is structured in five broad sections. Section I introduces the general topic of Web accessibility and the current situation with Web accessibility adoption in the society. Section II talks about issues faced by users at the two extremes of life, older persons and children, when interacting with the Web, and how design can alleviate these issues. These two user groups are traditionally underrepresented in the Web design community and, therefore, this book aims to raise awareness of the importance of considering these groups. Section III considers gender-related differences in Web interaction, and how design can appeal to a certain gender. Gender-related differences are very much recognized and highlighted in other areas, such as marketing. Research in this topic, however, is still rare and patchy. This section provides some guidelines and findings of the process of designing for a specific gender group. In Section IV, we include chapters that discuss cross-cultural and multilingual aspects of Web interaction. As Tim Berners-Lee stated, the power of the Web is in its universality, yet the majority of Web sites are aimed at people from Western cultures who speak English. This section presents the work in introducing a multilingual aspect in Web design and work in understanding the effect of cultures in Web interaction. Finally, in Section V, the chapters include studies that aim at facilitating equal Web access for people with specific disabilities. Again, as Tim Berners-Lee stated, the Web should provide access by everyone regardless of disability, and yet low conformance to Web accessibility guidelines was reported worldwide, some arguably are caused by the lack of awareness of the issues faced by Web users with disabilities. This section highlights the state-of-the-art studies on this issue.

The book includes 12 chapters from prominent international authors. The international character of the book is evident from the fact that it includes chapters from authors from Canada, Italy, Republic of Ireland, United Kingdom, and the U.S., encompassing charity organizations, higher education institutions, and medical centers, to name a few.

The following sections present an overview of each chapter.

Section I: Introduction and General Issues

Chapter I, *Web Accessibility and the Needs of Users with Disabilities* is written by Aspasia Dellaporta. It discusses Web accessibility, and focuses on the challenge of meeting the needs of a diverse audience with different types of disabilities, as well as outlining best practices. It reveals that Web accessibility problems do not only affect blind people, but other users with disabilities as well.

Chapter II, *Failing the Disabled Community?: The Continuing Problem of Web Accessibility* is written by David Kreps and Alison Adam. It discusses the current situation with Web accessibility provision, ranging from the legal view to a more practical view. It provides the caveats of automatic accessibility evaluation.

Section II: The Two Extremes of Life

Chapter III, *Designing Children's Multimedia* is written by Bridget Patel. It summarises young children's perspectives about '"'good" educational multimedia Web design. It uses a social-constructivist view of learning as the basis to perform user-centred Web design with young children. This chapter is complemented with a case study of using a child-centred participatory design approach with Year 2 children (6 and 7 year olds).

Chapter IV, *Bonded Design: A Methodology for Designing with Children* is written by Andrew Large, Valerie Nesset, Jamshid Beheshti, and Leanne Bowler. It presents a new methodology for designing information technologies called bonded design that is especially suited for design sessions where designers and children collaborate. The chapter is complemented with two case studies where designers work with elementary school students.

Chapter V, *Ageing and its Implications for Elderly Web Experience* is written by Syariffanor Hisham and Alistair D. N. Edwards. It discusses ageing related issues, and their implications for the Web experience of elderly users. The chapter includes a summary of the use of the Web among elderly users in Malaysia. The chapter concludes with some ideas concerning the cultural and demographic differences in determining new trends, directions, and opportunities in advanced Web design specifically for elderly users

Section III: Gender Issues

Chapter VI, *Gender Issues in HCI Design for Web Access* is written by Stefania Boiano, Ann Borda, Jonathan P. Bowen, Xristine Faulkner, Giuliano Gaia, and Sarah McDaid. It presents HCI models at different levels of abstraction, and how gender issues could impinge at each of these levels. The chapter contains some examples from the commercial and cultural fields in the form of design case studies of home pages for Web sites that exhibit gender-related orientation.

Chapter VII, *Interpreting the Female User: How Web Designers Conceptualise Development of Commercial WWW Sites to Satisfy Specific Niche Markets* is written by Noemi Maria Sadowska. It argues that the prevalence and accessibility of WWW makes it a powerful vehicle of change both within design practice and in terms of gender structures more widely. It presents an example of gendered Web portal design that targets female users.

Section IV: Cultural Issues

Chapter VIII, *From Computer-Mediated Colonization to Culturally-Aware ICT Usage and Design* is written by Charles Ess. It uses Hofstede's and Hall's theories to explain communication failures caused by differences between the values and preferences embedded in CMC (computer-mediated communication) and those of a given cultural group. It provides examples of successful online cross-cultural communication via CMC.

Chapter IX, *A Case Study: Creating and Designing a Bilingual Resource Web Site for Somali Immigrants* is written by Sauman Chu, Mauricio Arango, and Charles Earl Love Yust. It addresses the design and procedural variables of creating a bilingual Web site information portal for an audience of culturally diverse immigrants. It describes the design process of a bilingual Web site for Somali immigrants in Minnesota.

Section V: Accommodating Disabilities

Chapter X, *Web Site Design for People with Dementia* is written by Nada Savitch and Panayiotis Zaphiris. It describes design considerations when building Web sites for people with dementia. It also illustrates appropriate methodologies for working with people with dementia.

Chapter XI, *Comparing Comprehension Speeds and Accuracy of Online Information in Students with and without Dyslexia* is written by Sri Kurniawan and Gerard V. Conroy. It describes describing problems people with dyslexia experience with reading online material and some technological aids available to help them. It presents a user study that found that students with dyslexia are not slower in reading than students without dyslexia when the articles are presented in a dyslexia-friendly colour scheme, although they still made more errors in comprehension.

Chapter XII, *Implementing Accessible Online Learning for Blind and Visually Impaired Students: A Pilot Study* is written by Hugh O'Neill, Inmaculada Arnedillo-Sánchez, and Brendan Tangney. It presents a framework for the design of accessible online learning environments for blind and visually impaired students using a combined approach of WCAG and principles of universal design for learning. It is complemented with a case study of using objectivist instructional design theory to teach blind and visually impaired students how to write Web pages in HTML.

Acknowledgments

We would like to warmly thank the publishing team, especially Kristin Roth, our development editor, for all the support and encouragement in this process, and all of the authors for making this book possible through their very interesting contributions.

Sri Kurniawan, University of Manchester, UK

Panayiotis Zaphiris, Centre for HCI Design, City University, UK

Section I

Introduction and General Issues

Chapter I

Web Accessibility and the Needs of Users with Disabilities

Aspasia Dellaporta, Cimex Media Ltd., UK

Abstract

This chapter discusses Web accessibility, and focuses on the challenge of meeting the needs of a diverse audience with different types of disabilities, as well as outlining best practices. It presents the nature and need for Web accessibility, focusing on the UK legislation, and argues that e-accessibility goes beyond legal obligations offering life-enhancing opportunities and services, and promoting inclusion. The dynamics between the Web and its diverse audience are emphasized by giving an overview of the multiple facets of Web accessibility. It has been observed that accessibility is often discussed as affecting blind people only, and discussions frequently isolate a few aspects of it. The author hopes that, by demonstrating and offering ways of understanding Web accessibility and its multilayered nature, the ground will be laid for a more effective and inclusive approach towards Web accessibility as a process in Web design and development.

Introduction

Web accessibility is about being able to reach and use information and services regardless of the disability, and of the technology used. The primary focus is on people with disabilities with the secondary focus on people who use different browsers and technologies to access the Web.

Nowadays, not all people can afford broadband Internet connection, and not all people use Internet Explorer. There is a notable increase in the uptake of broadband Internet, but still, the market has not reached maturity levels: "At current rates of broadband adoption, there are on average a good eighteen months to two years of strong penetration increases across Western Europe before markets begin to mature" (Gower, 2005).

Although, the majority of Internet users seem to use Internet Explorer 6, Mozilla Firefox has become quite popular: "As of September 2005, estimates suggest that Firefox's usage share is around 7.6% of overall browser usage. Since its release, Firefox has slightly reduced Internet Explorer's dominant usage share" (Wikipedia, October, 2005). In addition, Firefox has become quite popular, especially among developers, for its advanced accessibility features, and it can be used as an aid for testing Web pages for accessibility, according to Lauke (2002). Also, the Opera browser comes with accessibility features such as page magnification, enhanced keyboard navigation, and style and colour customization by offering a set of style sheets that can be applied on a Web page (Opera.com, 2005). Web accessibility features are developed for different Web technologies recognizing the need to offer a good browsing experience to users with a range of abilities (Gunderson, 1997). This imposes the requirement for cross-browser as well as cross-platform compatibility. The latter will be presented.

Users can also access a Web site under constraining circumstances through a mobile phone or a public Internet terminal. A mouse may not be available, and the colours on the Web site may not be fully supported or properly displayed. The W3C WCAG 1.0 guidelines emphasize the variety of contexts in which people use the Web that need to be considered when designing and developing Web applications. More specifically, users:

- May not be able to see, hear, move, or may not be able to process some types of information easily or at all
- May have difficulty reading or comprehending text
- May not be able to use a keyboard or mouse
- May have a text-only screen, a small screen, or a slow Internet connection
- May not speak or understand fluently the language in which the document is written

- May be in a situation where their eyes, ears, or hands are busy or interfered with (e.g., driving to work, working in a loud environment)

- May have an early version of a browser, a different browser entirely, a voice browser, or a different operating system

It is important that a Web application can be accessed by people who use different technologies and under different circumstances, as previously discussed.

Moreover, the requirements of people with disabilities need to be considered when designing and building Web applications. Before considering their needs, it is important to look at the Disability Discrimination Act, the emphasis that is given on the rights of disabled people for accessing the Web, and the wider benefits for Web accessibility.

Legislation and the Need for Web Accessibility

Although the importance of Web accessibility is widely recognised-for example, in the U.S., Section 508 specifies that federal agencies must purchase electronic and information technology that is accessible (Thatcher, 2005)-the focus here is on the legislation in the UK. The Disability Discrimination Act (DDA) defines a disabled person as someone with "a physical or mental impairment which has a substantial and long term adverse effect on his ability to carry out normal day to day activities."

Part III of the Disability Discrimination Act gives disabled people important rights of access to everyday services, more specifically:

Duties under Part III are coming into force in three stages.

- Treating a disabled person less favourably because they are disabled has been unlawful since December 1996.

- Since October 1999, service providers have had to consider making reasonable adjustments to the way they deliver their services so that disabled people can use them.

- The final stage of the duties, which means service providers may have to consider making permanent physical adjustments to their premises, came into force in 2004.

Under the Disability Discrimination Act framework and more precisely Part III of the Act, the Disability Rights Commission (DRC) recently launched a formal investigation into Web site accessibility in the UK, which demonstrates aspects of the DRC legal strategy for 2003-2006.

The DRC, with its legal strategy (2003), aims to create a society in which all disabled people can participate fully as equal citizens. It promotes the rights of disabled people by deploying its statutory rights to maximum effect. It has defined a legal strategy, covering the period of 2003-2006, aiming at exploring creative ways of promoting the rights of disabled people as a whole, rather than simply enforcing individual rights.

The DRC pays particular attention to accessibility issues and information access through the Web for various reasons:

- The Web is a relatively new social environment and a very powerful one. It presents a unique opportunity for intervention in favour of disability rights at an early stage.
- The Web is a digital environment and much more flexible compared to physical environments. Therefore, adjustments to accommodate disabled people can be made at relatively reasonable costs.
- The Web can benefit disabled people greatly by providing access to information and services remotely; for example, from the user's own environment, overcoming physical barriers.

Summarizing, from October 1, 2004, service providers have to make reasonable adjustments in the areas of employment, access to goods, facilities, and services so that disabled people are not discriminated against, but they receive equal treatment to nondisabled people. This applies to both physical and electronic environments, with the latter presenting an interesting and beneficial aspect to disabled users environment.

Web Accessibility Benefits beyond Law Obligation

There are 10 million people with disabilities in the UK, with an estimated annual spending power of £50 billion (DRC, 2005). By making a Web site accessible, there will be an increase in sales, achieving a fast return on investment for having made reasonable accessibility adjustments. On the other hand, the Web is universal;

therefore, a large number of people with disabilities could reach a Web site from different parts of the world. Bilotta and Todd (2003) mention that in the United States, 19.4% or 48.9 million people have a disability, with half of them (24.1 million) considered to be severely impaired. Also, the same authors state that: "Between 15% and 30% of the population have functional limitations that can affect their ability to use technology products (50 million in US, 750 million worldwide). It is estimated that people with disabilities control a discretionary income of over $175 billion annually in U.S. alone."

By improving accessibility on a Web site, usability levels also improve significantly. The DRC investigation (2004) found that users with disabilities took 50% longer to complete a task on an inaccessible site; therefore, accessibility increases productivity. An accessible site is also a site that uses W3C standards-compliant HTML code and cascading style sheets for controlling the layout. This way faster download times are achieved, and there is easier control over the site's presentation, thus maximizing efficiency and ease of use. Moreover, accessibility means cross-platform compatibility. A device-independent display of information can be reached by a much wider audience; therefore, increasing profits, especially for e-commerce sites.

In 2002, Pilling, Barrett, Floyd, and AbilityNet, a UK charity giving information and advice to disabled people, conducted a survey to gather information on the views of disabled people with experience of using a computer. A convenience sample was used, and 193 people responded, from which 136 were Internet users.

The survey results state amongst other findings:

- *"Internet usage enabled respondents to communicate with others, and to reach a variety of information resources in spite of difficulties. These groups included those who were unable to leave their homes, those who found writing or reading common forms of print inaccessible, or those with speech impairments.*

- *Disabled Internet users who needed assistive devices to use a computer and the Internet found fewer Web sites that were easy to use and navigate than did those not using assistive devices."*

Jim Murphy MP (EU, 2005), in his forward to the eAccessibility of public sector services report in the European Union, places the user needs at the centre of electronic services, stressing that this is not just beneficial for the individual, but for the wider society. He also supports that inclusion needs to be built-in to public service design from the beginning so that opportunities in education, employment, health, and social life are enhanced for every individual.

The UK online Annual Report 2002 of the cabinet office states that 54% of services were available electronically by the issue date of the report, while the government, through the Cabinet Office and the e-Envoy, aims to make all government services available electronically by 2005 so that everybody can benefit from quick access to information and services.

In terms of benefiting the end users, the U.S. National Organization on Disability commissioned a survey in 2001 and found:

- Forty-eight percent of disabled people acknowledged that going online significantly increased their quality of life, compared with 27% of nondisabled people.

- Fifty-two percent with less severe disabilities and 34% with severe disabilities admitted that the Internet increased their ability to reach out and communicate with people who have similar interests and experiences, compared to 34% of the nondisabled online Americans.

- Fifty-two percent of the disabled interviewees said that the Internet helped them to be better informed about the world around them, compared to 39% of the nondisabled interviewees.

Windman (2001) mentions another benefit in accessibility, as expressed by Brown: "by making Web sites more accessible for those with disabilities could also make them more accessible to those with different learning styles such as auditory, kinesthetic and visual. Consequently, opportunities for teaching as well as lifelong learning would be enhanced."

In this section, it has been shown that there are numerous benefits to Web accessibility ranging from greater profits for e-commerce sites to increasing effectiveness and productivity, as well as benefiting both the individual and the wider society. It should not come as a surprise that Web accessibility is beneficial to nondisabled users too, and greatly increases opportunities for e-inclusion making a real difference in people's lives, especially for those with disabilities.

For ensuring optimum accessibility for a Web site, the needs of users with disabilities need to be taken into account, and studied from the beginning as part of the requirements' definition phase in design and development. According to Henry et al. (Henry, Law, & Kitch, 2001), "Accessibility is most efficiently and effectively implemented when included from day one of a project. Considering accessibility early in the project will increase the design impact and decrease the resource impact." In order to include accessibility effectively, a variety of user needs have to be considered.

In the sections that follow, the different needs of people with various disabilities are outlined, and guidelines for meeting them are provided.

Colour Blind Users

One in 12 people have some sort of colour deficiency (Henderson, 2002). Colour blindness is an eye condition affecting the perception of colour. A person with colour blindness will not be able to distinguish certain colours or shades of them. There are mainly three types of colour blindness: protanomally, deuteranomally, and tritanomally, affecting the perception of red, green, and blue respectively. A person with colour blindness, unlike the misleading name of the condition, can see colours and does not perceive the world just in black and white (Eyecaresource. com, 2002).

People with colour deficiency require good colour contrast on Web sites, particularly for foreground and background colours for text. They also benefit when designers use a variety of ways, not just colour, for conveying information on the Web (WAI WCAG 1.0, 1999). For example, colour should not be used as the only way to communicate location on the navigation menu: additional changes in size or shape should also be used. This way, if users cannot see the difference in colour, they understand where they are because the menu link appears in bold and it is bigger than any other link in the main menu. Certain combinations of colours such as red, green, brown, grey, and purple should be avoided to style items that are next to each other (Hesperian, 2005). User control of style sheets is also very important. Style sheets are files that control the presentation of Web pages. This way, presentation is kept separately from content. If a Web site uses style sheets to control all its presentation aspects, then users will be able to override them from their browser and apply their own style sheet. This is in line with the generally supported view that allowing for customisation is the most efficient way to ensure accessibility for a wide audience (Skillsforaccess.org, 2005).

Blind Users

The graphical nature of the Web means that poor Web accessibility has an adverse effect on blind users. There is a range of assistive software that blind users use on the Web. Some of them are:

- **Screen readers:** Software programs that speak the content on the screen. They read text, buttons, and menus as well as images, provided that the images have appropriate text descriptions attached to them. Screen readers offer a variety of customization options for audio.

- **Speech recognition systems:** Provide voice control and data entry, and the user does not have to use any other input devices.
- **Refreshable braille displays:** Provide tactile output of information represented on the computer screen.
- **Speech synthesizers:** Translate text input into audio input.

Screen readers are the most popular assistive software that blind users use in order to access the Internet. Theofanos and Redish (2003), in a research study they conducted with blind users to understand their Web behaviour, found that blind users are as impatient as sighted users when trying to find information, and they "scan information with their ears" the way sighted users scan information with their eyes. This means that they do not listen to a Web page from beginning to end, but they navigate around, skipping text and listening to information that they think may be relevant to what they are looking for. Although screen readers are very useful and powerful tools, they impose great demands on the user. According to Theofanos and Redish (2003), screen-reader users must understand the browser, the screen reader, and the Web site they are visiting, which imposes a great mental load on them. This means that blind users need to split their cognitive energy between the browser, the screen reader, and the site. Under these circumstances, it is not easy to acquire a good mental model of the screen reader environment as well as the Web site navigation and content structure. Thus, it is not surprising at all that many users do not know all the functionalities of the assistive software they use.

Guidance for meeting the needs of blind users on the Web:

- Blind people require appropriate text descriptions for images, diagrams, image maps, image links, videos, and animation. The only exception is when images are used for decoration or to support the layout of the page. Text descriptions are important for assistive technologies such as screen readers and Braille displays.
- Intuitive keyboard navigation is essential for a blind person as they do not use the mouse. The reason is quite obvious: the mouse requires hand and eye coordination, and blind users do not know where to move it or when to click it as they cannot see what is on the screen.
- Standards compliant well-structured code is equally important so that the screen reader can use it to communicate the structure of a Web page to the user.
- Data tables need to be coded with care so that data cells are associated with their respective header cells. Screen readers read in a serial form in a top-to-bottom, left-to-right fashion and therefore, a data table will not make sense unless properly coded.

- All form controls need to have clear labels associated with them so that the screen reader can communicate to the user what each form control is about.

- Tabbing from link to link needs to be intuitive and easy to understand. Creating a logical tab order and meaningful link names, avoiding "More" and "Click here," makes navigation more effective.

- Ways of skipping over navigation menus are essential so that the user can jump to the main content straight away, if they wish so, without having to listen to navigation links, which is tiring and frustrating.

- Audio descriptions need to be provided for videos if the video contains visual information that is not communicated through audio output and therefore, may be missed by blind users (Smith, 2003).

- Clear and easy-to-understand navigation structures can greatly enhance the user's experience so that blind users can easily find their way around a Web site.

Partially Sighted Users

The technical definition for partially sighted is that one's best-corrected visual acuity is no better than 20 out of 70 in either eye. This is better than just perceiving light (BraillePlus.net, 2004). For using the Web, different customisation options and technologies can be employed by partially sighted users ranging from using specialist software such as screen magnifiers to customising the operating system and browser settings. Partially sighted people mainly use magnification software to magnify a Web page, change colours both foreground and background, and customize the appearance of the cursor so that it can be easily perceived. According to RNIB (2005), the principle behind magnification software is that the image on the standard computer screen can be artificially enlarged, meaning that only a part of the content can be seen at a time. The scale of magnification can be up to 16 times, whereas magnification up to 32 times can also be available. However, the magnification degree has an impact on the ease of navigation; information access with great magnification being hard to manage. Screen magnifiers can offer a variety of ways for magnification. They can magnify the whole screen and show only a part of the screen at a time, they can have only a specific part of the screen magnified or follow the mouse, offering mouse driven magnification and focus.

Partially sighted users also require screen-reading compatibility, as they often prefer to listen to a page while navigating it. For this reason, some magnification software has embedded screen-reading functionalities. The use of clear and high-quality images on Web pages, particularly for functional images such as image maps and graphical buttons, is important so that they remain clear enough when magnified. However, the use of images as text needs to be avoided because text on images is not flex-ible, and users cannot customize it to suit their needs (RNIB, 2005). It would be a misconception to think that every partially sighted user uses magnification software. Some people prefer to customize their operating system and browser instead. So the coding of the page itself should allow for such settings to take place, that is, to allow for customizable colour schemes with style sheets and customizable text, as well as having a Web site layout that flows nicely on different screen resolutions. In terms of customising the operating system, there are, for example, several screen enhancement features integrated within Windows (RNIB, 2005):

- High-contrast colour schemes
- Large standard fonts
- Modifying the screen resolution
- Customisation options for the mouse pointer and the cursor

Also Mac OS X offers a variety of accessibility features too (Apple.com, 2005):

- Voice-over with speech and audio cues and talking alerts
- Zoom capabilities for enlarging the screen
- Magnification for QuickTime video
- Screen movement customisation when using the mouse
- Cursor scaling and customisation
- Contrast and colour adjustment controls

In addition, for accommodating the needs of partially sighted users, the following need to be taken into account:

- Using pop-up windows wisely and avoiding them in favour of other methods and techniques. The fact that a partially sighted user cannot have a full view of a Web page means that they may not notice a pop-up window that has opened on a different part of the screen than the one they are looking at (Jensen, 1998). Using audio alerts for pop-up windows/messages could also help.
- Making good use of CSS for styling the presentation of a Web page and speci-fying both background and foreground colours in CSS.
- Using standard styles for links; for example, underlined text so that the partially sighted user does not miss the link because of its appearance.

- Implementing a good colour contrast, especially between text and its background, and avoiding text on background images.

- Structuring information into short pages: a short page is much easier to use when greatly magnified than a long page that is likely to become very long with magnification and thus difficult to use and navigate. When long pages cannot be avoided, then breaking them with extra navigation links could help so that information can be easily reached. Many people find it difficult to read scrolling text, and constantly moving gifs can be distracting.

- Rollovers and expandable JavaScript menus can be problematic if the user has to click on an area and the menu expands away from what they initially clicked.

- Grouping of controls and content in a visual and intuitive way.

- Using clear labelling and positioning of form controls so that it is clear which form control a label refers to.

- Consistent word spacing and consistent presentation and layout in general.

- Offering a range of colour schemes for customisation.

The category of partially sighted users covers a variety of visual impairments; therefore, there are a variety of needs that fall under it.

Velleman (2005) talks about visual efficiency as a combination of visual memory, perception, cognitive, and motivational factors. Because of the different mix of this visual efficiency for partially sighted users, there can be great differences between this user group and their visual possibilities. This presents the need for customization offering a range of settings when looking at addressing the needs of partially sighted users on the Web.

Mobility-Impaired Users

There are three levels of mobility impairment including slightly impaired mobility, intermediate impaired mobility, and severe impaired mobility (Deng, 2001). The first level can occur as a result of aging and overuse of upper limbs such as repetitive strain injuries. The second level may include weakness and skeletal impairments, amongst others. At the third level, users experience lack of muscular control that may be partial or may affect the whole body. People with upper limb disorders such as arthritis and repetitive strain injury use the keyboard to navigate the Web. They find it hard to use complex navigation mechanisms designed for mouse users such as frames, rollovers, and JavaScript mouse events. They also benefit from the provision of keyboard shortcuts for frequently used controls. This applies for blind users too as they cannot use the mouse. Adequate seating and positioning is also important because this affects computer access, particularly for mobility-impaired users. The user, in order to access the computer and activate input devices, needs to sit in a way that is comfortable to them and close to the technology being used (University of Washington, 2005). Adjustable keyboards, monitors, and desks can significantly contribute to a pleasant and efficient computer use, as well as appropriate desk room for accommodating a wheelchair. Mobility impaired people may use a variety of assistive devices such as:

- Alternative keyboards
- Trackballs
- Head controlled pointing systems that translate head movements into mouse movements
- Switches
- On-screen keyboards
- Speech recognition software

Designers and developers can accommodate the main needs of mobility-impaired people by (Deng, 2001):

- Using a logical tab order (using the tab key from the keyboard to navigate from link to link) mapped to the layout of the controls and the layout of information on the screen
- Using keyboard mapping for speeding up keyboard interaction and enhancing alternative input methods
- Avoiding conflicts with the operation of assistive software such as screen readers, and exploiting the built-in accessibility features of operating systems
- Providing multiple methods for access via the tab key as well as the use of shortcut keys
- Defining hot keys for more functionality for example, allowing the user to go backwards from link to link
- Ensuring that access keys and hot keys for frequently used functionalities are reachable using one hand, for people using one hand only
- Avoiding repetitive key presses that would be uncomfortable for users with repetitive strain injuries
- Placing frequently used links and functions on the first navigation level without requiring the user to navigate a lot to reach them

Deaf Users

There is a growing concern for deaf people accessing the Web, as the use of audio and multimedia content on Web sites is becoming increasingly popular. The Web is moving from a text-based interface to a multimodal environment with the increasing use of multimedia; this environment, despite being more interesting and engaging, presents barriers to deaf people (Paciello, 2005). Deaf people cannot access audio output. When using audio to communicate the system state for example, other means such as text need to be used so that the same information can be accessed in an alternative format. People with hearing impairments require synchronized captioning for video clips and transcripts for audio clips. According to the US Department of Education (2000), captioning not only gives information access to people with a hearing loss, but also to those with literacy needs. Captions also benefit new readers and people who are learning English as a second language (Association of Science Technology Centers, 2004).

There are two types of captions:

1. **Closed captions:** They appear only when the user's technology, for example media player, supports them. Using closed captions on videos means that the user needs to be aware of their existence and knows how to turn them on and off. This is because closed captions are not embedded in the video, but are provided separately. If captions are preserved as text, users will be able to archive and index video content; this is lost with open captions (AccessIT, University of Washington, 2005). Also Clark (2004) supports that transcripts created from captions—using valid and semantic mark up—are a useful resource for searching and archiving information provided in a video.

2. **Open captions:** One distinct advantage of open captioning is that it is always on and always available and accessible (Clark, 2004). Also, open captioning has universal design benefits for people and does not only benefit those with hearing impairments. However, open captions, unlike closed captions, can loose their quality when the encoded video is compressed (AccessIT, University of Washington, 2005).

Also, when deciding what to choose, open or closed captions or even a combination of both (Clark, 2004), the Web application, the task as well as the context of use, needs to be carefully considered. Paciello (2005) offers some guidance on implementing captions:

- The user needs to be informed that captioning has been implemented (especially when using closed captioning) through a set of instructions on the homepage. This also could be added in the accessibility statement of a Web site.

- A textual captioning indicator is more accessible for deaf blind users than an image or icon. If this is provided, then appropriate alternative text needs to be used.

- Simple language needs to be used, along with short sentences.

Also Smith (2003), mentioning Section 508 and W3C WCAG 1.0 guidelines for multimedia and audio, emphasizes that captioning needs to be:

- *Synchronized* with the audio being played
- *Equivalent* in value and meaning to the spoken words or sounds
- *Accessible* in terms of being readily available to those who need it

Because there is a range of different captioning styles that are often divergent, there is a need to explore best practices and to choose a consistent style to follow that applies to the audio content being captioned and the task that it supports (Clark, 2004). However, captioning is not always enough to make content accessible to deaf people as, for many people who are deaf, their first language is Sign Language and not English. According to Byrne (2004), the most effective way to make content accessible to Sign Language users is to provide a Sign Language version of all content. This option can be very costly, and current research focuses on the development of signing avatars (virtual humans) so that it is easier and more cost effective to provide Web content in sign language. Providing captioning and using Sign Language alternatives are the most effective methods to make audio content accessible for hearing impaired users. An integral part of producing accessible content for audio is not only to follow existing guidelines and best practices, but also to constantly review and to test captioning or Sign language content with hearing impaired users (Skillsforaccess.org, 2005).

Cognitively Impaired Users

People with cognitive impairments or learning disabilities are the largest disability group. These impairments affect memory, perception, problem solving, and conceptualisation. Attention deficit disorder and dyslexia are some examples. Although the user needs are quite diverse within this group, cognitively impaired people can greatly benefit if a few provisions are made on Web sites such as:

- Clear and simple layout and language,
- Consistent navigational schemes with the key navigation on the same location for every page,
- Use of images and illustrations to supplement text content,
- Grouping of information in small and logical chunks, and
- Lack of distracting visual and audio elements.

It may seem that there is a conflict between the needs of cognitively impaired and blind users as blind users do not need images and illustrations, whereas cognitively impaired users benefit from them. However, the use of images is compatible with the requirements of both user groups as long as adequate alternative text is provided for the images.

Dyslexia is a common form of cognitive impairment, and a brief overview of it and the challenges it presents is given.

The British Dyslexia Association gives a comprehensive definition of dyslexia:

Dyslexia is best described as a combination of abilities and difficulties that affect the learning process in one or more of reading, spelling and writing. Accompanying weaknesses may be identified in areas of speed of processing, short term memory, sequencing and organisation, auditory and/or visual perception, spoken language and motor skills.

Rainger (2003) describes the difficulties that dyslexic users may face at two levels.

At the first level, problems with visual processing that lead to slow visual object recognition and low visual concentration levels as well as over-sensitivity to light, meaning that dyslexic users can be affected by both the look of a graphical user interface (GUI) and the visual readability of the content.

At the second level, dyslexic users experience problems with short term and working memory, structure, and sequencing. This has obvious implications on the structure of information affecting the accessibility of information architecture.

As a result, the more complex and cluttered a site is, the more difficult it is going to be for a dyslexic user to find their way around, navigate deep in the site, and find their way back. This imposes the requirement not only for laying out content clearly using "white space," reducing information density, and grouping navigation mechanisms, but also for simplifying site structures.

Deaf Blind Users

According to Sense (2005), a UK charity for deaf blind people and for those with associated disabilities, there are 40 deaf blind people per 100,000 in the population. In addition, there are overall 23,000 deaf blind people living in the UK. Someone is called deaf blind when neither their sight nor hearing can compensate for the impairment of the other sense: in other words, they cannot function as a deaf person or a blind person (Sense, 2005). Some people may have nearly complete loss of both senses, where others may have some remaining hearing or vision. People who experience total loss of both senses use refreshable Braille displays to access the Internet. The Braille display transforms all the textual content of the Web page into Braille tactile output. That is, any images or multimedia that do not have appropriate textual descriptions cannot be accessed.

There are different grades of deaf blindness (Deafblind UK, 2004). A deaf blind person may have little remaining sight and thus prefer to read text in large print, customize the text size on a Web site, or use magnification software. For those with no remaining vision, accessing information in a tactile form by reading Braille or Moon with their fingertips is essential. However, those who have a little hearing left may access information using audio; for example, by listening to audiotapes and using a screen reader for accessing the Web. According to Deafblind UK (2005), "deaf blind people remain second class citizens due to the widespread lack of knowledge and the misconceptions surrounding their disability." The design and development of technologies considering the needs of disabled people can greatly enhance the way deaf blind people interact with their environment.

Elderly Users

By 2020, half the adults in the UK will be aged 50+. By 2050, those aged 65-84 will number 1.3 billion globally (Coleman, 2005). According to Nielsen (2002), by 2010, American seniors (aged 65 and over) will spend about $25 billion per year on e-commerce purchases, based on current trends. Also, elderly users go online mainly to find health information, to plan personal travel, and for e-mail. Nielsen (2002) conducted a study with 20 elderly users on 20 U.S. sites, and with 4 elderly users on 4 Japanese sites, and concluded that current Web sites were twice as hard to use for seniors as they were for younger users. The same author supports that "seniors are affected more by usability problems than younger users. Among the obvious physical attributes often affected by the human aging process are eyesight, precision of movement, and memory." The main ageing-related functional impairments can be grouped into two general categories (Zaphiris & Kurniawan, 2005):

1. Vision-related impairments (decline in static acuity, dynamic acuity, contrast sensitivity, colour sensitivity, sensitivity to glare, decrease in visual field, and decrease in processing visual information), and

2. Psychomotor, attention (declines in selective and divided attention), memory and learning, intelligence, and expertise impairments.

At first glance, it may seem that age-related impairments may not pose significant difficulties in using the Web if we look at them individually. However, taken together, as they frequently occur, they may have a cumulative effect that makes Web interaction more difficult for older people (Zaphiris & Kurniawan, 2005).

General guidance for meeting the needs of elderly users on the Web includes (Nielsen, 2002; U.S. Department of Health and Human Services, 2001):

- Support for larger font sizes than those younger users prefer.
- Sites mainly aimed at target seniors should use at least 12-point type as the default.
- Large text for hypertext links and large enough clickable areas and controls.
- Adequate spacing between links and controls to avoid accidental activation.
- Avoidance of the requirement for precise mouse movements that is often caused by hierarchical and pull down menus.
- Using simple and explicit navigation mechanisms that are easy to learn and use, as well as using clear labels for navigation.
- Left justifying and double spacing text.
- Writing in simple language as well as using positive statements and active voice.
- Providing a text version for multimedia files such as captioning, video, and audio.
- Providing a site map that easily communicates the site structure.
- Using good colour contrast with plain backgrounds, particularly for text.
- Including a site guide that demonstrates to the user how to use the site, as well as offering a telephone number to talk to a person if the user needs to.
- Using error messages that are easy to notice as well as providing clear guidance of what the error is and how to recover from it.

Accessibility Testing Methods

It is fundamental to study the needs of users with disabilities and age-related impairments at the requirements stage of the project lifecycle; however, more techniques have to be employed at different stages to ensure that a Web site is truly accessible and useful.

The most widely used methods include:

- **Guidelines and best practices:** This often includes W3C accessibility guidelines, Web standards best practices, as well as guidelines and findings from research papers and Web blogs.

- **Audits:** Expert reviews using assistive software and performing a series of manual checks in the code as well as using automated tools on representative pages. In the case of dynamic Web sites managed with the use of a content management system, both the page templates and the extent to which the system produces accessible code and content need to be assessed (W3C WAI, 2005).

- **Testing using automated evaluation tools:** The W3C WAI (2005) recommends testing Web pages with at least two different automated tools, and comparing their results to ensure that they are valid. Automated tools perform a series of checks in the code of a Web site against W3C and Section 508 guidelines.

- **Browser extensions such as Firefox Web Developer Extension and other plug-in evaluation tools such as AIS Toolbar for Internet Explorer:** These tools are used to identify components of a Web page; to facilitate the use of other online accessibility applications such as the W3C Mark up Validation service, as well as linking to free automated testing tools. Another useful feature includes the use of simulations that help the user understand how users with certain disabilities experience aspects of the Web. These tools also provide links to references and additional resources for Web accessibility.

- **User testing:** This method involves a range of users with disabilities: setting tasks for them and observing how they use the Web site. The problems they encounter are analyzed and recommendations for addressing them are provided.

Each of these methods has its strengths and weaknesses; however, when carefully combined they can be very effective. For example, automated tools can process many Web pages quickly, and the evaluator can get an overview of some of the main issues that can be identified this way. Manual checks are very useful to assess many Web accessibility aspects (such as the presence of good alternative text for images) and making recommendations for addressing them; however, they are time consuming and they assume a very good knowledge on the behalf of the evaluator. Browser extension and plug-ins are very convenient tools, but they cannot replace the use of assistive software, and they are not aimed to be used as such.

User testing is essential. It combines elements of usability and accessibility testing, and can identify problems that cannot be found using any other method. However, user testing requires a good sample of users, good knowledge of user testing methodologies, and avoidance of the risk to base recommendations on the preferences of one user. A combination of methods and techniques used in a systematic way is required for producing accessible Web sites.

Henry and Grossnickle (2004) talk about incorporating accessibility into user-centered design following a process of creating widely accessible products. Vanderheiden's and Tobias' (2000) approach has the same basis and is described with the term "universal design":

Universal design is the process of creating products (devices, environments, systems, and processes) which are usable by people with the widest possible range of abilities, operating within the widest possible range of situations (environments, conditions, and circumstances), as is commercially practical.

The European Union, in 2005, conducted an accessibility evaluation study that initially tested the accessibility of 436 government Web sites across the EU using automated tools. This was then followed by manual testing across a sample of them. The study revealed that only 3% of the 436 online public service Web sites assessed achieved basic accessibility compliance with W3C WAI WCAG 1.0.

It is becoming evident that a more systematic and thorough approach to Web accessibility is required for the development of accessible Web sites, an approach that spans from the requirements to the implementation stage of a Web project.

Conclusion

Examining the needs of users with disabilities helps to develop more useful and usable systems for everybody. Therefore, good design for people with disabilities results in good design for all (Vanderheiden, 2002).

All too often focus is placed on one user group that is mostly disadvantaged by poor Web accessibility. Moreover, very frequently there is a focus on accessibility in a prescriptive way, describing solutions without addressing and understanding the user needs that lie behind:

Many designers and developers are introduced to accessibility because of regulations and the need to comply with the law. In such cases, the motivation for accessibility is often limited to meeting standards and guidelines. Many times this puts the focus on the technical aspects of accessibility and the human interaction aspect is lost. (Henry, 2002)

Focusing on specific users and giving prescriptive solutions are very important in order to promote accessibility and stimulate interest, but they can also distract from the broader and deeper user needs for accessibility.

But accessibility is not limited to disability.

Vanderheiden and Henry (2003) give an interesting dimension to disability by seeing it as an intersection of the user's own abilities and their environment's characteristics for accommodating these abilities:

People experience disabilities ... not just because of their abilities or functional limitations, ... but rather as a result of the intersection—of a person's abilities and—the requirements of their environment.

Designers, developers, information architects, and usability specialists shape the Web on a daily basis. The requirements of this dynamic e-environment towards its users undergo constant change both at a technical and conceptual level, and this imposes great demand on every professional to update their knowledge by researching user needs in various contexts of use. The extent to which people will experience disabilities when using a Web site will depend on their abilities but above all, it will depend on how well the Web application has been designed to meet their needs.

Understanding user needs is important so that we can provide and maintain accessibility while knowing how to balance trade-offs between different user groups when designing Web sites and implementing accessibility. However, understanding the user needs and requirements is only the beginning. Web sites are built by people, and they need to be aware of the user needs, the latest accessibility standards, and best practices. Above all, accessibility needs to be treated as a process in Web design and development, and not a product itself.

References

AccessIT, University of Washington. (2005). *What is the difference between open and closed captioning?* Retrieved September 13, 2005, from http://www.washington.edu/accessit/articles?50

Apple.com. (2005). *Mac OS X accessibility features.* Retrieved September 15, 2005, from http://www.apple.com/accessibility/vision/

Association of Science-technology centers. (2004). *What captioning is and who uses it.* Retrieved September 15, 2005, from http://www.astc.org/resource/access/medcaption.htm

Bilotta, J., & Todd, L. R. (2003, March). *Constructing an accessible Web experience: Equity and enhancement through design.* Retrieved September 15, 2005, from http://www.imtc.gatech.edu/csun/stats.html

BraillePlus.Net. (2004). *Partially sighted definition.* Retrieved September 16, 2005, from http://www.brailleplus.net/visually_impaired_resources/Glossary/Partially_Sighted/

The British Dyslexia Association. (2005). *Frequently asked questions.* Retrieved October 3, 2005, from http://www.bda-dyslexia.org.uk/faq.html

Byrne, J. (2004). *Web accessibility for deaf people - Adding captions or providing transcripts isn't always enough.* Retrieved September 15, 2005, from http://www.mcu.org.uk/show.php?contentid=86

Cabinet Office. (2002). *The UK online annual report: Transforming businesses, transforming government, transforming opportunity.* Retrieved September 16, 2005, from http://archive.cabinetoffice.gov.uk/e-envoy/reports-annrep-2002/$file/indexpage.htm

Chong, C. (2002). *Making your Web site accessible to the blind.* Retrieved September 18, 2005 from http://www.nfb.org/tech/webacc.htm

Clark, J. (2004). *Best practices in online captioning.* Retrieved September 18, 2005, from http://www.joeclark.org/access/captioning/bpoc/introduction.html

Clark, J. (2004). *Best practices in online captioning, closed captions and open captions together.* Retrieved September 18, 2005, from http://www.joeclark.org/access/captioning/bpoc/CC-and-OC.html

Coleman, R. (2005). *About inclusive design.* Retrieved September 20, 2005, from http://www.designcouncil.org.uk/

DeafblindUK. (2005). *Accessing information.* Retrieved October 01, 2005 from http://www.deafblind.org.uk/deafblindness/accessinfo.html

DeafblindUK. (2005). *End the exclusion of deaf blind people.* Retrieved October 1, 2005, from http://www.deafblind.org.uk/news/2005awarenessweek.html

Deng, Y. (2001). *Accommodating mobility impaired users on the Web.* Retrieved September 25, 2005 from http://www.otal.umd.edu/uupractice/mobility/

Disability Rights Commission (DRC). (2004, April). *Formal investigation report: Web accessibility.* Retrieved September 15, 2005, from http://www.drc-gb.org/publicationsandreports/report.asp

Disability Discrimination Act (DDA). (2005). *Definition of disability*. Retrieved September 15, 2005, from http://www.pcs.org.uk/Templates/Internal.asp?NodeID=897276

Disability Rights Commission (DRC). (2005). *Disability Discrimination Act: What does it mean?* Retrieved September 16, 2005, from http://www.drc-gb.org/thelaw/thedda.asp

EU. (2005). *eAccessibility of public sector services in the European Union*. Retrieved September 25, 2005, from http://www.cabinetoffice.gov.uk/e-government/docs/eu_accessibility/pdf/eaccessibility(eu)_report.pdf

Eyecaresource.com. (2005). *Colour blindness*. Retrieved October 3, 2005, from : http://www.eyecaresource.com/conditions/color-blindness/

Frontpagewebmaster.com. (2005). *Accessibility and design—It's not all about CSS and standards*. Retrieved October 5, 2005, from http://www.frontpagewebmaster.com/m-281620/tm.htm

Gower, T. (2005). *Broadband uptake begins to plateau*. Retrieved September 15, 2005, from http://www.netimperative.com/2005/11/25/Broadband_plateau

Gunderson, J. (1997). *World Wide Web browser guidelines*. Retrieved September 25, 2005, from http://www.w3.org/WAI/UA/wai-browser-gl

Henderson, C. (2005). *Color vision statistics*. Retrieved October 5, 2005, from http://www.iamcal.com/toys/colors/stats.php

Henry, S. L. (2002). *Another –ability: Accessibility primer for usability specialists*. Retrieved October 15, 2005, from http://www.uiaccess.com/upa2002a.html

Henry, S. L., & Grossnickle, M. (2004). *Accessibility in the user-centered design process*. Retrieved 15/10/2005 from: www.UIAccess.com/AccessUCD/

Henry, S. L., Law, C., & Kitch, B. (2001). *Adapting the design process to address more customers in more situations*. Retrieved October 15, 2005, from http://uiaccess.com/upa2001a.html

Hesperian. (2005). *Types of colour blindness*. Retrieved October 5, 2005, from http://www.hesperian.co.uk/ia/ia_colourblind.asp

Jensen, S. H. (1998). *Telematics in the Education of the Visually Handicapped conference*. In Institute for the Blind (Denmark) NTEVH 98, Paris June 2-3 1998.

Lauke, P. H. (2005, September). *Evaluating Web sites for accessibility with the Firefox Web developer toolbar*. Retrieved October 15, 2005, from http://www.webaim.org/techniques/articles/evaluatingwithfirefox

Microsoft. (2005). *Resource guide for individuals with visual difficulties and impairments*. Retrieved October 18, 2005, from http://www.microsoft.com/enable/guides/vision.aspx

Murphy, J. (2005). Foreword. *eAccessibility of public sector services in the European Union – Executive briefing*. Retrieved September 25, 2005, from: http://www. cabinetoffice.gov.uk/e-government/resources/eaccessibility/exec_brief/fore-word.aspNational Information Library Service (NILS), Accessible Information Solutions (AIS). (2004). *Web accessibility toolbar EN 1.2—About*. Retrieved October 1, 2005, from http://www.nils.org.au/ais/web/resources/toolbar/index. html

Nielsen, J. (2002). *Usability for senior citizens*. Retrieved October 5, 2005, from http://www.useit.com/alertbox/20020428.html

O'Brien, N. Hughes, P. Holbrook, J., & Gooding, C. (2003, August). *DRC legal strategy 2003-2006*. Retrieved September 20, 2005, from http://www.drcgb. org/thelaw/lawdetails.asp?id=496&title=ls

Opera.com. (2005). *Opera features, accessibility*. Retrieved September 20, 2005, from http://www.opera.com/features/

Paciello, M. (2005). *Making the Web accessible for the deaf, hearing and mobility impaired*. Retrieved September 25, 2005, from http://www.samizdat.com/pac2. html

Pilling, D., Barrett, P., & Floyd, M. (2004, May). *Does the Internet open up opportunities for disabled people?* Retrieved September 25, 2005, from http://www. jrf.org.uk/knowledge/findings/socialcare/pdf/524.pdf

Rainger, P. (2003). *A dyslexic perspective on e-content accessibility*. Retrieved October 5, 2005, from http://www.techdis.ac.uk/seven/papers/dyslexia.html

RNIB. (2005). *Using a computer with low vision*. Retrieved October 10, 2005 from http://www.rnib.org.uk/xpedio/groups/public/documents/PublicWebsite/pub-lic_rnib002982.hcsp

Skills for Access UK. (2005). *Enable user customization in CSS*. Retrieved October 15, 2005, from http://www.skillsforaccess.org.uk/howto.php?id=92

Skills for Access UK. (2005). *Provide text equivalents for audio-general advice on captions*. Retrieved October 15, 2005, from http://www.skillsforaccess.org. uk/howto.php?id=103

Smith, J. (2003). *Captions*. Retrieved October 20, 2005 from http://www.webaim. org/techniques/captions/

Thatcher, J. (2005), *Web accessibility for Section 508*. Retrieved September 25, 2005, from http://www.jimthatcher.com/webcourse1.htm

Theofanos, F. M., & Redish, J. (2003). *Guidelines for accessible and usable Web sites: Observing users who work with screen readers*. Retrieved October 18, 2005, from http://www.redish.net/content/papers/interactions.html

University of Washington. (2005). *Working together: Computers and people with mobility impairments, disabilities, opportunities, internetworking & technol-*

ogy. Retrieved September 17, 2005, from http://www.washington.edu/doit/Brochures/Technology/wtmob.html

U.S. Department of Education. (2000). *Captioning guidelines from the US Department of Education.* Retrieved September 18, 2005, from http://www.sivideo.com/captudoe.htm

U.S. Department of Health and Human Services, National Institute on Ageing, National Library of Medicine. (2001). *Making your website senior friendly: A checklist.* Retrieved October 25, 2005, from http://usability.gov/checklist.pdf

U.S. National Organization on Disability. (2001). Cited in *Does the Internet open up opportunities for disabled people?* Retrieved September 26, 2005, from http://www.jrf.org.uk/knowledge/findings/socialcare/524.asp

Vanderheiden, C. G., & Henry, S. L. (2001, January). Everyone interfaces. In C. Stephanidis (Ed.), *User interfaces for all: Concepts, methods, and tools* (Human Factors and Ergonomics Series). Mahwah, NJ: Lawrence Erlbaum Associates.

Vanderheiden, C. G., & Henry, S. L. (2003, April). Designing flexible, accessible interfaces that are more usable by everyone. In *CHI Conference Proceedings.* Lauderdale, FL: ACM Press.

Vanderheiden, C. G., & Tobias, J. (2000, July 28-August 4). HFES 2000 Conference San Diego, CA, Human Factors and Ergonomics Society.

Velleman, E. (2000). *Center on Disabilities, Technology and Persons with Disabilities 2000 Conference Proceedings.*

Wikipedia. (2005, October). *Mozilla Firefox.* Retrieved September 20, 2005, from http://en.wikipedia.org/wiki/Firefox#Web_development_tools

Windman, R. (2001). *ROI on accessibility.* Retrieved September 18, 2005, from http://www.eweek.com/article2/0,1759,1505488,00.asp

World Wide Web Consortium (W3C), Web Accessibility Initiative (WAI). (1999, May), *Web accessibility content guidelines* (WCAG) 1.0. Retrieved September 25, 2005, from http://www.w3.org/TR/WCAG10/

World Wide Web Consortium (W3C), Web Accessibility Initiative (WAI). (2005). *Evaluation approaches for specific contexts.* Retrieved October 24, 2005, from http://www.w3.org/WAI/eval/considerations.html

World Wide Web Consortium (W3C), Web Accessibility Initiative (WAI). (2005). *Involving users in Web accessibility evaluation.* Retrieved October 27, 2005, from http://www.w3.org/WAI/eval/users

Zaphiris, P., & Kurniawan, S. (2005). Research derived Web design guidelines for older people. In *ASSETS 2005 Conference* (pp. 129-135). Baltimore: ACM.

Chapter II

Failing the Disabled Community:
The Continuing Problem of Web Accessibility

David Kreps, University of Salford, UK

Alison Adam, University of Salford, UK

Abstract

The focus of this chapter is Web accessibility for disabled people, given that much of the Web remains inaccessible or difficult to access. The topic of disabled people's Web access is introduced through a consideration of disability discrimination legislation and a description of how the law applies to Web accessibility. There is a tension between the active burdens the legislation demands and the relative passivity of approaches towards disability discrimination that still prevail. This is exacerbated by the widespread acquiescence to automatic software checking. The history of the development of the World Wide Web in terms of accessibility is briefly described. This reveals the familiar tension between a "free market" approach and regulation that does not readily support social inclusion through accessibility. A table of detailed points showing where automatic tools cannot perform an adequate check against the W3C standards is presented followed by a narrative expanding our claim for the poverty of automatic approaches.

Introduction

...most Web sites are inaccessible to many disabled people and fail to satisfy even the most basic standards for accessibility recommended by the World Wide Web Consortium. It is also clear that compliance with the guidelines and the use of automated tests are only the first steps towards accessibility: there can be no substitute for involving disabled people themselves in design and testing... (DRC, 2004)

The words of Bert Massie, chairman of the UK's Disability Rights Commission, represent an indictment of the continued problems of Web accessibility, automatic tools, and the exclusion of disabled people from design, signalling a continuing digital divide between the disabled community and the rest of society.

The concept of the digital divide has become something of a mantra for those concerned with the accessibility of ICTs. As studies are undertaken on accessibility in terms of gender, class, age, disability, and so forth, our understanding of the ways in which accessibility to new ICTs is much more than just having technology available becomes increasingly sophisticated. At the same time, the use of the World Wide Web for the provision of goods, services, information, and education has grown exponentially in the last 10 years. It seems incontrovertible that access to the Web could be immensely beneficial for disabled users, over a wide range of applications, especially those whose impairment affects vision or mobility.

In this chapter, we consider the issue of Web accessibility for disabled people. We argue that much of the Web remains inaccessible resulting from the interplay of a number of factors. In the following section, the topic of disabled people's Web access is introduced through a consideration of disability discrimination legislation, and how the law applies to Web accessibility.

This issue is exacerbated by the widespread acquiescence to automatic software checking, where it is assumed that software can do everything necessary to pass all the appropriate accessibility checks. Our analysis continues in the next section, which describes the history of the development of the World Wide Web in terms of the development of HTML and XML. Although the absence of regulation of the Internet has permitted an incredible explosion of creativity, the "free market" of Internet expansion and Web usage does not promote an active programme for social inclusion. Despite this, the active attempts of Berners-Lee and the W3C has resulted in a set of Web accessibility standards that have been accepted by the European Parliament. The next section details a table of detailed points showing where automatic tools cannot perform an adequate check on the accessibility of a Web site, and the narrative following this expands our claim for the poverty of automatic approaches. We close by suggesting ways forward from the current impasse.

Legislation and Accessibility

In several Western countries, legislation has been enacted to ensure that individuals are not discriminated against on the grounds of disability, gender, race, and, more recently (at least in the UK), age. For the purposes of this chapter, we shall be focusing on the UK and the wider EU, with reference also to the U.S. and Australia. Each of these regions has legislation in force to prevent discrimination against the disabled; this legislation is widely interpreted as mandating the use of accessibility techniques on the Web. The standards described, like the reach of the Internet itself, are, however, global.

In the U.S., the Rehabilitation Act of 1973 was updated in 1998, and "Section 508" states specifically that Federal agencies' electronic and information technology should be accessible to people with disabilities (http://www.Section508.gov). Section 508 lists a range of guidelines for Web authors similar to, but neither as exhaustive nor as strict as, those adopted elsewhere. They do, however, represent an overt legal requirement in contrast to, for example, UK legislation that does not even mention the Web, leaving it to others to interpret the meaning and scope of the term "services."

In Europe, as part of the "Lisbon 2010 objective of making the European Union the most competitive and dynamic knowledge-based economy in the world," (EU-Parliament, 2003), a series of action plans have been implemented including the eEurope Action Plan 2002, 2005, and iEurope 2010. The first of these action plans was closely followed by EU Council and EU Parliament resolutions (EUParliament, 2002) mandating accessibility standards for all public Web sites, and in keeping with this new focus, the EuroAccessibility Consortium, founded in April 2003, brought organisations from across the Union together to prevent fragmentation in understanding and implementation of the guidelines, with the aim of setting up a Web Accessibility Certification Authority and Quality Mark for the EU, based upon the W3C Guidelines (http://www.euroaccessibility.org). The eEurope Action Plan 2005 included the plan to achieve "an information society for all," and, consequently, an eInclusion agenda for both social and regional inclusivity in the information society (EU, 2005).

At a national level, within European nation states, legislation on disability discrimination, as it relates to the provision of services, has also been interpreted as including services delivered electronically. In the UK, the Disability Discrimination Act (DDA 1995) came into force in phases over a period of almost 10 years, the most important phase for Web accessibility being October 1, 1999. This was the date when provisions in Part 3 of the Act came into force, making it unlawful to discriminate against disabled people by refusing them service, providing service on worse terms, or providing a lower standard of service. It also requires service providers to make reasonable adjustments to the way they provide their goods, facilities, and services to make them accessible. The owner of a public-facing Web site is a "service provider" under the terms of the Act and must therefore comply with the law. The DDA revised Code of Practice on Rights of Access to goods, facilities, and services was published in February 2002 (DRC, 2002); chapters two and five deal specifically with accessibility of Web sites. The revised Code of Practice "deals with the duties placed by Part III of the Disability Discrimination Act 1995 on those providing goods, facilities or services to the public" and "makes it unlawful for service providers ... to discriminate against disabled people in certain circumstances" (DRC, 2002, p. iii).

This Code of Practice was written by the Disability Rights Commission, the UK Government body charged with protecting and championing the rights of disabled people in the UK. In section 2.17 of the Code, under the subheading "What services are affected by Part III of the Act," the following sentence appears: "An airline company provides a flight reservation and booking service to the public on its Web site. This is a provision of a service and is subject to the Act." Additionally, in sections 5.23 and 5.26, the list of auxiliary aids and services "which it might be reasonable to provide to ensure that services are accessible" for those with hearing and visual impairments, respectively, includes, in both cases, "accessible Web sites" (DRC, 2002). Hence, although UK legislation does not explicitly mandate accessible Web sites, the examples clearly signal that we are to understand the Web's role in the provision of services, and make due consideration as to accessibility.

The original 1995 Act was not the end of the story in the UK, however. The Act included an exemption for the education sector. Accordingly, in 2001, the Special Educational Needs and Disabilities Act (SENDA), which came into force with respect to "student services" in September 2002, required that the Web sites (Internet and intranet) of HE institutions should also apply accessibility practices. Recently completing its passage through the UK Parliament, furthermore, the Disability Discrimination Act 2005, which comes into force from December 2006, will strengthen and supersede the former Act in several respects, in particular with regard to the public sector. It will include a new duty on local authorities to "promote equality of opportunity for disabled people" (UK Parliament, 2003). The Bill includes "a duty to take steps for the purpose of making an auxiliary aid or service available to any such disabled persons." This duty to make information available in an accessible format underlines the provisions in the Code of Practice, mentioned previously, that lists auxiliary aids and services.

It is in this respect that an accessible Web site, however, becomes of critical importance to any organisation in its attempts to comply with disability legislation. The UK government Web site that acts as a resource for disabled people- http://www.disability.gov.uk, now merged with the disability section of http://www.directgov.gov.uk-carried the advice that "Putting documents onto a Web site designed to be accessible to disabled people, and publicising this, will go a long way towards making your information accessible" (http://www.disability.gov.uk, 2004).

In summary then, in the UK at least, but by implication also across the whole of the EU, where similar legislation is either already or soon to be put in place, it might be said that not only is it a legal requirement that Web sites be accessible, but that making information available through an accessible Web site is a recommended means of complying with the legal requirement to make information accessible to disabled people in a general sense. For public sector organisations, this is of paramount importance. For businesses working with or alongside the public sector, the implication of the new duty on public authorities to promote equality of opportunity, furthermore, is that the accessibility of their own Web sites will be of no small importance in the assessment of any tender for services they might make.

Tension between Legislation and Current Approaches toward Accessibility

Hence, significantly, the UK DDA mandates an active approach towards removing disability discrimination. It is not enough to provide goods and services and hope that disabled people will access them. We are mandated to take active steps to ensure accessibility, and this applies to those who provide goods and services through the medium of the Internet, just as much as to those who use more conventional means.

Throughout the world, disability legislation is relatively new, and there have been very few court cases, as yet, that specifically test the legislation in regard to Web site accessibility. So far, the Australian Disability Discrimination Act (1992) is the only legislation, globally, that appears to have been tested in court with regard to Web accessibility. In the case of Maguire vs. The Sydney Organising Committee for the Olympic Games, the court found that the Committee had been in breach of the Australian Act by failing to provide a Web site to which Mr Maguire (a blind Australian) could have access (DRC, 2004).

The chairman of the UK Disability Rights Commission, Bert Massie, however, stated in his introduction to a recent DRC report that "the industry should be prepared for disabled people to use the law to make the Web a less hostile place." These are strong words; they explicitly urge disabled people to look to the law if their needs are not met. It is to be expected, then, that the coming years will see test cases in the UK and, more widely, in Europe. The Royal National Institute for the Blind (RNIB) in the UK have made it known (Isolani, 2003) that they have been in private contact with several blue chip corporations, who have naturally undertaken accessibility retrofits of their Web sites in exchange for silence and the avoidance of legal action. No one, it seems, wishes to be seen to be discriminating against disabled people.

All in all, this means that there are now, in many cases, legal obligations. Alongside this, there is an increased awareness of equality and diversity issues. Additionally, there is a clear business case for more inclusivity in corporate practice. According to the Employers' Forum on Disability 2001, based on figures from the Labour Force Survey of 1998, there are 6.2 million disabled people of working age in the UK, equal to 18% of the working population, and a market worth some £40bn annually. There are equal opportunity policies in a growing number of UK organisations that make specific reference to the equality of opportunity for disabled people.

The active demands of the legislation contrasts with a fairly passive approach towards discrimination that, at best, sometimes centres around the catching-up type described previously. There is a clear tension here between a passive approach towards increasing awareness with a concomitant generalized will towards equality and diversity that we now see becoming prevalent in many Western countries and an engagement with very active measures that are required for compliance with legislation, and for offering genuine equality of opportunity for disabled people. Nowhere is this tension more clearly manifest than in regard to the question of Web accessibility for disabled people.

The Story of HTML

In this section, we consider how the contribution of the development of the Web, and attempts to regulate it, have contributed to the accessibility problems outlined previously.

Hypertext markup language (HTML) has something of a chequered history. In its earliest days, it was a new tool created by Tim Berners-Lee at the CERN laboratories in Switzerland to assist in data sharing between the computers at the centre. Based upon SGML, it was a miniature, simplified version of that highly complex mark-up language.

But Berners-Lee soon had other plans for it. Taken up by the World Wide Web Consortium (W3C)—the body established by Berners-Lee in 1994 to try to marshal the phenomenal growth of the Web his mark-up language had spawned—HTML was to undergo a profound reinvention (W3C, 2004).

HTML 3, a formal recommendation of the W3C in the mid-90s, contained a wide range of new visual formatting properties in response to the increasing interest in what could be achieved presentationally on the Web. Yet, following this, while Netscape and Microsoft vied for control of the Web with their own, proprietary, unwieldy new versions of HTML, and others busied themselves with ever more complex and cumbersome plug-ins visitors to Web sites were increasingly encouraged to download and install into their browsers, the W3C began creating a new foundational language for the future of the Web: extensible markup language (XML) (W3C, 2004).

XML is at the heart of Berners-Lee's concept of the semantic Web; his wish, through the universal application of rigorously quality processed international standards for code languages, to see machines talking to one another on our behalf. Thus, the trajectory of the W3C's versions of HTML lifted the language from its SGML origins and shifted it across to this new, XML foundation, first through the publication of HTML 4, and then XHTML. Both these new kinds of HTML, published in the late 1990s, came in two flavours: strict and transitional. The former flavour had stripped out all of the visual formatting and presentational elements introduced in HTML 3, paring the language down to a more robust version of the earlier, more structural HTML 2. Visual formatting was now to be achieved exclusively through the use of a new W3C technology, cascading style sheets (CSS). The transitional flavour of these new versions of HTML allowed Web designers to continue using older, HTML 3 visual-formatting code until such time as the makers of browsers had caught up, and were properly supporting the use of CSS. The differences between HTML 4 and XHTML 1.0 were minor, constituting mainly in some more rigorous rule-based practices in the latter than in the former, geared toward making the code more XML friendly. Finally, in the summer of 2001, XHTML 1.1 was published, with no transitional version. The transition from SGML to an XML basis for HTML was complete.

Parallel with these developments, the W3C undertook an exercise, entitled the Web Accessibility Initiative (WAI) that, in 1999, published its Web Content Accessibility Guidelines (WCAG). As part of the initiative, alongside stripping out the visual formatting from HTML, new elements and attributes were introduced into the code to help make it more accessible to disabled people. "The power of the Web is in its universality," as Tim Berners-Lee famously stated, "Access by everyone regardless of disability is an essential aspect." Thus, HTML 4 and XHTML 1.0, published the same year, contained these elements in both strict and transitional flavours, as does the now completely XML based XHTML 1.1.

The WAI also published, in the following years, the Authoring Tool Accessibility Guidelines (ATAC), and User Agent Accessibility Guidelines (UAAG). (W3C, 1999) It is these standards for those making Web sites, the software tools many use to make them, and the browsers through which they are accessed, that have, since 1999, been increasingly applied by organisations around the world, and have been accepted by governments in numerous countries as the de facto global standards for Web accessibility. The battles between Netscape and Microsoft came to an end, and the makers of browsers now pride themselves on their support for, and compliance with, the standards set by the W3C.

The WCAG provide a set of guidelines for creating Web pages that are accessible to all, regardless of sensory, physical, or cognitive ability. To provide Web developers with a graded approach to the implementation of accessibility, three "levels" have been defined: Level A, Level AA, and Level AAA. The first level, Level A, covers items on Web pages that must be made accessible in order for individuals with disabilities to access the content at all. The second level, Level AA, includes items on Web pages that should be made accessible to allow a wider group of users to access the content. The third level, Level AAA, describes items on Web pages that can be made accessible to allow the widest amount of individuals with disabilities to use the site. For the full WCAG, visit the W3C Web site at http://www.w3.org/TR/WCAG10/full-checklist.html. Most governmental directives specify Level AA as the minimum requirement.

The EU Council and Parliamentary resolutions specify the W3C's Web accessibility standards mandating compliance, Europe-wide, with WCAG Level AA.(CouncilofEurope, 2003) Indeed, the EU recommendations are not only for the adoption of the WAI Guidelines, but for the use of XHTML and XML in the construction of Web pages. The e-Government agenda across Europe, as evidenced in such mandatory standards for the UK public sector as the e-Government Interoperability Framework (e-GIF)(eEnvoy, 2004), similarly require use of XHTML, XML, and compliance with the WCAG Level AA for all public Web sites. The EU, in short, have adopted this part of the W3C's project of the semantic Web wholesale, preferring to side with Berners-Lee's nonproprietary, nonprofit-making association of experts, rather than the likes of, say, Microsoft or AOL. The European Parliament, in its June 2002 resolution on public Web sites, makes frequent reference to "pure standards like (X)HTML and XML," calls the WAI Guidelines "the global standard for the designing of accessible Web sites," and makes specific criticisms of what it calls, "producer-dependent solutions" (EUParliament, 2002).

In this brief history, we are describing a classic tale of "free market" profit making vs. nonprofit making nonproprietary regulation. In European terms, the pendulum has swung markedly towards regulation and standardisation. Given the active approach that disability discrimination legislation requires, this would seem to be a very positive move in achieving accessibility. Unfortunately, these positive moves are undermined both by the quantity of old style HTML sites still in existence and, additionally, by the reliance on automatic checkers.

The Poverty of Automated Approaches

Automated approaches to checking Web pages against these guidelines have proliferated, as described previously, in response both to Web page complexity, and to the general interest, the world over, in technological solutions to human problems. In this section, we describe in more detail the types of accessibility problems for which they are unsuccessful. Such programmes include A-Prompt (one of the better ones), Bobby, LIFT, and many others (WAI, 2004). The W3C maintain a list of such tools on their Web site (WAI, 2004), but are careful not to endorse any of them and, despite providing the best and most definitive tool for checking that

Web pages validate to their own published formal grammars for HTML and CSS, the W3C do not provide their own software tool to check Web pages against their accessibility guidelines.

Given all the arguments we have made, we, among others, believe that the guidelines simply cannot be properly tested in an automated manner and that, for many of them, only a human check is possible. Publications of the UK Government (http://www.cabinetoffice.gov.uk/e-government/resources/handbook/introduction. asp) and Disability Rights Commission support this view (see Table 1). Web Aim, the Web Accessibility in Mind project, based at Utah State University, publicises its own tools and advice with the statement, "It is impossible for any program to fully check Web accessibility. Human judgment is needed" (Connecticut, 2004). As Peter Blair says on the Web Aim site itself, "Web accessibility requires more than just accessibility tools; it requires human judgment" (Blair, 2004).

Not focussing on any one particular tool, the following table is a detailed list of issues that automatic software accessibility packages cannot deal with in a satisfactory way, along with the human check that is actually required.

Table 1 shows some of the guidelines that cannot be tested satisfactorily by automated software in general. Some two thirds of the guidelines below are required to achieve the favoured Level AA.

Table 1. Automated software failings

Issue	WC AG	Guideline Text (abbr)	Explanatory remarks	Automated Software Failing	Human Requirement
Imagery	1.1	Provide a text equivalent for every nontext element.	Visually impaired people use speech synthesis software that reads out the text on Web pages. "Screen readers" and "voice browsers" are perhaps the most commonly known "assistive technologies" used by disabled people to surf the Web. The IMG element of HTML is used to place an image on a Web page. The ALT attribute of this element was introduced in HTML 2 for Web authors to provide a text equivalent for images. The RNIB recommend five words (e.g., ALT= "dog leaps for a stick." Speech synthesis software reads the ALT text.	Will accept ALT=image. jpg in the code, as a valid ALT attribute.	Alternative text for graphics and imagery must be meaningful, and only human comprehension can provide meaningful ALT text.

Table 1. continued

Issue	WC AG	Guideline Text (abbr)	Explanatory remarks	Automated Software Failing	Human Requirement
Imagery	1.1	Provide a text equivalent for every nontext element.	If the dog is leaping for a stick over a canal, and the paragraph of text below the picture is about how funny it is that the dog gets wet, it may be necessary to describe the picture in more detail. The LONGDESC attribute of the IMG element, introduced in HTML 4, allows Web authors to provide the URL of a page where a longer description may be found.	Cannot tell if graphic requires LONGDESC.	Human comprehension of a page is required to decide whether a longer description of a graphic is needed.
Text	3.5	Use header elements to convey document structure and use them according to specification.	Speech synthesis software enables users to "skim" pages in a similar way that sighted users "scan" pages. The software reads out only the headings and subheadings until a keypress stops the "skimming" process and the software reads out the paragraphs beneath the subheading selected. The HTML elements <H1> to <H6> create headings and subheadings, and <p> denotes a paragraph.	Can only detect absence of <H1> – <H6> in code and recommend a human check. Cannot detect when a heading or subheading has been placed in a <p>.	For headings and subheadings to be meaningful, human comprehension of a page of text is required, and human selection of headings made for appropriate mark-up.
Text	3.6	Mark up lists and list items properly.	Speech synthesis software enables users to select different tones and genders of voice for reading out different elements including headers and subheaders, links, and lists. The HTML elements <UL>, <OL>, and <DL> denote unordered (bulleted), ordered (numbered), and definition (question and answer) lists.	Can only detect absence of <ul>,<ol>,<dl>, etc. Cannot detect when a list has been placed in a series of paragraphs or in a table, which is a frequent practice.	Marking up lists appropriately requires a human understanding of what is a list and what is not.
Text	4.1	Clearly identify changes in natural language of a document's text.	Speech synthesis software needs to be told when, for example, a French phrase appears in a paragraph of English text. "C'est la vie" will only be pronounced in an intelligible way if the appropriate language identifiers are used in the code.	No automated accessibility checking software (currently available) contains full dictionaries of multiple languages to scan for such changes.	Changes in natural language must be accurately identified by human comprehension – particularly for names that are unlikely to appear in dictionaries.

Table 1. continued

Issue	WC AG	Guideline Text (abbr)	Explanatory remarks	Automated Software Failing	Human Requirement
Text	4.2	Specify the expansion of each abbreviation or acronym in a document where it first occurs.	New elements in HTML 4 included the <abbr> and <acronym> elements designed to allow the expansion of abbreviations and acronyms in the code so that speech synthesisers could be set to read out the expansion, and browsers for sighted users could enable those with learning difficulties to see the expansion of acronyms and abbreviations in a tooltip brought up by placing the cursor over the relevant text.	Can only check for absence of <abbr> or <acronym>. Without full dictionaries, cannot determine whether abbreviations or acronyms are used. Cannot tell what some abbreviations or acronyms may be when there is more than one possible expansion.	Providing the expansion of ABBR and ACRONYM requires comprehension – e.g., is "Prof" Professor or Professional? Providing abbreviation for acronyms such as UNESCO requires human knowledge of common usage.
Text	13.8	Place distinguishing information at the beginning of headings, paragraphs, lists, etc.	The practice of "frontloading" promotes comprehension for all users of the Web. For those using speech synthesis software, who cannot scan the content of paragraphs for distinguishing words before deciding to listen to it, knowing the gist of a paragraph in the first sentence is an important time saver.	Cannot check for this.	Placing distinguishing information at the beginning of content in headers and paragraphs (front loading) requires human comprehension.
Forms	10.2 and 12.4	Associate labels explicitly with their controls. For all form controls with implicitly associated labels, ensure that the label is properly positioned.	Forms on Web pages enable interaction for a wide range of purposes, from simple feedback to complex transactions. Speech synthesis software reading out the text beside form fields, so that visually impaired users know where to input their details, rely upon new elements in HTML 4 to ensure that the right labels are clearly associated with their corresponding input fields. A poorly coded form, whilst clear to sighted users, might easily lead a visually impaired user to type the expiry date of their card into the security id input field, their post code into the county field, and so on.	Can only check for the absence of <label> element and <for> attribute in html forms.	Human comprehension is required to correctly associate labels with their form controls.

Table 1. continued

Issue	WC AG	Guideline Text (abbr)	Explanatory remarks	Automated Software Failing	Human Requirement
Links	13.1	Clearly identify the target of each link.	Speech synthesis software, in addition to text skimming, can also gather all the hyperlinks in a Web page and read them out first – a valuable time saving device for users wishing to find the right page before listening to the text. Links that simply say "Click here" are, in this case, quite useless. Link text should, therefore, always be substantive.	Can only test for appearance of "click here" or "more" in <a> elements, and recommend human check.	Clearly identifying the target of links requires that link text should be substantive and meaningful – requiring human comprehension.

The W3C has not provided any automated check based upon these Guidelines, presumably, if we accept the arguments above, because it cannot. This reinforces the need for a human check, and bears out the quote, at the beginning of this chapter, that indicates that there is no substitute for involving disabled people in the design and testing of systems.

How Automated Approaches have been Counter-Productive

But the problem is not only that automated approaches to checking Web pages for accessibility are insufficient and unable to substitute for a human check: it is that the existence and proliferation of such software has, in certain respects, actually hampered the global project of making the Web more accessible. The development of the Web and the rise of the W3C and WAI might seem to militate against this, but the W3C cannot provide automatic checks and, in any case, much old illegal code remains. Therefore, we claim that automatic approaches may even have a negative effect and, in this section, we give an example.

Levels A, AA, and AAA of the Web Accessibility Initiative have been used by a very popular tool called Bobby (CAST, 2004). Now Bobby, recently withdrawn and replaced with a new tool called WebXact, was a very useful tool insofar as it could quickly and effectively show how inaccessible a Web page is, but it was all too often misunderstood. Many organisations, including disability organisations (!), seemed falsely to believe that simply passing the Bobby test would satisfy their Web accessibility obligations. Witt and McDermott, in their research study of international higher education institutions, found that "39% of institutions met with Bobby Priority 1 Approval, 1.5% with Bobby Priority 2 and 1.5% with Bobby Priority 3. It must be noted that the majority of these institutions did not, however, satisfy the relevant WAI approval" (Witt & McDermott, 2004). They conclude, and we concur, that "It is apparent… that some Web sites have been observed to display the Bobby or WAI icons even though they are not compliant."

For the makers of such Web sites, the measure of accessibility was whether or not their pages can attain the Bobby Approved icon. The Bobby icon represented an achievable standard and a tangible, cost-effective reward for efforts made towards Web accessibility. But it was really quite patronizing for disabled visitors to Web sites to be told that, because it was a Bobby Approved page, it was accessible to all. As we have seen above, where the alternative text on an image says "photo1. jpg, 5100bytes," the page would have successfully attained the Bobby Approved icon. A fully accessible page run through the WebXact automated testing engine now generates the following report: "This page complies with all of the automatic checkpoints of the W3C Web Content Accessibility Guidelines. However, it does not comply with all of the manual checkpoints, and requires manual verification"(http://www.WebXact.com).

The Bobby test did not in any way ensure "real" accessibility. Firstly, "Bobby Approved" was based on passing some of the WAI Level A checkpoints alone. If a site is to be truly accessible, it should pass the WAI Level AA checkpoints. Bobby did test for these WAI Level AA and the Level AAA checkpoints, but compliance was not part of getting the icon. Worse, because of the confusion created around the different levels and standards, and the relative marketing success of Bobby against the WAI, what was achieved was, in fact, an increase in ignorance of what real accessibility—the WAI defined standards—actually entails. As Witt and McDermott assert from their own study, "End users may find the use of these various logos confusing. A page that is declared as Bobby Level x or A-prompt Level x may not necessarily be WAI Level x compliant. Users may not know or understand what is meant by compliance with a formal grammar such as HTML 4.01. The use of older logos such as the Bobby 3.2 logo confuses the situation further."

It is a commonplace experience amongst Web developers tendering for work in the Public Sector in Europe, where the WAI Level AA benchmark is mandated for all Web sites, to find the specifications in the Invitation to Tender (ITT) actually listing

Bobby Approved as the required benchmark of accessibility—the authors have seen such an ITT from a UK Metropolitan Borough Council. In this case, a tool that cannot possibly do the job of all the checks required is actually listed as the benchmark. If the authors of such tender documents are confused about what is required, then it is no wonder that, as the UK Disability Rights Commission reveal in their report, "The Web: Access and Inclusion for Disabled People - A formal investigation" (DRC, 2004), 81% of the 1,000 Web sites included in the investigation failed "to satisfy the most basic Web Accessibility Initiative category" - Level A.

In his introduction to this report, Bert Massie, chairman of the DRC, had this warning: "Organisations that offer goods and services over the Web already have a legal duty to make their Web sites accessible to disabled people. Our investigation contains a range of recommendations to help Web site owners and developers bring down the barriers to inclusive design. But where the response is inadequate, the industry should be prepared for disabled people to use the law to make the Web a less hostile place."

So the Bobby icon, despite its best intentions, ends up promoting social exclusion because it cannot possibly provide all the checks automatically; it will necessarily end up approving many sites that have serious accessibility problems. The Bobby icon prolongs the agony for those trying to surf the Web across the social barriers of discriminatory code. That its "heart" may be in the right place is no excuse. Many Web pages with the Bobby Approved icon (and no other) are, unintentionally, paying lip service to inclusivity, and are attracting respectability to themselves with the minimum of effort.

CAST, the makers of the Bobby software, themselves, recommend that Web developers use Bobby only as a first step to ensure accessible Web page design. It might be more accurate to say that Bobby can be used to identify definite inaccessibility rather than to verify accessibility. Indeed, the guidelines for UK Government Web sites handbook, (http://www.cabinetoffice.gov.uk/e-government/resources/handbook/introduction.asp) state clearly, "a successful 'Bobby Approved' should not be regarded as an endorsement of accessibility." Similarly, the DRC Report highlighted the shortcomings of automated validators, and the importance of a human check. The report points out that "automated tools cannot check the performance of a Web site against all 65 Checkpoints, since some require human judgement," and that in many cases "automated tools can only give 'warnings' highlighting those aspects that should be checked manually." The report concludes with a series of recommendations, the sixth of which reads: "In accordance with the Guidelines, Web site developers should not rely exclusively on automated accessibility testing" (DRC, 2004).

Humans are needed to make sense of the world, and though the inclusivity is laudable, the attempted reliance upon an automated approach is an attempt not to have to make the effort after all.

Conclusion and the Way Forward

In this chapter, we have attempted to give a fair portrait of the exceedingly complex, somewhat troubled and multifaceted picture of disabled people's access to the Web. In painting this portrait, we draw upon a full spectrum of intellectual resources—legal, technical, historical, political, and social-signalling that the richness of this issue is best understood across this wide spectrum. Drawing upon legislation and its implications for Web accessibility, we note the tension between the active approach demanded by disability discrimination legislation, and the more passive approach that is still being taken towards inclusivity. This reinforces the view of the chair of the UK Disability Rights Commission that disabled people must be involved in the design and testing of Web sites. Considering the history of how the World Wide Web has developed, this reveals the traditional tension between free market and regulation. The acceptance of Web accessibility standards by the European Parliament indicates a positive move, yet the inability of the W3C to provide automated checks and the proliferation of old code militates against the success of these initiatives. In criticising the poverty of automation, we list, in detail, some of the many checks that cannot be automated, and that require a human check. Taking the popular Bobby icon as an example, we show how having a badge of respectability can actually be counterproductive.

Given the complexities of Web accessibility, we should not expect simple solutions.

However, if we want to get beyond passive and ineffective approaches towards accessibility, given, in any case, that the legislation demands it and pressure groups such as the DRC will actively press for testing the legislation, we should heed the calls of these groups, coupled with a clear need for human intervention rather than automatic checking, to involve disabled people much more directly in the design and testing of Web sites.

References

Blair, P. (2004). *A review of free, online accessibility tools*. Retrieved 2004, from http://www.webaim.org

CabinetOffice. (2003). *The guidelines for UK government websites*. TSO.

CAST. (2004). *Bobby*. Watchfire Corporation. Retrieved 2004, from http://www.watchfire.com/bobby/

Connecticut. (2004). *Accessibility tools*. State of Connecticut Web Accessibility Committee. Retrieved 2004, from http://www.cmac.state.ct.ud/access/tools.html

Council of Europe. (2003). *Council resolution on the implementation of the eEurope 2005 Action Plan*. Retrieved 2005, from http://www.eu.int/information_society/eeurope/2005/doc/all_about/resolution.doc

DRC. (2002). *Disability Discrimination Act: Code of Practice* UK Act of Parliament 2008_223. London: Disability Rights Commission. Retrieved 2005, from http://www.drc-gb.org/thelaw/practice.asp

DRC. (2004). *The Web: Access and inclusion for disabled people*. London: Disability Rights Commission. Retrieved 2005, from http://www.drc-gb.org/library/webaccessibility.asp

eEnvoy. (2004). *eGIF v6. eGovernment Interoperability Framework*. UK: Office of the eEnvoy. Retrieved from http://www.govtalk.gov.uk/documents/e-gif-v6-0.doc

e-Government Unit. (2005). eAccessibility of public sector services in the European Union. Retrieved 2005, from http://www.cabinet.gov.uk/egovernment/resources/eaccessibility/content.asp

EU. (2005). *eInclusion*. Retrieved 2005, from http://www.europa.eu.int/information_society/soccul/einc/index_en.htm

EUParliament. (2002). *European Parliament resolution on the Commission communication eEurope 2002:*Accessibility of public Web sites and their content. (COM(2001) 529 – C5-0074/2002 –2002/2032(COS)). Retrieved 2005, from http://europa.eu.int/information_society/topics/citizens/accessibility/web/wai_2002/ep_res_web_wai_2002/index_en.htm

EUParliament. (2003). *Council resolution on the implementation of the eEurope 2005 Action Plan*. Retrieved 2005, from http://www.eu.int/information_society/eeurope/2005/doc/all_about/resolution.doc

EuroAccessibility. (2003). Retrieved 2005, from http://www.europaccessibility.org

Isolani. (2003). *Weblogs: Web Accessibility*. Retrieved 2005, from http://www. isolani.co.uk/blog/access/MoreDetailOnRnibLegalAction

UK Parliament. (2003). *Draft Disability Discrimination Bill*. Retrieved 2006, from http://www.opsi.gov.uk/ACTS/acts2005/20050013.htm

W3C. (1999). *Web content accessibility guidelines 1.0*. WAI - Wendy Chisholm, Trace R & D Center, University of Wisconsin – Madison; Gregg Vanderheiden, Trace R & D Center, University of Wisconsin – Madison; Ian Jacobs, W3C. Retrieved 2004, from http://www.w3.org/WAI

WAI. (2004). *Evaluation, repair, and transformation tools for Web content accessibility*. Retrieved 2005, from http://www.w3.org/WAI/ER/existingtools.html

Watchfire. (2005). Retrieved 2005, from http://www.webxact.com

Witt, N., & McDermott, A. (2004). Web site accessibility: What logo will we use today? *British Journal of Educational Technology, 35*(1), 45.

Section II

The Two
Extremes of Life

Chapter III

Designing Children's Multimedia

Bridget Patel, University of Cambridge, UK

Abstract

This chapter's overarching aim is to elucidate young children's perspectives about, and contribute to, a better understanding of what makes "good" educational multimedia Web design. Focusing on Web design from the child's perspective has the potential to illuminate the multifaceted sociocultural-technological context in which they learn. Underpinning the chapter is a social-constructivist view of learning applied to Web design for young children. The chapter covers (1) "engagement" as a key criterion for successful design; (2) how children make meaning in a Web-based environment; (3) theoretically grounded models of multimedia design including learner-centered design, activity theory, and models of participatory design with children. The chapter is informed by, and reports on, a qualitative case study using a child-centered participatory design approach with Year 2 children (6 and 7 year olds).

Introduction

The nature of our communicational and technological systems is changing. In the postindustrialized West, the everyday lives of children are colored by an aural and visual array of information, messages, and narratives. Like a wildly flowing river, it rushes by in sound bites, digital bytes, cartoons, Weblogs, e-zines, e-mails, musical ring tones, t-shirt insignias, and advertisements, merging into a vast communicational stream of which children are very much a part. Carrington (2005) illuminates this sociocultural phenomenon of contemporary childhood with reference to the Japanese term "Shi Jinrui," for "New Humankind," to illustrate just how different this generation of young is to previous generations (Wilks, 2002, cited in Carrington, p. 11). That our terminology to describe current communicational technologies is fraught with the precedent "new" (new media age, new literacy studies, new humankind, etc.) bespeaks that this is an area deserving fresh approaches to children's communicative practices as they relate to the new media environment, specifically, and the wider sociocultural mosaic of our times.

This chapter discusses and analyzes the communicative practices children use when working in the new media environment, and how the designer can take account of these in designs for children. It explores a group of seven-year-olds' views about digital multimedia, their narrative texts, and their design ideas for multimedia storytelling. Children bring with them to the interface a different set of expectations, knowledge, abilities, and practices, and designing for children brings with it a different set of demands. The child's perspective is discussed by way of child-identified features of multimedia design that contribute to an engaged child-user experience. Further to this discussion is the way in which children make meaning in computer-mediated environments, bringing together the visual, aural, textual, and navigational elements of multimedia design and content. The notion of learner-centered design is examined to see how its principles align with, and can be applied to, designing children's multimedia (Reeves, 1999; Soloway, 1996a). Activity theory is considered as a framework for conceptualizing educational multimedia (Nardi, 1996). Lastly, innovative participatory design approaches with children are discussed and illustrated by recent research studies (Druin, 1999a; Kress & van Leeuwen, 1996; Marsh, 2005; Pahl & Rowsell, 2005).

The Study

In a rural Church of England school, the mixed Year One/Year Two class had just about finished six weeks of geography and literacy work based upon The Katie Morag picture books by Mairi Hedderwick. Their weeks of cross-curricular work:

Figure 1. Grace's story

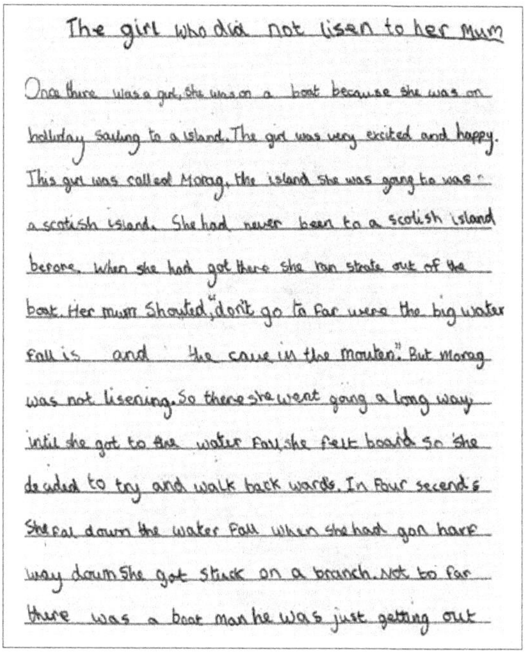

> The girl who did not lisen to her Mum
>
> Once there was a girl, she was on a boat because she was on holliday sailing to a island. The girl was very excited and happy. This girl was called Morag, the island she was going to was a scotish island. She had never been to a scotish island before. When she had got there she ran strate out of the boat. Her mum Shouted, "don't go to far were the big water fall is and the cave in the mouten." But Morag was not lisening. So there she went going a long way intil she got to the water fall she felt board so she decided to try and walk back wards. In four seconds She fal down the water fall when she had gon half way down she got stuck on a branch. Not to far there was a boat man he was just getting out

looking at landscapes, journeys, Scottish island life, and the conundrums of Katie Morag's character, culminated in story writing. Each child's text was analyzed. Five pupils were chosen for inclusion in this pilot case study based on the textual analysis of their written narrative texts (one of whom was absent for too many sessions to include in analysis). The selection criteria included children who wrote (a) traditional, linear story structures, (b) spatially, visually organized story structures and (c) story structures with elements of linear *and* spatial structuring. Each child's text represented a different degree of multimodality (the use of multiple modes of communication in a book, a page, a screen, etc.; see Figures 1 and 2). The stories can be seen along a spectrum from dense text temporally ordered and cohered to the highly multimodal, spatially ordered and cohered, where the story can be seen as taking place through the interplay of the child's drawings and words (Bearne, 2003b; Jewitt, 2003; Kress & van Leeuwen, 1996; Pahl & Rowsell, 2005; United Kingdom Literacy Association, 2004).

Children's narratives reflect deeply embedded cultural understandings of (school and home) literacies. They form an interesting, evaluative entry point into that which

Figure 2. Naomi's story

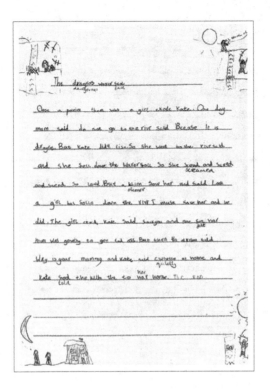

drives and forms their communicative practices. This data was triangulated with participatory observations of children using multimedia in the classroom, and a participatory design activity inspired by the work of Allison Druin (1999) in which children made models of storytelling machines. The study concluded with children writing a second story, one to be told with their storytelling machines. The addition of story writing and text analysis extends the reach of a methodology tradition from human-computer interaction into the field of literacy. This practice reflects the real-world interconnectedness of narrative content and narrative presentation. This exploratory case study is underpinned by a social-constructivist view of learning, and has as its framework the "single case (embedded) design" (Yin, 2003).

Terms and Definitions:
Building Bridges on Shifting Ground

There is a huge discomfort with the current terminology used to talk and write about the nature of communicational practices in the digital age. An agreed vocabulary has yet to emerge. A wobbly bridge connects communication of similar ideas between disciplines. As if there is no concrete foundation supporting the structure of this conversation, each discipline has built its own bricks, inventing terminologies to offer a means of understanding. These have been insightful, formative but, at times, fractured, fragmented, and overlapping. Kuutti (1999) remarks on the situation in the information systems field: "Currently, each researcher tends to use his or her own framework and concepts, which rarely are integrated or even comparable to any marked extent" (Kuutti, 1999, p. 372). Technologies, forms, and mediums of communication are in flux; naturally, ideas about these new forms are in flux, too. Certainly in the context of a discussion about children, educational ideals about the best way forward in rebuilding ("reform"ing) a curriculum around constantly shifting ground acquiesce to this state of flux. A malleable frame of reference is a natural fit to such an interdisciplinary, flexible, and potentially rich site of creative, communicative development. Knowing one's point of viewing and purpose then provides the kind of exacting measures necessary to progress knowledge about the way communicational practices are transforming and being transformed by new technological tools available in our society. My approach in this chapter is one of practical experience in multimedia design, and evidence from educational studies and studies in human-computer interaction theoretically underpinned by developmental psychology, semiotics, and socioculturalism. The intention of this chapter is not to develop a terminology suitable to sustain the current discourse, but to tease out the meanings of relevant existing terms.

Multimodal texts communicate through the interplay of images and words. The Katie Morag stories that provided grounding for the children's unit of work are a good example of this definition of multimedia. The opening page of all the Katie Morag picture books is a detailed map of the island with labels of each and every important place, like Granny Island's house and the Post Office. The picture books are beautifully illustrated with watercolor landscapes that speak anew to the story each time they are looked at closely. *Multimedia* is a term used since the 1950s in manifestly varying ways. It refers to "the use of two or more media to present information" (Green & Brown, 2002, p. 4). Adopted herein is the more specific term *digital multimedia* to "refer to any combination of media that can be interpreted, stored and displayed by a computer" (Green & Brown, 2002, p. 4). The wide range of modes of communication simultaneously at work when children interact with multimedia brings to bear, in this chapter, a discussion of visual literacy, digital literacy, and challenges to traditional notions of literacy. *Communicative practice* is a way of describing the multimodal meaning-making process engendered by digitally mediated tools, such as computers, television, and mobile phones and hand-held devices (Marsh, 2005; Street, 1997).

Of course, "new media" is composed of both new (as in Macromedia's Flash movies) and old media (video, text, audio, and voice-over recordings) bound by the shared distinction and affordances of digitized technology (Marsh, 2005; Norman, 2004). When done well, the new and old are crafted and assembled together in coherent on-screen multimedia designs.

Multimedia Design: Dimensions of Engagement

Children's Views, Children's Voices

Sara (age seven): I like [BBC's Web site] Blue Peter because you can print out things to make. I like going to those kinds of Web sites where there's a TV show.

Sara likes intertextuality. The connection between a television show and a Web site appeals to her. She used this particular Web site (BBC's Blue Peter) as a resource for activities away from the computer. Sara is also an articulate child who is able to identify and describe the characteristics of multimedia that she likes. She recognized that it is the intertextual relationship, the thematic link between the two media that she enjoys. Sara's opinion speaks to my question of: What makes good multimedia? What do children like about the multimedia they use, play, and learn with? What multimedia features do they find motivating? What don't they like? What frustrates, confuses, or bores them? Children's opinions and views about multimedia offer one perspective on answering these questions: the child's perspective. The data in the case study reported here were collected to capture the child's perspective and amplify children's voices, for it is children whom are at the center of learning, especially at school, the site of the study. If our goal is for children to be engaged in learning, they should be given engaging learning tools.

A few themes emerged from my participant observations and conversations with Sara, Grace, Naomi, and Caroline around which the children's interests coalesced. All four children reported that their favorite thing to do on the computer was to play games. Here are some snippets of our conversations.

Sara

Bridget: Do you use the computer at home?

Sara: Yes. I play games. Solving problems kind of games.

Bridget: What games do you play?

Sara: Zoombinis. You use the keyboard for steering. I got to level three, but couldn't do the steering on level four. More things come up and faster.

Naomi

Bridget: What sorts of things do you like to do on the computer?

Naomi: Games on the Internet.

Bridget: Where do you play them?

Naomi: At home.

Bridget: How often do you do that?

Naomi: A couple of days a week.

Grace

Bridget: How often do you use the computer?

Grace: Not a lot. My sister uses it all the time.

Bridget: When you do get to use it what do you do on it?

Grace: Play a game or two games. Not like the Cbeebies games. I don't like the Cbeebies games.

Bridget: What games do you like?

Grace: Golf, on the computer.

The children in this study had a preference for computer game playing activities. They all enjoyed problem-solving games in which they took the role of the main character and had to overcome challenges (whether it be driving a ball into a hole across sandpits and water traps, or maneuvering a boat through dangerous waters). As Sara's remark shows, the children in the study also liked companion Web sites to TV shows, like BBC's Blue Peter. They expressed dislike for Web sites geared to a younger audience (such as BBC's Cbeebies).

Table 1. Dimensions of engagement

Control	Interactivity	Design and content

•User control
•Scaffolding support
•Social experience
  and collaboration
	•Challenge through
	  game like activities
	• Expressive tools
	• Role play, goal setting,
	  creating
	• Immediacy, feedback
	  and rewards
		• Aesthetically pleasing
		  and inherently
		  interesting
		•Combine media to
		  explain, inform, and
		  reduce text
		•Attention grabbing
		  entertainment and
		  information
		•Ease of use: clear,
		  easy to read, familiar
		• Humourous and fun

Dimensions of Engagement

A substantial body of research in human-computer interaction employs the term "engagement" as a key criterion upon which to judge the quality of a children's multimedia product and the experience it has to offer. Risden, Hanna, and Kanerva (1997) reported intrinsically motivating factors for children when "playing" their favorite computer activities. "Ease of use" was found to be a "critical determinant" of engagement, followed by "familiarity," "control," and "challenge." Hanna, Risden, Czerwinski, and Alexander (1999) originate the term *dimensions of engagement*. It provides a clear metaphor for the multifarious features that contribute to meaningful reading and playing of multimedia texts (Bearne, 2003a; Mackey, 2003). When talking about *children's* engagement, in very simple terms, we mean the features of multimedia that grab children's attention, keep their attention, and enable them to learn things and have fun in the process (Hanna et al., 1999). Table 1 reports those engaging features of multimedia that children testify to and demonstrate through their computer play. I aggregated the elements of this list from studies conducted with children aged 6 to 14 years. In addition to the work of Hanna et al. (1999), findings from the following studies are included: (1) A study in which Year Six pupils, aged 10 and 11, were multimedia authors for their peer group and younger pupils (Years Two and Three) at their school (Atherton, 2002). The 30 students who collaborated on the project developed two sets of guidelines for designing multimedia for children, one for each target audience. (2) An experimental study with children aged 9 to 14 showed that although children see potential in multimedia, they often find the designs of multimedia applications unappealing. The resultant "Engaging Multimedia Design Model" reflects the importance of six contributors to engagement, including simulation interaction (such as role play), construct interaction (such as creating, modeling, building), immediacy (actions appear on the visual interface), feedback (rewards, support), goals, and previous experience. Interestingly, time spent playing led to more engaged interaction (Said, 2004).

The dimensions fall into roughly three categories: control, interactivity, and design and content. Children want the independence of being in control of the experience, but the support of help and guidance when they need it, and the interdependence of working together with friends and peers. They are not engaged in solitary activity, but rather it becomes a social experience where they collaborate with friends and peers. Interactivity is important. Children want to create. They favor expressive tools, game-like challenges where they can set goals and be "in role," as in playing a character in a story. Like adults, children are discerning; aesthetics *and* functionality are important to them. They are well attuned to the nuances of good design, and have a preference for visual material, clearly and interestingly presented. Data from my case study show that humor and affect also play important roles in engaging children.

The Play Dimension

Sitting at the row of computers, Grace and Naomi are searching for dress patterns to print out for their next topic of work. As they wonder, play, and search, they collaboratively invent stories and scenarios about the photographs they see. Yes, they are being silly, chortling at how the pictures and poses are "weird," adding dialogue to go along with the funny poses of people in the photo, but what they are also doing is bringing humor to an otherwise humorless interface. It illustrates the importance of entertaining children with the material we give to them, using humor and fun to motivate their learning. Kress and van Leeuwen (1996) point out how different the notion of reading is today from that which was prevalent in textbooks from the 1930s. In comparing an image from a textbook of today and a text from the 1930s they remark, "Students of science are no longer addressed in the hierarchically complex structures of scientific writing, with its specific demands for cognitive processing. They are addressed, seemingly, as people whose interests need to be solicited and *won*, who need to be entertained, humored; a very different notion of reading ..." (Kress & van Leeuwen, 1996, p. 30).

There is a thin line between what is classed today as entertainment and education. It is important to think through the user's experience and if the purpose is educational, the educational gains that a multimedia design allows. I also argue that the reverse is true. When educational purposes inform your design, it is necessary to think through the elements of entertainment, like fun, humor, and playfulness that the specific multimedia design offers. Engagement is the first key step into learning. Fun, humor, and playfulness engage children in learning. These are the kinds of things that give educational multimedia their "child appeal." The extensive body of literature in developmental psychology supports this idea of play as children's hard work and the center of their early learning experiences (Piaget, 1950; Vygotsky, 1978). By using children's play, likes, and dislikes as a foundation for educational multimedia, it becomes grounded in child-centered educational practice. "Children's play, like everyday literacy practices, draws meaning from being situated within cultural histories, values and practices and this generates engagement, involves networks, and is consistently related to the everyday lives of people in their communities" (Hall, 2000, p. 191).

This view meets with scrutiny from research into educational effectiveness as the most enjoyable, the most well liked may not necessarily reflect the most effective practice (Burnett, 2002). Perhaps a good question to ask is how to use "child-appeal" to motivate and *retain* attention, so children answer both the call of fun and the call of learning.

Children's Multimodal Meaning Making

What resources do children draw upon to engage with multimedia? Children's hands, eyes, and minds are in coordinated action that involve physical dexterity and manipulation of mouse, keyboard, cursor, and other hardware tools that act upon the interface, literate abilities in reading and interpreting the visual designs and textual elements of interfaces, and navigational understanding underpinned by conceptual development.

Child Development, Cultural Conventions, and the Visual Interface

Multimodality (the use of multiple modes of communication in a page, a book, a screen, etc.) is not new. That is something that has been reiterated in the literature many times over (Atherton, 2002; Jewitt, 2003; Kress & van Leeuwen, 1996). Ironically enough, for something as engrained in human nature and people's sense making of images, pictures put to words, and words to pictures, our sense making, when mediated by the computer, is distinctly *different*. Why is it that human sense making is distinctly different with computers than with other older tools and traditional media? We can flip back and forth through on-screen pages, but it does not foster enhanced comprehension achieved through the kind of flipping and text scanning that we do with books and magazines. The ability exists in the technology and is within our physical capabilities (hitting the back button of a browser, acting on the digital representation of a text), but our minds have not evolved to the cognitive sense making of the reading paths of new media. It is the physicality of the tools themselves. It is how they feel and work in coordination with our bodies and how our bodies work in coordination with the tools: how we bend; move our arms, wrists, and fingers; the position we sit; kinesthetic feedback; and what is in our visual field of perception. From then on, it is what they render in meaning, concretely, figuratively, aesthetically, and so on. Our bodies and our minds, together, make sense of the communicated world.

Children's development, together with their understanding of the cultural conventions used in and surrounded by visual interfaces, affect what they do with multimedia

Table 2. Implications for visual interface design based on children's development

Child development	Visual interface design implications
Physical development	
Imprecise cursor positioning	Physically active screen area larger than visible screen area
Haphazard, ineffiecient page-scrolling	Minize page scrolling
Difficult coordinating drag-and-drop	Use point-and-click
Conceptual development	
Confused by alphabetic indexes with letter spans e.g. A-C, D-F, etc.	Avoid letter spans in alphabetic index
(Novices) favor one search strategy instead of best-fit strategy	Scaffold search options, e.g. simple search and guided search interfaces
Difficulties thinking of search terms	Scaffold for age-appropriate conceptual development
Difficulties plotting a reasonable path through new subject area	Clear navigation, scaffold level of guidance through the content
Compositional abilities	
Recognise coherent designs, but use of typeface and size naïve	Use legible, consistent typography, model good design practice, create typographic tools and activities for children to experiment with.

(Norman, 1999; Norman, 2004). For example, experimental evidence shows that a point-and-click interaction style is more efficient, effective, and motivating for children than drag-and-drop style (Inkpen, 2001). Table 2 presents a view of visual interface design implications for children aged four to seven based on their physical and conceptual development, and their compositional abilities when working in the digital environment, as reported in the literature and evidenced in this case study. The focus here is on the general skill level of young children. The scope is not large enough to discuss individual differences brought about by special needs some children may possess, but presents us with a limited understanding as to why interaction styles make a difference to children.

Reading Screens

A significant body of work has been carried out that describes the interconnectedness of multimodal design elements such as linguistic, visual, audio, gestural, and spatial at play in children's meaning making of multimedia texts (Cope & Kalantzis, 2000; Kress, 2003; Kress & van Leeuwen, 1996; Mackey, 2003). Kress (2003) reiterates the limitation to communicational practices of assuming the dominance of language in meaning-making practices in the digital age. The affordances of new technologies offer innovative delivery and development of story, but also require a broader skill set in order to engage with and construct story, one that is inclusive of wider visions and definitions of literacy (NESTA Futurelab, 2005; United Kingdom Literacy Association, 2004).

In this way, multimedia can be read as a text (Bearne, 2003b). A multimedia text is first and foremost a visual composition. The visual is the main entry point into the material (as opposed to the linguistic, in a written text; although in some instances their may be an auditory opening, as in a musical intro). The visual whole created by the combination of various multimodal parts is the first element a "reader," "viewer," or "user" perceives. This is the Gestalt principle that "the whole is greater than the sum of its parts" (Arizpe & Styles, 2003; Lester, 1995; Ruth, 1995). The visual composition of a page organizes the user's attention to specific aspects of the page. Compositional elements such as similarity, proximity, contrast, figure-ground, visual hierarchy, color interaction, and metaphor and graphic icons affect how users both read and navigate the page and construct meanings, whether intended or not (Ruth, 1995). It is, as Kress and van Leeuwen (1996) point out, "a semiotic unit, structured not linguistically, but visually" (Kress, & van Leeuwen, 1996, p. 185). Their theoretical interpretation of visual design offers an especially useful vantage point on the design of multimedia for children, as it is rooted in examples of children's early drawing and writing. These examples are windows into children's reception and production of social meanings communicated through their texts.

Figure 3. Trouble on the Island by Caroline

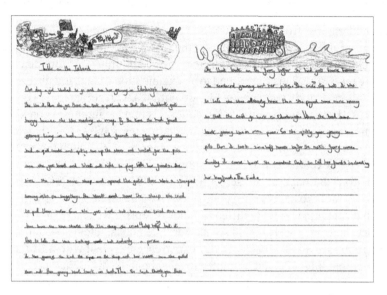

Kress and van Leeuwen (1996) show how images in the west can be seen as organized around vertical and horizontal axes, and their positioning around these axes produce meaningful relationships. The vertical axis produces a left and right relationship where the left depicts the Given, something understood and accepted in society. The right depicts the New, that thing that the image is proposing to the viewer, and proposing the viewer to accept. This is the Given-New relationship. The horizontal axis separates the Ideal on the top portion of an image and the Real on the bottom portion. The idealized world, idea, or concept is represented above the realistic, the practical, the everyday world as we know it. Intriguingly, screen two of Caroline's second text (Figure 3), is a good example of these theoretical constructs.

A main criticism in looking at any particular multimedia product or page design as a multimedia text is that the term oversubscribes rules of a grammar, or the likeness of a set of structured governing rules as we have in language use, to a set of multi-modal features. The argument is that artwork, images, graphics, and navigational elements such as icons, and so forth, are not, by nature, describable through words, nor can their meanings be contained within a set of explicated rules or systems of meaning (Burnett, 2002).

Writing Screens

What do children take from their reading of multimedia texts, and what evidence can be found of influences in constructing their own multimedia texts? Barrs and Cork (2001) look at the threads woven into young children's writing taken from their reading repertoire. This can extend to an examination of multimedia texts. The children in this case study were given A1 card outlined with six screens. The screen format was used as a way to evaluate the children's understanding of concepts underlying on-screen visual communication without being inhibited by the variation in technical skills like typing and drawing with a mouse (with which this group had less school-based experience). Where was this particular group of children located in the shift from the page to the screen (Jewitt, 2003; Kress, 2003)? They were asked to write a story to be told with their storytelling machine. Prior to writing, we had a group discussion about the different kinds of stories we read and see, and the various places in which we read and see stories, like books, television, and so forth They were reminded about some previous experience they had with a British Film Institute storyboarding unit, and prompted to talk about the different kinds of media through which stories are presented. They were told that they could do anything they wanted to with their stories, they did not have to fill the space with writing only, but they could if they wanted to, and that they could draw if they wished.

The children's stories were analyzed in terms of characterization, use of picture as related to story, text cohesion, language and style, sense of reader, and focus of story. Caroline's first text, despite its exactingly detailed drawings, could be read as lacking in coherence (Figure 3). Analyzed in the traditional sense using the Qualifications and Curriculum Authority's literacy assessment focuses, Caroline's performance would be rated lower than her peers. Given a second reading of the assessment focuses, one that widens its scope to analyzing texts as multimodal compositions, Caroline *would* excel (United Kingdom Literacy Association, 2004). For example, her second drawing works like a text-cohesive device tying the action of the previous page to the action of the following page, and the wavy seawaters spanning across the page margins function like a filmic fade. The text is a storyboard, with a clear beginning, middle, and end!

Caroline's second text, *The Kitten and Cat Family*, confirms this reading as she excels in the screen-shaped paper narrative (Figure 4). Again, the drawing is incredibly detailed. The first picture sets the scene. Rising action is depicted as families board an airplane, leaving their cats behind and alone. The tail of the plane is either vibrating or the propeller is whirling around, signaling motion. The written word cleverly and explicitly characterizes Ebony, the pet kitten, by her indelible black fur. This characterization drives the story's events. In screen two, all the action is contained in the visual: Ebony swings from the ceiling, shouts "go away" in frustration, climbs the stairs, takes a bath, sleeps in bed. All the different rooms of the

Figure 4. The Kitten Family and Cat Family by Caroline

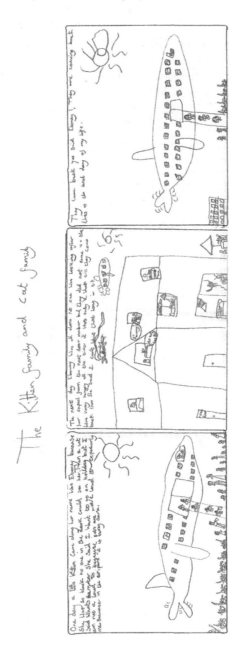

house, and outside sitting at the patio table, illustrate how Ebony is spending the long, lonesome week. The written is a window into the character's feelings, while the drawings actually tell the story of what is happening. The airplane in screen two is smaller, distant, as is the sun. There is a great deal of, and emphasis on, perspective in these drawings. The flying cat above the house acts as a cohesive tie (from the written to the pictorial and vice versa) for her wishful dreams that she could fly to be with her family. In screen three, a cloud appears to be trailing away from the sun as if to say, "the cloud is lifting; the bad times are coming to an end." Again, the written text reveals the inner state of being of the character, "this is the happiest day of my life!" and the pictorial is where the story unfolds, with a plane landed and people walking down the steps where a line of cats greets them.

Caroline's texts are visual. Additionally, the influences of personal identity and history contribute to her narratives. Biographical data regarding frequency of screen-based media use and narrative experience would make it possible to draw further conclusions.

There is not enough pilot-study data to draw conclusions about children's computer-mediated writing practices, though the main study aims to gather data to speak to this. In his discussion of two- to four-year-old children's on-screen writing, Merchant (2005) builds upon Clay's (1975) classic principles of writing. That is, those characteristics of writing and words children come to understand through their early and emergent writing. Merchant expands these paper- and pencil-based principles to the digital age to see if they hold true for children's on-screen writing. Interestingly, many of them do[2] and even more interesting are those that do not, such as the *space concept:* particular conventions govern the placing of words and the use of space. There are cultural conventions largely applied to the design of space on a screen, just as there are on the page. On the page, we would think about margins, line spacing, and other formatting conventions children learn through their experiences with narrative and informational texts. On the screen, the use of

Figure 5. Timeline: Theories and practices informing design

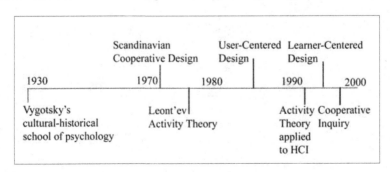

space is restricted by the physical display size of the screen, and broadly follows conventions of a landscape orientation. Moreover, the cultural conventions guiding space on the screen are more implicit than explicit. The *message concept,* a written message can be read and understood by others. In a computer-mediated message, there are potential nonlinear reading paths (as in hypermedia); unidirectional communication is displaced; time, place, and audience of the interaction is wider, which exacerbate individuals' naturally varied responses to a message. Merchant (2005) also proposes new principles such as the *gaze principle*—knowing where to "direct one's gaze" as actions on a keyboard appear on the screen; *selection and pressure principles*—writing with a keyboard requires you to select letters and know how long and how hard to press a letter's key; and *rhythmic principle*—young children play with the sounds produced by their typing in a rhythmic way.

So why focus on children's contemporary communicative practices? What concern is this to a designer of children's multimedia? How does knowing about children's development with computer-based tools affect designs? User frustration was high when system design lacked contextualized user data. As Figure 5 shows, purposeful methods for integrating a multidisciplinary knowledge base have since evolved.

[Software] applications that target children aim at the child's intellectual curiosity, at eagerness for new concepts and knowledge, and at the patterns for learning to distinguish between appearance and reality. In other words, children do more than reflect what is presented to their senses. They reconstruct it to fit their worlds, and they don't simply make a copy of it. The challenge for designers of children's applications, then, is to enable children to reconstruct and build on their own images of the world, to support the development of their reasoning, and to surpass repetition and rote learning of static concepts. A major goal of our society is to have people who discover, who are creative and inventive. To achieve this goal, we need children who are active, who learn early to find out things by themselves, partly by their own spontaneous activity and partly through the materials we design for them.
(Brouwer-Janse, Fulton Suri, Yawitz, de Vries, Fozard, & Coleman, 1997, p. 36)

Models of Multimedia Design

System design was technology-centered up until the mid-1980s, at which point (Norman & Draper, 1986) *user-centered system design* (UCD) took to center stage (Reeves, 1999; Soloway & Pryor, 1996). The mid-1990s saw an ideological progression from user-centered design to learner-centered design (LCD) applied to educational technology, underpinned by a socioconstructivist epistemology acknowledging the *"gulf of experience"* learners must cross in bridging their current knowledge with that of the learning domain (Ardito et al., 2004). Applying the concept to designing children's multimedia means using knowledge a child already possesses to introduce new and unfamiliar ideas; sometimes whole paradigms. It has ramifications to the design of *Web site* navigation, interface design, and the multimedia content itself, both in terms of the mode of delivery of the content and how the content is structured for the learner.

Learner-Centered Design

"From edutainment to context-sensitive help systems, the need to support learners is well recognized" (Soloway et al., 1996, p. 189). Drawing on the work of user-centered design, Soloway (1996) outlined three main tenets of learner-centered design: growth, diversity, and motivation. Growth is seen as a primary goal of education. Thus, designs for learners should enable growth. Before the question, *How does one design for growth,* can be answered, the question of *How do people grow? How do they learn?* must be addressed. As Ardito et al. (2004) put it: "It is necessary to rely on an educational theory driving the designer." Learner-centered design is steeped in constructivist learning philosophy, whereby learning is seen to occur when people make meaning by actively engaging in authentic, culturally valued tasks (Soloway et al., 1996). Diversity acknowledges the social milieu of our times, and children's wide-ranging developmental abilities, cultural mores, practices, and individuality (a principle that can be seen through Caroline's writing). Designing for diversity also means, in educational terms, *differentiation*. In other words, scaling the language usage, topic scope and depth, presentation, information visualization, and activity in developmentally appropriate terms. Motivation—though lacking in a unified model or theory—is specified here in the reflection that a learner's motivation should not be taken for granted.

Reeves' (1999) conception of learner-centered design emerges from the cognitive approach whereby principles of cognition are applied to the design of information-rich environments. It is a way to manage the complex information a user meets in an *interactive information field* (such as a product, information system, or a workspace), the computer-mediated system being a major example. The information age has brought about *cognitive complexity* whereby the efficient use of artifacts becomes unclear; cluttered by environmental factors and societal forces. There are three conceptual tools to help learners manage cognitive complexity. *Understandability* is derived from usability, as understanding a product or system. In LCD, it comes with the added caveat that both the (1) design of a technology and (2) content delivered by such a technology must be *easy* and apparent to understand. Design elements that help beginners and novices understand *how* to use an artifact bring about *learnability*. *Scaffolding* builds in learning supports that assist the learning process.

The role of corporate capital in the development of educational resources has been cited as an inherent weakness of the learner-centered design approach (Burnett, 2002). Although the economic argument has validity, it does not negate the *principles* of learner-centered design, but may speak to the (im)possibility of their fruition in developing multimedia materials for children. There is not scope in this chapter to dissect, in full, the kinds of political power structures alluded to and whose questions might benefit from a historical perspective on curricular reform movements[3]. There are economic forces driving the development of educational materials. Schneider (1996) argues that designs for formal learning and adult purchasers are "the greatest obstacles to employing such tools," (Schneider, 1996, p. 74). From learning goals beneficial to children and helpful to teachers, curricular objectives become selling points beneficial to corporations. In terms of all teaching and learning, children's views, abilities, natural curiosities, inclinations, and likes should be valued and designed into learning experiences. In LCD terms, that would be designing for growth, diversity, and motivation.

Reeves (1999) emphasizes "the interaction of learner and artifact as *a single cognitive unit*," (emphasis added) (Reeves, 1999, pp. 7-8). It is this latter focus on the unit of learner and artifact that differentiates the approach to participatory approaches. Participatory approaches explicate the role of environment, context, and /or workspace with an emphasis on collaboration. LCD acknowledges the role, but focuses on the cognitive strategies and modes of thinking people draw on during an interaction. It is more based upon intrinsic factors and the inner working of the mind in conjunction with a learning tool. Its greatest contribution is in enhancing our conceptions and practices in scaffolding, and adding engaging, motivational elements to multimedia design, although it is somewhat limited in its consideration of how technology is received into the social fabric of a context (Norman & Spohrer, 1996).

Activity Theory: A Framework for Conceptualizing Educational Multimedia

Amidst the breadth and depth of cognitive theorizing on the human-computer dyad lays the previously underexplored contextual influence of the social environment (Kuutti, 1996). Activity theory (AT) is an analytic theoretical framework for viewing HCI. It offers a way of visualizing the end user (child learner) within a holistic picture of the sociocultural system in which the child interacts with technology. A system that is inclusive of the child, cultural tools like computers and language, and the context of use; where social communities, rules, and norms play a part.

Activity theory stems from the cultural-historical school of psychology based on principles of human development sketched by Vygotsky, Leont'ev, and El'konin (Brostrom, 1999). Vygotsky outlined young children's mental development in evidence arising from their play activity (Vygotsky, 1978). One of Vygostsky's key contributions to developmental theory was the notion of the *zone of proximal development*. Human learning inhabits a *zone of proximal development* where people can achieve greater growth with guidance or assistance than on their own. In Vygotsky's own words, it is "the distance between the actual developmental level as determined by independent problem solving and the level of potential development as determined through problem-solving under adult guidance or in collaboration with more capable peers" (Vygotsky, 1978, p. 86). This is because of the socially mediated nature of learning. Internalization is a social process; people learn by doing.

Leont'ev (1978, 1981) grounded activity theory's principles on this earlier work of Vygostky. According to AT, learning can be analyzed in an activity system. Activity itself is the unit of analysis whereby the use of cultural tools (computers, books, language, etc.) shapes human thought, development, and behavior. Humans, in turn, shape cultural tools.

For example, children in this case study were observed in a lesson where they learned how to use a programmable floor turtle. Their goal was to build a maze, out of plastic and wooden bricks, ending in a towering wall. Their challenge was to program the turtle to maneuver through the maze and crash the tower of bricks at the end. To succeed, the children needed to understand ninety-degree angles, along with the operation of which arrow buttons to press to get the turtle to move in the right direction and to a specified distance.

The lesson progressed from a discussion of the kinds of words we use when we give instructions. Children chimed in with, "bossy," and explained how it is important *not* to ask a question like "Would you please do this?" but instead to say in a strong voice "Do this!" The class discussed how to "talk to" or program machines (all kinds of machines, like washing machines, microwaves, etc.). The children agreed that machines needed clear instructions. The teacher led a demonstration of the programmable floor turtle to the group. A student illustrated a right angle with his arm outstretched perpendicular to his body. He then turned four ninety-degree angle turns. The physical use of his body led to a conceptual tool the children put to use in meeting their overall challenge.

Within an activity system, there is: a subject (an individual), and an object (the motivating goal). There are also cultural tools that make activity possible, and social norms and values that govern (or at least influence) the relations within the system (Kaptelinin, 1996). Figure 6 shows this activity system through the case-study example listed.

There is a hierarchy in human activity that is tied to motivation. For instance, the children in this case study were motivated by first- and third-person problem-solving games guided by a narrative and intertextuality. Perhaps it is the likeness of these elements of multimedia play to elements of young children's motivation arising in their natural, spontaneous play. Young children develop through role-playing familiar, everyday scripts. For them, play is motivated not by a concrete outcome,

Figure 6. An activity system: Seven-year-olds programming a floor turtle

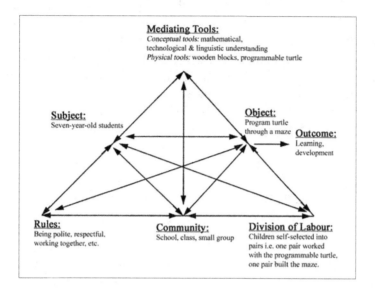

but in the emotions and meanings realized through the process of play itself (Hak-karainen, 1999; Leont'ev, 1981). "The motivating object is symbolic exchange relations between people" (Hakkarainen, 1999, p. 248). As they grow, they can step into invented scripts governed by external rules, as in a narrative game. They are taking on new developmental challenges whilst acting in a familiar sphere. Intertextuality provides another connection of the script to the child's social world. The narrative is woven into the social fabric of the child's world, and is connected to his/her experiences in a range of social settings.

Some evidence does show that certain strategies motivate children in a digital environment. Supplemental (content and context relevant) cuing animations and sound effects have been shown to enhance user comprehension, whereas incidental (irrelevant, off-topic) animations can interfere with comprehension (Labbo & Kuhn, 2000). In one instance of this case study, children's verbal and gestural exchanges centered around sharing invented stories of pictures found on the Internet. They were motivated by this playful social interaction. Elements of social human interaction, like praise, enhance learners' positivity and perception of learner control (Reeves & Nass, 1996). Choice of interaction style, such as point-and-click or drag-and-drop, impacts motivation (Inkpen, 2001). The keyboard enables another style of interaction. It may have motivating or demotivating effects for children. Sara commented on how it was difficult to steer through her favorite game using arrows on the keyboard. Children in other studies have played rhythmically with the sounds produced by their typing. This is an area that lends itself to further investigation, but provides certain pieces of motivational findings upon which designs can be built.

The activity theory model has its roots far deeper than is possible here to delve. But when activity becomes the unit of analysis in designing educational multimedia, it is possible to design for "use" mediated by people, cultural tools, and embedded value systems. Participatory design models can gather data that address AT's theoretical framework.

Models of Participatory Design with Children

Pioneer of *cooperative inquiry*, Allison Druin, shaped the practice of designing technology *with* children. Since its inception over a decade ago, the practice has grown and received substantial attention in the field of HCI such that variant methods and numerous studies have been conducted on the basis of its principles. Its roots can be traced along the timeline in Figure 4, with theoretical influences from Scandinavian contextual inquiry to today's model of cooperative inquiry (Druin, 1999a). The case study reported here is just one example. Others variations on Druin's original technique include, among others, curriculum-focused design and informant-based design (Rode, Stringer, Toye, Siimpson, & Blackwell, 2003; Scaife & Rogers, 1999).

Cooperative Inquiry

Cooperative inquiry (Druin, 1999a, 1999b; Druin, Bederson, Boltman, Miura, Knotts-Callahan, & Platt, 1999) places children in the role of designer amongst an intergenerational team of professionals. It is a democratic approach that gives voice to the child. Envisioned and practiced by Druin, it is typically constituted through a team of people working with a group of children. It is composed of three techniques. The first, *contextual inquiry,* is participatory observation of children, in their natural context, working with technology. In the second technique, *technology immersion*, children opt into weeklong technology-intensive sessions, much like a summer camp. It concludes with *participatory design,* in which children collaborate with a design team and use low-tech modeling, arts-and-crafts materials like crayons, yarn, and clay, to articulate and prototype their technology needs and wants.

The success of cooperative inquiry can be seen through the Kidpad and Pad++ software (among others) born from the approach (Druin et al., 1999). These were originally conceived as storytelling technologies. The methodology and approach has been both emulated and modified in this pilot study. This pilot study's original research aim was to identify what children find engaging about educational multimedia they use in schools, and how their sociocultural experiences of communications technologies influenced their writing. Child-centered design was used in this case study as a way to access children's underlying knowledge about communications technology, and identify what children like, want, and what they find engaging in technology. Children and adults see things differently. Child-centered design can make a contribution to what designers, technologists, and educators regard as "quality" educational multimedia through making explicit that which children regard as quality. The decision to include cooperative inquiry as part of the pilot study methodology emerged from the nature of the research aim (Cohen, Morrison, & Manion, 2004; Yin, 2003). Contextual inquiry and participatory design sessions were used, while technology immersion did not fit this particular research aim or context. The norm is for design *teams* to carry out the inquiry. Here the method was adapted and tested for its usefulness with a sole researcher. Some of Druin's contextual inquiry techniques were not possible to carry out as a single researcher in the classroom.

Druin recommends that more than one adult should always be on a team, otherwise it becomes "school-like." The classroom was the context of the study, and had the reverse effect on the children. It became less school-like because they were free to create as and how they wished (albeit within the parameters of the activity). Working in such an open-ended, exploratory way is something students do not often get a chance to spend three hours on, during a typical school day. Despite claims that when carried out in the classroom, creative freedom is constrained, my experience was the opposite (Cooper & Brna, 2004; Rode et al., 2003). Instead of viewing the classroom as a constraint on creativity, the research was a creative opportunity. In addition to concerns over creativity, there is the practical issue of logging the large amounts of simultaneous data being generated. I was both interactor and notetaker. Ten years ago, Druin's team found video cameras a hindrance. To fulfill these competing demands, I used the video setting on a small digital camera that did not disrupt children at work with flashes. Although sometimes muffled by the cacophony of the large group, the camera captured the sound and the interaction. Reflective listening in my conversations with children meant that I could reify their statements and ensure the sound recording was audible. The drawback of the camera was that it could only capture 3-minute video clips, so timing was an important issue that had to be remembered. Adult-adult interaction was made possible by the presence of the teacher, the teaching assistant, and myself, but it was of a different nature because of our different roles.

Figure 7. Storytelling machine

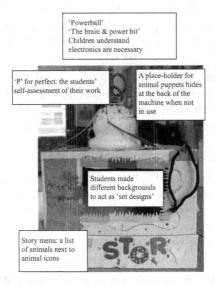

The model-building activity revealed children's technical understanding and imagination. Children wanted their machines to have characteristics of animals, in shape, functionality, and content (in the mix of materials were animal stickers that likely contributed to this). Some of their ideas were to make it look like a "sitting-up cat" or "half of a cat and half of another animal." They referred to machines with pet names. Another strong theme was that of designing affect into technology. For example, some children wanted stories to be read to them that made them feel sleepy and put them to sleep. Another group designed a sensor so that the storytelling machine could tell what kind of a mood you were in, to know which story to read. *Child:* "It can tell what kind of a story to read you because it can tell if you're happy or sad." One of the "machines" was actually functional in that the group used a "perceived affordance" to dub the user (Norman, 2004). *Child:* "This bit pretends that it can see the story. It's *pretending* to be a really good machine, but you put it (a book) through the mouth and a person runs 'round the back and reads it." Figure 7 shows the storytelling machine that children in this case study designed.

Curriculum-Focused Design

Rode et al. (2003) faced difficulties in porting Druin's out-of-school model directly into the classroom. Their aim was to develop tangible, user interfaces for collaborative use in schools equipped with radio-frequency ID tags. As a result, their work was situated within the English and Citizenship National Curriculum subjects, focusing on argument education to allow for curricular and classroom constraints and their revised methodology, called curriculum-focused design. They used a range of prototypes from "no-tech," such as *Web* page print outs, to "low-tech," for example, cardboard boxes, paper, and markers, to "high-tech," where RF-ID tag technologies were added.

Although very much akin to my case study design, Rode et al.'s (2003) main findings differed in the considerable hurdles they faced within the school context. The class teacher I worked with fit the research sessions into her planning to align with the objectives she was teaching. The teacher was comfortable and enthusiastic about low-tech prototyping, in contrast to Rode et al.'s experiences. This methodology fit well with her refreshingly interdisciplinary approach. The differences in our findings exemplify the variability in school contexts and pedagogical approaches where multimedia has a home. They also highlight the helpful and necessary role teachers play in school-based participatory design sessions. It furthermore highlights the different kinds of contributions made by members of a design team.

Informant-Based Design

The informant design framework, instead of relying on children in the main to drive the momentum and direction of a technology, emphasizes team members' roles in technology development for children (Scaife & Rogers, 1999). The Canadian Broadcasting Corporation's CBC4Kids' Storybuilder is a case in point. Five practices were used to evolve the *Web*-based environment for 8-10 year-olds to collaboratively tell their Canadian stories (Antle, 2003). User-centered and informant-based design were among these (Scaife & Rogers, 1999). Using the fundamental principle of informant-based design, the developers identified key points at which children's contributions would be the most valuable. So, amidst the team's work of examining "existing storytelling activities, creativity tools and storytelling styles," children were consulted at the early concept stage for a period of 12 weeks (Antle, 2003, p. 59). Their involvement was continued as usability testers at the prototype and beta phases (Antle, 2003).

Conclusion

Children's ideas about designs reported in this pilot case study point to a more holistic notion of interactivity that involves, in addition to sight and sound, sensitivity and responsiveness to human emotion, mood, and the sense of smell, as well as direct manipulation designed to raise affect in the user. They consistently ascribed social qualities to communicational technologies. Programmable toys, tangible technologies, and robots can all be seen to align with their ideas of engaging technological tools, and the compass point to future research directions.

The building of a theoretical knowledge base to guide design has led to user involvement in the whole design life cycle. Taking up a broad model in visualizing design can help to capture the intricacies of socially mediated factors at work. Communicative practices are one strand of these factors: the cultural tools involved in reading and writing, the symbolic communication that takes place through the medium of the screen, the affordances of multimedia and, more generally, the digital environment. It is hoped that overarching developmental guidelines provide an understanding of use and that these, in turn, can provide insight in the highly creative practice of design.

References

Antle, A. (2003). *Case study: The design of CBC4kids' storybuilder.* Paper presented at the Proceedings of the 2003 Interaction Design and Children, Preston, UK.

Ardito, C., De Marsico, M., Lanzilotti, R., Levialdi, S., Roselli, T., Rossano, V., et al. (2004, May 25-28). *Usability of e-learning tools.* Paper presented at the AVI, Gallipoli, Italy.

Arizpe, E., & Styles, M. (Eds.). (2003). Visual literacy: Processes, frameworks and models. In *Children reading pictures: Interpreting visual texts.* London: Routeledge Falmer.

Atherton, T. (2002). Developing ideas with multimedia. In A. Loveless & B. Dore (Eds.), *ICT in the primary school.* Buckingham: Open University Press.

Barrs, M., & Cork, V. (2001). *The reader in the writer.* London: CLPE.

Bearne, E. (2003a). Playing with possibilities: Children's multidimensional texts. In E. Bearne, H. Dombey, & T. Grainger (Eds.), *Classroom interactions in literacy.* Maidenhead: Open University Press.

Bearne, E. (2003b). Ways of knowing; ways of showing - Towards an integrated theory of text. In M. Styles & E. Bearne (Eds.), *Art, narrative and childhood.* Stoke on Trent, UK: Trentham Books.

Brostrom, S. (1999). Drama games with 6-year-old children: Possibilities and limitations. In Y. Engestrom, R. Miettinen, & R.-L. Punamaki (Eds.), *Perspectives on activity theory*. Cambridge: Cambridge University Press.

Brouwer-Janse, M., Fulton Suri, J., Yawitz, M., de Vries, G., Fozard, J., & Coleman, R. (1997). User interfaces for young and old. *Interactions, 4*(2), 34-46.

Burnett, R. (2002). Technology, learning and visual culture. In I. Synder (Ed.), *Silicon literacies: Communication, innovation and education in the electronic age*. London: Routledge.

Carrington, V. (2005). New textual landscapes: Information and early literacy. In J. Marsh (Ed.), *Popular culture, new media and digital literacy in early childhood* (pp. 14-27). Routledge.

Clay, M. (1975). *What did i write?* London: Heinemann Educational.

Cohen, L., Morrison, L., & Manion, K. (2004). *Research methods in education*. London: RouteledgeFalmer.

Cooper, B., & Brna, P. (2004). A classroom of the future today. In J. Siraj-Blatchford (Ed.), *Developing new technologies for young children*. Stoke on Trent, UK: Trentham Books.

Cope, B., & Kalantzis, M. (Eds.). (2000). *Multiliteracies: Literacy learning and the design of social futures*. London: RoutledgeFalmer.

Cuban, L. (2001). *Oversold and underused: Computers in the classroom*. London: Harvard University Press.

Druin, A. (1999a, May 15-20). *Cooperative inquiry: Developing new technologies for children with children.* Paper presented at the CHI'99, Pittsburgh, PA.

Druin, A. (Ed.). (1999b). *The design of children's technology*. San Francinsco: Morgan Kaufmann.

Druin, A., Bederson, B., Boltman, A., Miura, A., Knotts-Callahan, D., & Platt, M. (1999). Children as our technology design partners. In A. Druin (Ed.), *The design of children's technology*. San Francisco: Morgan Kauffman.

Green, T., & Brown, A. (2002). *Multimedia projects in the classroom: A guide to development and evaluation*. Thousand Oakes, CA: Corwin Press.

Hakkarainen, P. (1999). Play and motivation. In Y. Engestrom, R. Miettinen, & R.-L. Punamaki (Eds.), *Perspectives on activity theory*. Cambridge: Cambridge University Press.

Hall, N. (2000). Literacy, play and authentic experience. In K. A. Roskos & J. F. Christie (Eds.), *Play and literacy in early childhood: Research from multiple perspectives*. Mahwah, NJ: Lawrence Erlbaum Associates.

Hanna, L., Risden, K., Czerwinski, M., & Alexander, K. (1999). The role of usability research in designing children's computer products. In A. Druin (Ed.), *The design of children's technology*. San Francisco: Morgan Kauffman Publishers.

Inkpen, K. M. (2001). Drag-and-drop versus point-and-click mouse interaction styles for children. *ACM Transactions on Computer-Human Interaction, 8*(1), 1-33.

Jewitt, C. (2003). Re-thinking assessment: Multimodality, literacy and computer-mediated learning. In *Assessment in Education* (pp. 83-102). Carfax Publishing.

Kaptelinin, V. (1996). Activity theory: Implication for human-computer interaction. In B. Nardi (Ed.), *Context and consciousness: Activity theory and human-computer interaction*. Cambridge, MA: MIT Press.

Kress, G. (2003). Literacy in the new media age. 186.

Kress, G., & van Leeuwen, T. (1996). *Reading images: The grammar of visual design*. London: Routledge.

Kuutti, K. (1996). Activity theory as a potential framework for human-computer interaction research. In B. Nardi (Ed.), *Context and consciousness: Activity theory and human-computer interaction*. Cambridge, MA: MIT Press.

Kuutti, K. (1999). Activity theory, work, and systems design. In Y. Engestrom, R. Miettinen, & R.-L. Punamaki (Eds.), *Perspectives on activity theory*. Cambridge: Cambridge University Press.

Labbo, L, & Kuhn, M. (2000). Weaving chains of affect and cognition: A young child's understanding of CD-ROM talking books. *Journal of Literacy Research, 32*(2), 187-210.

Leont'ev, A. N. (1978). *Activity, consciousness, and personality*. Englewood Cliffs: Prentice Hall.

Leont'ev, A. N. (1981). *Problems of the development of the mind*. Moscow: Progress.

Lester, P. (1995). Digital literacy: Visual communication and computer images. *Computer Graphics, 29*(4), 25-27.

Mackey, M. (2003). Children reading and interpreting stories in print, film and computer games. In J. Evans (Ed.), *Literacy moves on: Popular culture, new technologies and critical literacy in the elementary classroom*. London: Routledge.

Marsh, J. (Ed.). (2005). *Popular culture, new media and digital literacy in early childhood*. Abingdon: RoutledgeFalmer.

Merchant, G. (2005). Barbie meets Bob the builder at the workstation: Learning to write on screen. In J. Marsh (Ed.), *Popular culture, new media, and digital literacy in early education*. Abigdon: RoutledgeFalmer.

Nardi, B. (Ed.). (1996). *Context and consciousness: Activity theory and human-computer interaction*. Cambridge, MA: The MIT Press.

NESTA Futurelab. (2005). I-curriculum: Policy and planning for digital literacies, *BETT*. London.

Norman, D. A. (1999). Affordance, conventions, and design. *Interactions, 6*(3), 38-43.

Norman, D. (2004). Affordance, conventions and design (part 2). Retrieved 7 July, 2005, from http://www.jnd.org/dn.mss/affordance_conventi.html

Norman, D., & Draper, S. (Eds.). (1986). *User-centered system design: New perspectives on human-computer interaction.* Hillside, NJ: Lawrence Erlbaum Associates.

Norman, D., & Spohrer, J. (1996). Learner-centered education. *Communications of the ACM, 39*(4), 24-27.

Pahl, K., & Rowsell, J. (2005). *Literacy and education: Understanding new literacy studies in the classroom.* London: Sage.

Papert, S. (1980). *Mindstorms: Children, computers and powerful ideas* (2nd ed.). New York: Basic Books.

Piaget, J. (1950). *The psychology of intelligence.* London: Routledge.

Reeves, B., & Nass, C. (1996). *The media equation: How people treat computers, television, and new media like real people and places.* Cambridge: Cambridge University Press.

Reeves, W. (1999). *Learner-centered design: A cognitive view of managing complexity in product, information, and environmental design.* Thousand Oaks, CA: Sage Publications.

Risden, K., Hanna, E., & Kanerva, A. (1997). *Dimensions of intrinsic motivation in children's favourite computer activities.* Meeting of the Society for Research in Child Development, Washington, DC.

Rode, J. A., Stringer, M., Toye, E., F., Simpson, A. R., & Blackwell, A. F. (2003, March 3). *Curriculum-focused design.* Paper presented at the Interactice Design and Children, Preston, UK.

Ruth, S. (1995). Visual literacy and the design of digital media. *Computer Graphics, 29*(4), 45-47.

Said, N. S. (2004). *An engaging multimedia design model.* Paper presented at the Proceeding of the 2004 conference on Interaction design and children: Building a community, Maryland.

Scaife, M., & Rogers, Y. (1999). Kids as informants: Telling us what we didn't know or confirming what we already knew? In A. Druin (Ed.), *The design of children's technology.* San Francisco: Morgan Kauffman.

Schneider, K. G. (1996). Children and information visualization technologies. *Interactions, 3*(5), 68-73.

Soloway, E., Jackson, S., Klein, J., Quintana, C., Reed, J., Spitulnik, J., et al. (1996, April 13-18a). *Learning theory in practice: Case studies of learner-centered design.* Paper presented at the CHI '96, Vancouver, BC Canada.

Soloway, E., & Pryor, A. (1996b). The next generation in human-computer interaction. *Communications of the ACM, 39*(4), 16-18.

Street, B. (1997). The implication of the new literacy studies for education. *English in Education, 31*(3), 45-59.

United Kingdom Literacy Association. (2004). *More than words: Multimodal texts in the classroom.* London: Qualifications and Curriculum Authority.

Vygotsky, L. S. (1978). *Mind in society: The development of higher psychological processes.* Cambridge, MA: Harvard University Press.

Yin, R. (2003). *Case study research.* London: Sage Publications.

Endnotes

[1]   Mackey (2003) further distinguishes between the concepts *engagement* and *immersion.*

[2]   For a fuller discussion, see Merchant (2005, p. 245).

[3]   Agalianos, A., Noss, R., & Whitty, G. (2001). Logo in mainstream schools: The struggle of the soul of an educational innovation. *British Journal of Sociology of Education, 22*(4), presents a historical case study of Logo, and how the implementation of the transformational learning theory espoused in *Mindstorms* (Papert, 1980) was socially shaped amidst the political context of its reception and use in schools in the 1970s. For a critical perspective on current educational technology see *Oversold and Underused* (Cuban, 2001) and Burnett (2002).

Chapter IV

Bonded Design:
A Methodology for Designing with Children

Andrew Large, McGill University, Canada

Valerie Nesset, McGill University, Canada

Jamshid Beheshti, McGill University, Canada

Leanne Bowler, McGill University, Canada

Abstract

This chapter presents a new methodology, called bonded design (BD), for design-ing information technologies. It is especially suited to work with children, where designers and children collaborate in an intergenerational team to develop a low-tech prototype, over a number of design sessions, using techniques such as group discussions, critical evaluation of existing technologies, brainstorming, and prototyping. BD is compared with other user-focused design methods, and its unique features identified. Two case studies are presented in which designers worked with elementary school students, within the BD framework, to design two Web portal prototypes intended for young students to find information for class projects. The successful evaluation (using focus groups and an operational study) of working portals developed from these prototypes validated BD as a means to design technologies for young students.

Introduction

It is hardly controversial to argue for user involvement in the technology design process: the issue rather is the extent of that involvement, and whether or not this is related to the kind of user. To be more specific, can young children play a meaningful role in design and if so, what should it be? A number of user-focused design methodologies have accommodated children in various ways and to various degrees in the design of technologies intended for use by children (Nesset & Large, 2004). In this chapter, a new such design methodology, bonded design, is explained and discussed in the context of two cases where it was used to design Web portals intended for elementary school students seeking information to support class projects. In the first case, the adult designers worked with a group of grade-six students (aged 11 to 12 years) from an elementary school, and in the second case with students (aged 8 to 9 years) from grade three of the same school. In both cases, the application of bonded design resulted in the development of two low-tech prototypes of Web portals, called *History Trek* (grade six) and *KidSearch Canada* (grade three). After discussing these two case studies, the chapter concludes by suggesting how bonded design might be applied to other user communities and other tasks.

User-Focused Design Methodologies

Bonded design did not emerge in a vacuum; various methodologies have been suggested to provide professional designers with input from their targeted user communities. The oldest and most conventional approach has been termed "user-centered design" (Nesset & Large, 2004; Scaife & Rogers, 1999; Scaife, Rogers, Aldrich, & Davies, 1997). It focuses upon the impact of technology on users; but traditionally, these users were only involved after the technology had been designed. In other contexts, user-centered design also has been understood by some authors to mean direct contact between users and designers throughout the design process (Rubin, 1994). Typically in user-centered design, users themselves have little or no control over the design process, meaning that they cannot initiate changes, but only reveal design shortcomings. From the designer's perspective, an advantage of user-centered design is that they can accomplish their work more quickly because they maintain control over the design process (Druin, 2002). Because users are not directly involved throughout the process, but only at the beginning and/or end, children can be involved quite easily, and in large numbers. For example, Druin (2002) cites a study conducted with 1,300 children, in 1991, at Vanderbilt University, where the children were watched and tested during the study, but did not themselves take part in the design process.

Contextual design calls for researchers to collect data from the users' own environments by observing them performing typical activities, but interaction between researchers and users is minimal. The intention is to reveal the details of, and motivations behind, people's work, and to use this as the basis for decision making (Beyer & Holtzblatt, 1999). The final phase in contextual design is to develop a low-tech prototype of the system for testing with users. The use in contextual design of such concrete techniques as low-tech paper prototypes and pictorial diagramming, as well as its emphasis on group (team) work, make it especially suitable for children.

Learner-centered design assumes that everyone is a learner, whether a professional or a student (Soloway, Guzdial, & Hay, 1994). It seeks to ensure that the design is adapted to the interests, knowledge, and styles of the learners who will use it: how will the learner learn by using it; how will it motivate a learner; how can it support different user approaches; and how will it accommodate learners as they change?

The premise behind participatory design is that users are the best qualified to determine how to improve their work, and that their perceptions about technology are as important as technical specifications (Carmel, Whitaker, & George, 1993). As Fleming notes: "Through this approach, users move out of roles such as observer, approver, 'knowledge repository'… and into roles such as peer co-designer, design owner, expertise contributor, and self-advocate" (Fleming. In Bilal, 2002, p. 208). According to Carmel et al. (1993), there are two governing themes for the implementation of participatory design principles: in *mutual reciprocal learning,* users and designers teach each other about work practices and technical possibilities through joint experiences; in *design by doing,* interactive experimentation, modeling and testing, hands-on designing, and learning by doing are employed. Although participatory design is suitable for design projects involving children, where their school or home can substitute for the adult workplace, any reluctance to involve children as active participants may lie in the disinclination of some professional designers to accept the notion that users, especially when children, are able to contribute to the process as true design partners (see, i.e., Muller & Kuhn, 1993).

Informant design was introduced specifically to address some of the perceived problems with user-centered and participatory design techniques when working with children. In conventional user-centered design, where users are involved only as evaluators or testers at the end of the design process, their feedback is based on reaction rather than initiation. Furthermore, it is the designers who translate and interpret the users' reactions, and this can sometimes be inaccurate (Scaife et al., 1997). The perceived problem with participatory design is its promotion of equality for all team members. Scaife and his colleagues considered this effective for a team of adult users who can view each other as peers, but infeasible when dealing with children who do not have the time, knowledge, or expertise to fully participate in the collaborative participatory design model (Scaife et al., 1997). In informant design, the designer tries to elicit suggestions from the children, and then lets them know if it is possible to incorporate them into the working design. Scaife and his colleagues considered informant design the best method "for the design of interactive software for nontypical users or those who cannot be equal partners (e.g., children)" (Scaife et al., 1997, p. 346). Its basic assumption is that in the design process, children are most helpful at suggesting ideas for the motivational and fun aspects of educational software.

Cooperative inquiry combines techniques from different design methodologies that have proven useful when working with children. Developed by Druin (1999) and her colleagues at the University of Maryland, it involves a multidisciplinary partnership with children, field research, and iterative low-tech and high-tech prototyping. Children are treated as full design partners alongside the adult designers on the intergenerational team. Professional designers and users (children) of the technology are partnered in intergenerational design teams, with the understanding that full participation of users requires training and active cooperation. The design team makes use of such contextual inquiry methods as brainstorming and interviewing, as well as working together in small groups, brainstorming about what is wrong with existing technologies, and developing low-tech prototypes (Druin, 2002). Druin first employed cooperative inquiry, in her work on KidPad, as a design approach that supports and encourages the creation, by children, of nonlinear stories (Druin, Stewart, Proft, Bederson, & Hollan, 1997). She created a team that was not only intergenerational but also, borrowing from the contextual design approach, interdisciplinary. Using cooperative inquiry, Druin and her colleagues have also designed the "International Children's Digital Library" (Druin, 2002; Druin, Bederson, Weeks, Farber, Grosjean, Guha, et al., 2003) and are working with young children (aged three to six years) on "The Classroom of the Future" (Guha, Druin, Chipman, Fails, Simms, & Farber, 2004).

Bonded Design

Essentially, bonded design assumes a team comprising designers and users. This team employs a variety of design techniques—a user needs' assessment, evaluating existing technologies, group discussion, brainstorming, prototyping (for example, drawings), and consensus building-to collaborate in producing a technology prototype. This is represented diagrammatically in Figure 1.

The intergenerational process used in bonded design can also be understood from another theoretical perspective, that of the zone of proximal development (ZPD), a sociocultural approach to knowledge development (Vygotsky, 1978). This theory argues that when an appropriate structure (or scaffolding, as Vygotsky calls it) is put in place, children are able to accomplish more complex tasks than if left to their own devices. In bonded design, the design techniques represent this scaffolding, which

Figure 1. Model of bonded design

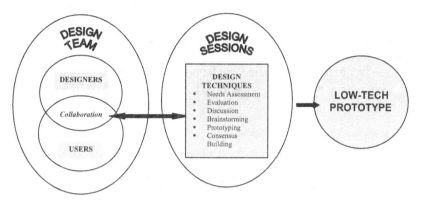

supports collaboration among team members. The relationship between bonded design and ZPD is discussed further in Bowler, Large, Beheshti, and Nesset (2005).

Design Team

In bonded design, the design team comprises two distinct groups: designers and users. It is assumed that the designers have a familiarity with the relevant techno-logical environment as well as the design process. For example, within the teams that developed the *History Trek* and *KidSearch Canada* Web portals, the designers were familiar with information retrieval, HCI principles, and the Web as an infor-mation resource. The other group within the design team, the users, were novices in terms of their technical knowledge, but nevertheless had a critical expertise to bring to the team: they were experts in childhood! The designers, of course, had once been children themselves, and furthermore, all had children of their own. Yet it is fallacious, if common, to believe that these two attributes allow adults to think like children and see the world through youthful eyes. If designers want to be con-fident that their product will meet the expectations and requirements of children, they better understand what these are, and the best way to do this, bonded design asserts, is to include children along with designers as collaborators throughout the design process.

If the design team is to work effectively and produce a low-tech prototype after a limited number of design sessions, it is important to restrict the size of the team. In bonded design, it is recommended that the team include between 6 and 10 members to facilitate consensus building while providing a variety of ideas. The *History Trek* team comprised 11 members—3 designers and 8 grade-six students (aged 11 to 12 years)—but the relatively large number of students was intended only to compensate for predicted absences through illness (the team met in the depths of a Montreal winter). A subsequent team that designed a low-tech Web portal prototype, called *KidSearch Canada,* only included nine members—three designers and six students from grade three (aged 8 to 9 years). The fact that the children within each team were similar in age facilitated collaboration and helped to speed up the design process (in contrast, for example, to Druin's cooperative inquiry teams, which often are a little bigger, and whose child members come from a wide range of ages).

Team Collaboration

Since collaboration is integral to the bonded design methodology, it is important to facilitate interaction among the team members. When working with children, this can present unique challenges that can be met in a number of ways: a casual environment where the team sits around one large table, name badges (first name only), and respect for and acceptance that each team member's (adult and child) contribution is worthy of consideration. In other words, the team should promote a collaborative environment rather than a traditional classroom setting with its teacher-student relationships. Even with these things in place, it cannot be assured that everyone will feel at ease in participating. It is the responsibility of the adults to ensure that the sessions are not dominated by one or two voices, and that the more reticent are at least encouraged to participate actively.

For bonded design to work most effectively, it is important, from the outset, to establish a collaborative team environment. An effective way to accomplish this is to involve everyone in the selection of a team name and logo. Once these have been chosen, they can be incorporated onto t-shirts to be worn by adults and children alike. This is an activity in which all can participate and indeed, on which all have an opinion.

Design Sessions

Bonded design assumes a limited number of design sessions in which the team works towards the completion of a low-tech prototype. When working with children, it is important that the duration of any session be limited so as to maintain their attention and avoid boredom. The sessions with the grade-six students extended for around 70 minutes, whereas those with the grade-three students, whose attention span was shorter, were only about 50 minutes.

Table 1. Timetable for History Trek *team sessions*

Session	Content
1	Introduction to project; project objectives; brainstorming on a team name; discussion of user questionnaire
2	Analysis of results of questionnaire survey; discussion of Web portal characteristics; pencil drawing by each team member of a Web portal screen
3	Discussion of drawings; identification of portal features; online critique of 8 Web portals (Alfy, Alta Vista, Ask Jeeves, Google, Fact Monster, KidsClick, Lycos Zone, Yahooligans!)
4	Review of progress; small group discussion of portal search options; whole group discussion of search options
5	Online information searches on 10 Web portals or digital libraries (Ask Jeeves, Google, Fact Monster, International Children's Digital Library, Internet Public Library Kidspace, KidsClick, PubMed, RefDesk, Web Brain, Yahoo) to review their search options; evaluation of these options
6	Discussion of e-mail & chat facilities; color drawings of a conventional portal
7	Discussion of help facilities; online critique of help facilities on 8 Web portals/digital libraries (Ask Jeeves, Google, Internet Public Library Kids Zone, KidsClick, Lycos Zone, MSN, Yahoo, Yahooligans!)
8	Screen layout design for conventional portal; discussion and online viewing of 3-D portals; color drawings of 3-D portals
9	Consensus building on design layout for one team conventional portal
10	Critique of HTML mock-up of conventional portal
11	Critique of version 1 of Photoshop conventional portal prototype; brainstorming on 3-D portal
12	Final review of conventional portal prototype; presentation by students of prototype to class teacher; completion of team questionnaire
13	Discussion of G3 team portal; discussion of 3-D portals

The sessions should follow a reasonably detailed schedule in which specific objectives are established for each session. When working with children, the adult designers retain a measure of flexibility to account for unforeseen circumstances, but nevertheless, it is critical that they set the agenda for the sessions ahead of time. In the design of *History Trek,* 13 sessions were undertaken; for *KidSearch Canada,* just 9 were sufficient (in both cases, normally held twice weekly). From a questionnaire-based survey of the students conducted at the end of the entire design process, a majority of students in both grades thought that the number of sessions had been just right, although a minority would have enjoyed additional sessions. The plan for the *History Trek* sessions is shown in Table 1, and is based upon a design matrix formulated by Large, Beheshti, and Cole (2002). To reinforce this plan and to focus the team, at the beginning of each session, the planned objectives were outlined on a white board, together with the objectives already met in earlier sessions.

Needs Assessment

Any design is intended, ultimately, to be used. An important preliminary step in the design process is to ascertain the needs that the design is intended to meet for any given user community. A needs assessment, where potential users are polled to elicit how and why they might employ the completed product, is an effective tool to achieve this objective. This holds true even when the users happen to be children. One way to undertake a needs assessment is to survey a user sample by questionnaire. This is exactly what the *History Trek* design team did immediately after the first session: the adult designers had developed a brief questionnaire focusing upon Internet usage, and the student team members were assigned the task of administering this questionnaire to their peers within the school. The analysis of the completed questionnaire responses provided a context for decision making throughout the design process. For example, the fact that respondents wanted to find information on the Internet as quickly as possible was taken into account in team discussions on the incorporation of portal features such as animation and/or games that may extend any online portal session.

A similar needs assessment was not undertaken by the *KidSearch Canada* team because at that time the researchers thought a questionnaire survey too challenging for the younger grade-three team members to administer, and their grade-three colleagues in the school to answer. In hindsight, and especially with the further experience gained from working alongside such students, their capabilities might have been underestimated, so long as the questionnaire itself was kept short and simple.

Evaluation

Evaluating any working examples of the intended product is a critical aspect throughout the design process. This evaluation may draw upon team members' prior knowledge of the product, or upon examination of examples within the design sessions. Any evaluation should be critical, and team members should be encouraged to identify strengths and weaknesses that can, in turn, inform their own preliminary designs. Furthermore, it is useful to focus such evaluations on specific components. For example, in the seventh *History Trek* session, the focus, when viewing, discussing, and evaluating various Web portals, was upon their help features. During the sessions for both teams, examples of existing Web portals were extensively examined and critiqued to identify both useful and useless design features.

Group Discussion

A free exchange of ideas lies at the essence of bonded design, but this is also where the interaction between designers and users can pose the greatest challenge. The designers must be willing to accept the ideas put forward by the users, even if they have reservations about their efficacy and feasibility of implementation. In the same vein, the users should be willing to draw upon the expertise that the designers inevitably bring to the task. At the heart of bonded design lies the belief that the users have things to tell the designers that the latter cannot grasp themselves. Equally, bonded design is posited on the fact that the users, by themselves, do not have the necessary knowledge to design independently. It is the very bonding of ideas from these two groups that constitutes the strength of this design methodology. In the case of *History Trek,* the designers would never have included six different retrieval devices, which the students advocated (and whose views were validated ultimately in the subsequent user evaluations of an operational version of the portal). Conversely, the students would have preferred an intelligent portal that directly responded to their questions without any further user interaction, but accepted the designers' advice that, in practice, such a capability could not be realized.

Brainstorming

Brainstorming is an activity that promotes creativity by encouraging all team members to contribute ideas on a topic. At this stage, all ideas are accepted as having merit, and are documented for later discussion. These ideas, however, are not always expressed verbally. For example, the students in both the *History Trek* and *KidSearch Canada* teams often expressed their ideas through drawing. Figure 2 shows a preliminary drawing from a member of the *History Trek* team in which various ideas are expressed, such as "Rate our Web site," a current events area, and a book rating and reviewing section.

Prototyping

Prototyping is a technique shared by many design methodologies (Beyer & Holtzblatt, 1999; Carmel et al., 1993; Druin, 1999, 2002; Scaife et al., 1997). It forms the bridge between discussion and brainstorming, on the one hand, and the completed prototype design. It can take various forms, but the most popular in participatory design methodologies is that of low-tech prototyping, where participants use paper,

Figure 2. Brainstorming drawing, History Trek *design team (Copyright © 2006 by McGill University. Used with permission)*

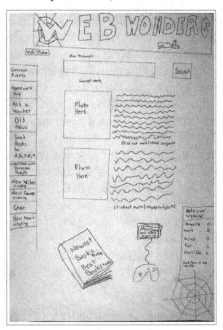

modeling clay, and other such materials to represent design ideas. In bonded design, prototyping is used iteratively throughout the sessions in order to produce a final low-tech prototype. Bonded design is particularly appropriate when working with children because they enjoy these types of prototyping activities, and very successfully accomplish them. Furthermore, children often can express their ideas more cogently through such activities, rather than attempting textual descriptions (Arizpe & Styles, 2003; Glynn, 1997).

In both the *History Trek* and the *KidSearch Canada* design teams, the preferred prototyping technique was to draw Web portal mock-ups on large sheets of paper. Initially, the team members sketched their own concepts of a Web portal before moving on to drawings that represented their ideas on specific components within a Web portal interface. A downside of drawing as a prototyping activity is that it can absorb the children's attention for long periods of time within a session. This tendency is especially prevalent when the children are encouraged to produce colored drawings rather than pencil sketches. Figures 3 and 4 show examples taken from the initial prototyping session of *History Trek:* the first drawing was contributed by an adult team member, and the second by a grade-six student member. Figure 5 is a similar example, but this time from a grade-three student in the *KidSearch Canada* team. These drawings represent early attempts at representing ideas for a complete portal interface.

Figure 3. Portal prototype drawing, adult, History Trek Team (Copyright © 2006 by McGill University. Used with permission.)

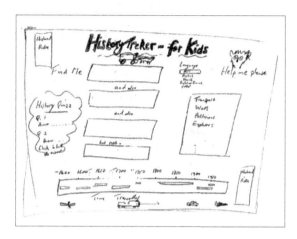

Figure 4. Portal prototype drawing, grade-six student, History Trek Team (Copyright © 2006 by McGill University. Used with permission.)

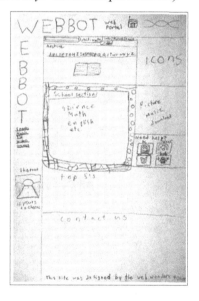

In these early prototype drawings can be identified features that found their way into the completed, low-tech prototypes, as well as ideas that never made it. For example, the adult drawing (Figure 3) introduced the idea of information retrieval through a scrollable timeline, where an event can be found by its date. All three drawings also incorporated an alphabetical search that appeared in both the completed prototypes.

At the same time, other early ideas were rejected as the portal design slowly developed; for example, *History Trek* did not incorporate a music downloading capability (Figure 4), and *KidSearch Canada* opted for a quite different design metaphor than the teddy bear greeting users with open arms (Figure 5).

As the design sessions progressed, the team members worked on the design of specific components within the portal interface, as outlined in Table 1 (Design sessions). Figures 6 and 7 show, respectively, a drawing of a hit display screen from a *History Trek* grade-six student, and two retrieval devices—a keyword search box and an alphabetical search within the design metaphor of a computer monitor and keyboard—by a grade-three student working on *KidSearch Canada*. These features in the two drawings, undertaken at a relatively advanced stage in the sessions, can be identified, albeit in modified form, in the completed portal prototypes.

Figure 5. Portal prototype drawing, grade-three student, KidSearch Canada Team (Copyright © 2006 by McGill University. Used with permission)

Figure 6. Results display, grade-six student, History Trek team (Copyright © 2006 by McGill University. Used with permission)

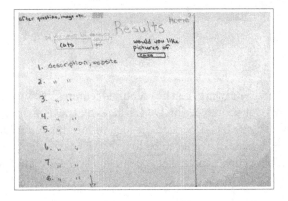

Figure 7. Retrieval devices, grade-three student, KidSearch Canada team (Copyright © 2006 by McGill University. Used with permission)

Consensus Building

In any team environment where individuals are required to work together to reach a common goal, consensus building must take place. In the early stages of bonded design, team members are encouraged to think independently, and to formulate and express their own design ideas. Brainstorming is an effective way to generate a rich pool of ideas, but at some point, these disparate ideas must coalesce into a unified design as a prelude to the completion of the low-tech prototype. Building such a consensus can be especially challenging when children are involved, as they tend to an egocentric view of the world; a willingness to embrace alternative viewpoints comes only with maturity (Piaget & Inhelder, 1969).

Before brainstorming begins, it is important to establish evaluation criteria. One way to achieve this is through an initial user needs assessment, as it can identify design objectives and serve as a valuable basis on which to construct consensus. After brainstorming, when trying to reach consensus, the team has to find which options best match the evaluation criteria. By matching options to predetermined evaluation criteria, there is less chance that the opinions of one or two people will dominate. Another method is to remind team members of the agenda set for the planned sessions, and to keep track of progress so that they know they are involved in an ongoing building process. An effective way to achieve this is to visually map tasks to be accomplished with tasks already completed at the outset of each session.

In both the *History Trek* and *KidSearch Canada* teams, attempts to build a consensus proved to be the most difficult stage in the entire design process. As difficult as it was, consensus was reached more rapidly on important issues (and especially concerning the retrieval aspects of the portal) than in areas of minor importance

Figure 8. Buttons in grade-three student design, KidSearch Canada team (Copyright © 2006 by McGill University. Used with permission)

such as the selection of a name for the team or choosing the color of the team's t-shirt—decisions that, in fact, had nothing to do *per se* with the portals' design, but which were taken very seriously by the child team members. Of course, for these seemingly small decisions, no criteria had been established by techniques such as a user needs assessment or agenda development. Opinions on screen layout and color were more varied, but again consensus was reached, probably helped by the decision to incorporate personalization into the portal that would allow users to select, for example, different color combinations (although in the operational portals this particular personalization option was not included).

Consensus building was more challenging with the younger students in the *KidSearch Canada* team than with their older counterparts in the *History Trek* team. The grade-three students demonstrated a strong sense of ownership over their own individual ideas, and wanted to see them realized in the finished portal. They would be satisfied, however, so long as some aspect of their own design concepts had been incorporated into the emerging group design. For example, one student complained that his drawing had not been utilized in the team portal, but was totally reassured when it was pointed out that two buttons (Back and Forward) present in one of his drawings (on the right-hand side of Figure 8) were to be incorporated into the portal low-tech prototype.

The Low-Tech Prototype

The final step in the bonded design process is the development of a low-tech prototype. By this term is meant a design that is completed but nonoperational. For

Figure 9. HTML mock-up of History Trek (Copyright © 2006 by McGill University. Used with permission)

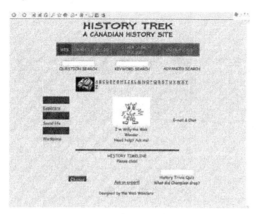

Figure 10. History Trek low-tech prototype (Version 1.0) (Copyright © 2006 by McGill University. Used with permission)

example, both the *History Trek* and *KidSearch Canada* teams were able, successfully, to produce Web portal designs that subsequently have been converted into working, high-tech prototypes. Once the two teams had reached consensus on a design, this was reflected in a rough mock-up developed for each team by an adult team member. The *History Trek* mock-up was done using HTML, and the *KidSearch Canada* mock-up was hand drawn. After team discussion and some design modification, the mock-ups were converted by a professional artist into on-screen representations that, in turn, were critiqued by the teams before the final versions of the low-tech prototypes were accepted. Each mock-up, along with its final low-tech prototype, is shown in Figures 9 to 12. The actual features included in the two low-tech prototypes are discussed in Large, Beheshti, Nesset and Bowler (2004).

Figure 11. Mock-up drawing, KidSearch Canada (Copyright © 2006 by McGill University. Used with permission)

Figure 12. KidSearch Canada low-tech prototype (Version 1.0) (Copyright © 2006 by McGill University. Used with permission)

It is interesting to observe that even at a late stage in the *History Trek* sessions, design modifications were still taking place as a result of discussion and consensus building. Although the HTML mock-up in Figure 9 has resemblances to the low-tech prototype (Figure 10), the design clearly continued to evolve through the two more iterations before arriving at its final state. In contrast, the mock-up drawing of *KidSearch Canada* shown in Figure 11 is very similar to the final low-tech prototype shown in Figure 12, although more detail was still to be added and the bookshelves, for example, redesigned.

Bonded Design from the Child Designer's Perspective

At the end of the design sessions for both teams, the student members were asked to complete a short questionnaire about their experience. Although the researchers had certainly gained the impression that their young collaborators enjoyed the experience, it was important to verify (or refute) this assertion. All seven (of the eight) students from the *History Trek* team who answered the questionnaire said they would recommend their friends to volunteer for a similar team. Overall, they enjoyed their experience and learned from it. From the sessions, they liked best of all drawing portal mock-ups; when asked what they enjoyed least, three answered "nothing," and two said looking at existing portals on the Web. What did they learn from their experience? The following quotes are representative of the general feedback from the student team members about their experiences.

- *[It] takes a lot of people to build a Web portal*
- *It isn't as easy as it seems to make a Web portal*
- *It's hard to design a Web portal and try to agree on everything*
- *It's rewarding to see the final outcome*
- *I had a lot of fun and I learned a lot of new things*

What about the younger students in the *KidSearch Canada* team? They said they liked just about everything they did: learning more about Web portals, looking at Web portals on the computer, drawing design ideas, and talking about ideas. To quote from their responses, they learned "that computers are cool," "how to design in a team," and "to be a good friended (sic)," the last comment gratifyingly from the student who had found socialization within the team difficult.

Bonded Design as a User-Focused Design Method

Bonded design is a means of bringing together, for design purposes, a team that unites in diversity. Adult design experts collaborate with child users who are experts in being children. As such, it draws upon facets of the other user-focused design methods outlined at the beginning of this chapter. From conventional user-centered design it takes the most basic premise, involving users. From contextual design were borrowed the ideas of drawing paper prototypes, and a similar process to what it terms *work redesign* in the use of a white board to set out a map at the beginning of each session for what had already been accomplished and what remained to be done. Participatory design provided the concept of peer co-designers, drawings (low-tech prototyping), hands-on activities, and "learning by doing." Informant design supported the approach of seeking new and creative ideas rather than merely confirming what the adults already knew. Bonded design also shares aspects of learner-centered design in that it provides a learning environment for all team members, children and adults alike. In designing Web portals for children, as in learner-centered design, all team members were learners, and the team's objective was to ensure that the design was adapted to the interests, knowledge, and styles of its target users.

Bonded design, above all, shares many characteristics with cooperative inquiry. It emphasizes an intergenerational partnership in working towards a common goal, and embraces the idea that children should play an active role in design from start to finish, rather than merely being evaluators or testers at the end of the design process. It does question, however, the nature of the cooperation between adults and children within the team. In this respect, it shares some of informant design's reservations concerning the extent to which true equality can exist within an intergenerational team (Scaife et al., 1997). At the same time, bonded design differs importantly from informant design in its inclusion of children throughout the design process and as full team members, rejecting the opinion that children are most helpful at suggesting ideas only for motivational and fun aspects.

Essentially, then, bonded design is situated between cooperative inquiry and informant design. It shares the former's belief in the ability of children to work as partners in all aspects of the design process, but has reservations about the extent to which full and equal cooperation can occur across the generational divide, and in these respects, therefore, has similarities with the latter. The relationship in terms of user involvement throughout the design process between bonded design and other related design methodologies is graphically represented in Figure 13.

Figure 13. User involvement continuum

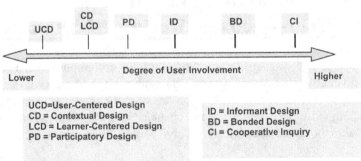

*Figure 14. Results display screen, KidSearch Canada (Version 3.1) (Copyright ©
2006 by McGill University. Used with permission)*

Bonded Design as a Design Technique

Bonded design arose from the authors' intention to design Web portals that would
appeal to children, as well as providing them with an effective tool for information
retrieval. A previous study (Large, Beheshti, & Rahman, 2002) had shown that children
around the age of 12 years like the idea of a portal especially designed for their user
community, but were critical of several children's Web portals then available. This
study, as well as others (Bilal, 2000, 2001, 2002; Large & Beheshti, 2000; Large
et al., 2004), also strongly indicated that, in general, children were not using such
children's portals. Bonded design was employed with two intergenerational teams
to design two Web portals, *History Trek* and *KidSearch Canada,* that could be used
by elementary school students to find information for class projects. The hope was
that by involving children closely in the design, portals would emerge that really
met the user community's needs and would, therefore, be utilized by them.

At the end of the design sessions, both the low-tech prototypes were converted into
working, high-tech portal prototypes. The programming language used was PHP,
the database software was MySQL Standard 4.0 for Windows, and the development
software was Macromedia Dreamweaver MX.

The two high-tech portals currently are operational (but password protected and
therefore not available to the general Web user). During the process of implementing
the high-tech portals, small modifications were made to the low-tech prototypes that
emerged from the two intergenerational design teams. In some cases, the modifications were a result of problems in realizing design features due to technical or time

limitations. For example, the e-mail and chat features envisaged by the designers of *History Trek* were not implemented in the working portal. In other cases, modifications were made after preliminary testing by small numbers of grade-six and grade-three students during the building process. For example, both the unlabelled keyword and alphabetical search features on *KidSearch Canada* were labeled (respectively "Put in your search words" and "Search by letter") to clarify their purpose. The *History Trek* design team had worked on other screens than the search screen shown in Figure 10, and such screens were developed for both completed portals (including results display screens and help screens). An example of a results display screen is shown in Figure 14. In order to provide keyword, question, topic, alphabetic, and timeline retrieval features, many additional screens are incorporated in the working portals alongside limited personalization features (on *History Trek,* four versions of the mascot, Willy, are available, and on *KidSearch Canada,* a choice of screensaver is available on the displayed computer screen). The portals also incorporated features such as spell checking and synonym control, requested by the design teams, to simplify their use by young students. Reflecting their design in Montreal, Quebec, the teams wanted the portal interfaces to be available in French as well as English versions, and this has been provided in the working portals.

The high-tech prototypes have been evaluated by children in three elementary schools. Two methods were used for this evaluation: focus groups (Large, Beheshti, Nesset, & Bowler, 2005), and operational classroom use. In each case, the portals searched a database of links to almost 2,500 Web sites on Canadian history, in either English or French, that were appropriate in subject content and literary style for elementary school students (Bowler, Nesset, Large, & Beheshti, 2004). Twelve focus groups, each comprising four students from either grade three or grade six, used the portals to find answers to four questions and in so doing, expressed their opinions on the portals: their first impressions, their likes and dislikes, their suggestions for improvements, and comparisons with existing "adult" portals on the Web. Both portals also were used over several weeks by two classes of grade-three and grade-six students to find information for a class project on Aboriginal Peoples in Canada; the students were observed when using the portals in the school's computer lab, and were interviewed individually at the end of the project.

The evaluations demonstrate that it is worthwhile to employ the bonded design approach when designing Web portals for children: both *History Trek* and *KidSearch Canada* were popular with their young users and overall, were effective tools for them to use when seeking information on the Web. The portals responded very well to their affective needs. For example, they liked the design motif of the Canadian flag for *History Trek* and the metaphor of the child's study for *KidSearch Canada,* expressing their satisfaction in such terms as "cool" and "really attractive." They approved of the multiple retrieval devices incorporated into *History Trek,* although neither portal entirely solved their retrieval problems. More attention, for example, needs to be directed at the ways in which the hierarchical subject index, accessed from the topics menu, is constructed, if students are to easily select the correct topic. In fact, the indexing for the two portals was undertaken by the designers alone after the intergenerational team's design work had been completed, rather than in the spirit of bonded design, where children themselves would also have been involved. In the same way that the portals' interfaces benefited from the child users expertise, so, in all probability, would the indexing. The students also approved of portals that are developed for specific subject fields rather than the universe of knowledge, and in almost all cases, said that when seeking information on Canadian history, they would prefer to use *History Trek* or *KidSearch Canada* in preference, say, to Google, MSN, or Yahoo.

For those who have not worked closely with children, it may be hard to accept that a design team can function with members who are so young. In particular, eyebrows might be raised at the prospect of including students from grade three who are only eight- or nine-years' old. Yet it is possible to accomplish this, and with children who were not especially chosen for their roles but were volunteers from a public (that is, state) school. The children were able to contribute their ideas (as were the adults), and the completed low-tech prototypes reflected the teams' thinking as a whole, rather than being imposed by the adults. Of course, the children could not have achieved this alone, but nor could the adults. If the children drew upon the adults' familiarity with information retrieval in a Web environment, the adults drew just as heavily upon the children's familiarity with childhood.

Bonded design is a method that involves users intimately in the design process. It does not simply ask users to test and respond to prototypes presented by professional designers (although it does turn to users for evaluations of the completed prototypes), but rather it incorporates members of the target user community into the decision making that lies behind the completion of these prototypes. In this way, users do not simply react to designs that are presented to them, but they help to create these designs. Such an approach provides an opportunity to accelerate the design process; instead of designing and testing over multiple iterations, as would be the approach in participatory design, bonded design over a limited number of design sessions can arrive at a low-tech prototype that has "bonded" the designers' professional expertise with the users' expertise in being users to get the best out of both constituencies. As such, it is particularly appropriate when designing technologies for children. In order for designers to create for children, it is essential that children themselves be consulted, and bonded design is an ideal way to achieve this. Children really are able to cooperate with adult designers through discussion, drawing, (or other forms of "hands-on" design activities), and brainstorming, to reach a consensus on a design that satisfies the demands of the latter while meeting the special desires of the former. At the same time, bonded design, in its emphasis on bonding together two disparate groups within one design team, is a method that could also be applied in other intergenerational contexts (senior citizens come immediately to mind) or with other specialized user communities (such as members of a particular profession). Shortly, it will be employed to design a Web portal using an intergenerational team comprising designers and grade-six students from Singapore; the objective here will be to explore the methodology's applicability to other cultural communities, as well as any cultural effects upon the portal design itself (for a discussion of cultural influences in interface design see, for example, Fernandes, 1995; Nielsen, 2000). Bonded design could also, of course, be applied to tasks other than Web portal design. In this way, it can demonstrate its robustness as a design methodology, able to take its place alongside other established approaches to technology design.

Acknowledgments

The research, from which bonded design emerged, was supported by the Social Sciences and Humanities Research Council (Canada). The authors owe a great debt of gratitude to the school board, principals, teachers, and especially the students who participated in the two design teams or the evaluation studies.

References

Arizpe, E., & Styles, M. (2003). *Children reading pictures: Interpreting visual texts.* London: Routledge Falmer.

Beyer, H., & Holtzblatt, K. (1999). Contextual design. *Interactions, 6,* 32-42.

Bilal, D. (2000). Children's use of the Yahooligans! Web search engine: 1. Cognitive, physical and affective behaviors on fact-based search tasks. *Journal of the American Society for Information Science, 51*(7), 646-665.

Bilal, D. (2001). Children's use of the Yahooligans! Web search engine: II. Cognitive and physical behaviors on research tasks. *Journal of the American Society of Information Science and Technology, 52*(2), 118-136.

Bilal, D. (2002) Children's use of the Yahooligans! Web search engine. III. Cognitive and physical behaviors on fully self-generated search tasks. *Journal of the American Society for Information Science and Technology, 53*(13), 1170-1183.

Bowler, L., Large, A., Beheshti, J., & Nesset, V. (2005, June 2-4). Children and adults working together in the zone of proximal development: A concept for user-centered design. *Data, Information, and Knowledge in a Networked World*:

Proceedings of the Canadian Association for Information Science, London. ON, Canada. CAIS. Retrieved August 7, 2006, from http://www.cais-acsi. ca/2005proceedings.htm

Bowler, L., Nesset, V., Large, A., & Beheshti, J. (2004). Using the Web for Canadian history projects: What will children find? *The Canadian Journal for Information and Library Science, 28*(3), 3-24.

Carmel, E., Whitaker, R., & George, J. (1993). PD and joint application design: A transatlantic comparison. *Communications of the ACM, 36*(4), 40-48.

Druin, A. (1999). Cooperative inquiry: Developing new technologies for children with children. *Proceedings of the SIGCHI Conference on Human factors in Computing Systems* (pp. 592-599). New York: ACM Press.

Druin, A. (2002). The role of children in the design of new technology. *Behaviour and Information Technology, 21*(1), 1-25.

Druin, A., Bederson, B. B., Weeks, A., Farber, A., Grosjean, J., Guha, M. L., et al. (2003). The International Children's Digital Library: Description and analysis of first use. *First Monday, 8*(5). Retrieved August 7, 2006, from http://www. firstmonday.org/issues/issue8_5/druin/index.html

Druin, A., Stewart, J., Proft, D., Bederson, B., & Hollan, J. (1997). KidPad: A design collaboration between children, technologists, and educators. In S. Pemberton (Ed.), *Proceedings of the SIGCHI Conference on Human Factors in Computing Systems* (pp. 463-470). New York: ACM Press.

Fernandes, T. (1995). *Global interface design: A guide to designing international user interfaces.* Boston: Academic Press.

Glynn, S. M. (1997). Drawing mental models. *The Science Teacher, 64*(1), 30-32.

Guha, M. L., Druin, A., Chipman, G., Fails, J.A., Simms, S., & Farber, A. (2004). Mixing ideas: A new technique for working with young children as design partners. In A. Druin, J. P. Hourcade, & S. Kollet (Eds.), *Proceedings of Interaction Design and Children 2004: Building a Community* (pp. 35-42). New York: ACM Press.

Large, A., & Beheshti, J. (2000). The Web as a classroom resource: Reactions from the users. *Journal of the American Society for Information Science, 51*(12), 1069-1080.

Large, A., Beheshti, J., & Cole, C. (2002). Architecture for the Web: The IA matrix approach to designing children's portals. *Journal of the American Society for Information Science and Technology, 53*(10), 831-838.

Large, A., Beheshti, J., Nesset, V., & Bowler, L. (2004). Designing Web portals in intergenerational teams: Two prototype portals for elementary school students. *Journal of the American Society for Information Science and Technology, 55*(13), 1140-1154.

Large, A., Beheshti, J., Nesset, V., & Bowler, L. (2005, June 2-4). Web portal characteristics: Children as designers and evaluators. *Data, Information, and Knowledge in a Networked World: Proceedings of the Canadian Association for Information Science*, London. ON, Canada. CAIS. Retrieved August 7, 2006, from http://www.cais-acsi.ca/2005proceedings.htm

Large, A., Beheshti, J., & Rahman, T. (2002). Design criteria for children's Web portals: The users speak out. *Journal of the American Society for Information Science and Technology, 53*(2), 79-94.

Muller, M., & Kuhn, S. (1993). PD. *Communications of the ACM, 36*(6), 24-28.

Nesset, V., & Large, A. (2004). Children in the information technology design process: A review of theories and their applications. *Library and Information Science Research, 26*(2), 140-161.

Nielsen, J. (2000). *Designing Web usability.* Indianapolis: New Riders.

Piaget, J., & Inhelder, B. (1969). *The psychology of the child.* New York: Basic Books.

Rubin, J. (1994). *Handbook of usability testing: How to plan, design and conduct effective tests.* New York: Wiley.

Scaife, M., & Rogers, Y. (1999). Kids as informants: Telling us what we didn't know or confirming what we knew already. In A. Druin (Ed.), *The design of children's technology* (pp. 27-50). San Francisco: Morgan Kaufmann.

Scaife, M., Rogers, Y., Aldrich, F., & Davies, M. (1997). Designing for or designing with? Informant design for interactive learning environments. *Conference Proceedings on Human Factors in Computing Systems* (pp. 343-350).

Soloway, E., Guzdial, M., & Hay, K. (1994). Learner-centered design: The challenge for HCI in the 21st century. *Interactions, 1*(2), 36-48.

Vygotsky, L. S. (1978). *Mind in society: The development of higher psychological processes.* Cambridge, MA: Harvard University Press.

Chapter V

Ageing and its Implications for Elderly Web Experience

Syariffanor Hisham, University of York, UK

Alistair D. N. Edwards, University of York, UK

Abstract

This chapter discusses ageing-related issues and their implications to the Web experience of elderly users. Particular emphasis is placed on ageing in a developing region, highlighting some cases from Malaysia. The first section consists of a brief review regarding ageing functional abilities and their implications for Web interaction. Examples are given based on studies by other researchers in this area, covering major age-related impairments, namely visual and mental impairment. The potential benefits of the Internet and the elderly user as an ideal partner is examined. The second section presents more examples of the Internet as a platform for elderly people to pursue self-fulfilment. This can be achieved through the available facilities, including communication, services, personal enjoyment, and lifelong education, that facilitate an independent life and valued membership of society. The third section investigates some of the barriers that inhibit elderly users in utilising

Web features. These include issues regarding interface design, assistive devices, and software aids for elderly users. A summary of the ICT penetration among elderly users in Malaysia is included after the three main sections. Finally, the chapter is concluded with some ideas concerning the cultural and demographic differences in determining new trends, directions, and opportunities in advanced Web design specifically for elderly users.

Introduction

Internet evolution has driven economic and social change remarkably in many developed countries such as the U.S., UK, and Japan. It continues to progress and reshape society in many ways including communication, education, and Internet technology itself. This principle has penetrated the public consciousness both in developed and less-developed regions such that the Internet is greeted as a tool to improve quality of life. The Internet is a product of computer technology that continuously expands and is well accepted by the public, including some older people. The United Nations has estimated a global population of 629 million people aged 60 years or older in 2002, and is projected to grow 2 billion by 2050, when the majority of the world's elderly (54%) will reside in Asia, while Europe will have the next largest share at 24% (United Nations, 2002). In this digital era, the Internet was seen as a new potential platform that could benefit the ageing population securing their social and economic viability. The United Nations (2002) distinguishes three global regions: *developed, developing* (those which are making progress on development), and *least developed.* The ageing population has increased, particularly in developing and least developed countries. There are differences, though, between regions in the number and proportion of elderly people. Referring to Figure 1, in more developed regions, almost 20% of the elderly population was aged 60 or older in the year 2000, and by 2050, this proportion is expected to reach 30%. In the less developed regions, only 8% of the population is currently aged over 60; however, by 2050, the elderly will make up nearly 20% of the population (United Nations, 2002).

The increase in the elderly population is the result of the demographic transition resulting from rising levels of fertility and lower mortality rates. The rate of change has been greater in developing countries than in developed countries, so that developing countries have had less time to adapt to the consequences of population ageing. Also, globalization has been mainly led by the developed countries, so that the use of information and communication technology (ICT) has spread unevenly between the developed and less developed regions. As a result, many less developed countries are not only struggling with the consequences of ageing, but also in bridging the socioeconomic gaps with developed countries. Hence, in spite of the globalization

Figure 1. Proportion of aged 60 or over, 2000-2050 (Adapted from United Nations, 2002)

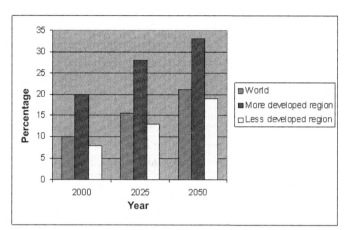

challenges, ICT offers great potential benefits in bridging the digital divides, as well as establishing socioeconomic development in less developed regions. Rapid developments in Web technology and the Internet have profoundly affected the way people lead their daily lives. The computer user population is broadening due to rapid growth in Web and Internet services.

Today, the Internet has become an essential resource for communication, information, education, and entertainment, as well as a platform for business transactions. Useful and efficient functionalities of the Web have encouraged elderly users to participate, and many of them, in turn, have demonstrated their willingness to embrace computer technology as part of their lives. Elderly users are largely to be found in Europe, the United States (U.S.), and Japan, with only minimal use in other countries. However, Malaysia is an example of a developing country that began ICT programmes for elderly users, as early as 2003, with pilot projects *Warga Emas Networks* and *Eagle Nest* to cater to both social and economics needs. The success of these projects contradicts the common belief that elderly users are resistant to change and unaware of the information age. As for many developing countries, ICT is a platform to change the societal perception of elderly from being a burden population to a potential knowledge force population. The use of ICT facilitates accessibility and affordability of information, as well as services for elderly to remain independent and active in society.

This chapter discusses several issues concerning the effects of ageing on Web interaction. Though many of the examples given are based on the earlier publications and researches by the researchers in the UK and U.S., some new examples, also included, are based on a Malaysian case study. This case study refers to the pilot projects, the *Warga Emas Networks* and *Eagle Nest,* that were organised in collaboration with The Malaysian Institute of Microelectronic Systems (MIMOS) and the former Ministry of National Unit and Social Development of Malaysia. Related examples and data were also taken from interviews with older adults at senior citizens centres, and a survey of awareness and usage of computers by senior citizens in Malaysia that was conducted in September 2005 by the first-named author. It is hope that the examples, based on the Malaysia scenario, will have broader significance. Most existing work on elderly users and the Internet primarily focuses on the elderly users in more developed regions such as UK, U.S., and Japan. There are a number of new factors introduced when one considers the situation in developing regions, including to cultural differences, demographic variables, and applicable legislation.

Referring to the World Wide Web (WWW), the user survey (Cultural Issues Questionnaires) conducted by the Graphics, Visualisation and Usability Center, Georgia Institute of Technologies, Atlanta, has shown that cultural preferences and biases affect user satisfaction and performance while browsing the Internet. For example, some Middle Eastern and European respondents stated that American images make the computer harder to learn, while Asian and American respondents believe American images have no effect on learning. What is more, Asian respondents suggest that if the Web sites were designed for their language and culture, more people would be willing to use the Web (Barber & Badre, 1998). Though the survey was not specifically targeting elderly users, nevertheless, it showed that cultural differences and biases exist among the Internet users regardless of their age group. Those dissimilarities, especially in the ageing group, would be new challenges and prospective areas for future research and trends in universal Web design.

What do we Need to Know about Ageing?

Gregor, Newell, and Zajicek (2002) states that the elderly can be categorised into three different groups:

- Fit elderly who do not appear—nor would consider themselves—disabled, but whose functionality, needs, and wants are different to those they had when they were younger.

- Frail elderly who would be considered to have one or more disabilities, often severe ones, but in addition, will have a general reduction in many of their functionalities.

- Disabled people who grow older, whose long-term disabilities have affected the ageing process, and whose ability to function can be critically dependent on their other faculties, which may also be declining.

To accommodate elderly populations, it is necessary to understand age-related differences in sensing, processing, and acting on information. It is also essential to apply the knowledge base to ensure that Internet and the Web are easy to use, and that interaction with them is a positive experience for elderly users. With an understanding of the functional abilities of older people and their implications to their activities, the Web designer would be able to design a proper interface to suit the elderly needs. As well as understanding the psychological changes associated with ageing, it is also crucial to understand how restricted functional abilities affect elderly people when browsing the Web. A brief review of age-related impairments and their implications for elderly people's activities on the Internet are discussed in this section.

Ageing and Restricted Functional Ability

It is in the nature of the ageing process that older people experience one or more related impairments that affect the individual's functional abilities. The two most common functional abilities associated with the elderly in this regard are *perception* and *cognition*. Perception is a process of receiving information from the outside world, followed by mental activities, such as reasoning and problem solving, known as cognition. Perceptual abilities refer to the visual, auditory, and olfactory senses that combine to construct a mental image. Abilities falling within the cognitive classification represent mental processes that individuals use in performing complex tasks such as recognition of information and awareness. There are two general type of cognition: *experiential* and *reflective*. Experiential cognition is a state of mind in which humans perceive, act, and react to their surroundings effectively and effortlessly. It acquires certain level of expertise and engagement, for instance, having conversation or driving a car. In contrast, reflective cognition involves thinking, comparing, and decision-making that lead to new ideas and creativity (Preece, Rogers, & Sharp, 2002). Cognition involves range of interdependent processes: attention, perception and recognition, reasoning, memory, and learning. A decline in cognitive abilities constitutes the important aspect of the ageing process. Cognitive abilities are concerned with an individual's capability to memorise visual input, to carry out reasoning using the input, and to recognise the information. The ability to memorise and retain new information is essential in accomplishing computer tasks (Jacko & Vitense, 2001). The locus of the problem for older adults seems to be in transfer of information from short-term memory to long-term memory (Hunt, 1993).

Short-term or working memory has limited capacity that requires the information to be held in "chunk" form and to be refreshed frequently.

Although most elderly people do not experience severe visual impairments, they may experience declines in eyesight that do affect their ability to perceive and comprehend visual information (Czaja & Lee, 2002). Visual images, captured through the eyes, generate mental models that are stored in the long-term memory for use by the reasoning process, and for retrieval as information. The failure of this process to function correctly inhibits the individual's ability to gain access to the information. Zajicek and Hall (2000) state skills are not affected because certain types of memory are unaffected by ageing, and others have shown that age associated memory impairment (AAMI) is associated with damage to different areas of the brain, such as the hippocampus or the frontal lobe. A distinction is drawn between *crystalline* and *fluid* memory. Crystalline memory refers to fixed, prelearned, and unchanging knowledge and skills, whereas fluid memory is described as the ability to solve problems for which there are no solutions derivable from formal training or cultural practices. The importance of memory changes for elderly users is that while the crystalline memory is relatively unaffected, the fluid memory is more likely to be subject to AAMI.

Ageing is also associated with changes in motor skills, including slower response times, declines in ability to maintain continuous movements, disruptions in coordination, loss of flexibility, and greater variability in movements (Czaja & Lee, 2002). Thus, elderly users tend to take longer to process incoming information, and typically require more time to respond.

Given that there are age-related declines in perceptual and cognitive abilities, the use of the Internet is likely to be challenging for elderly users. The following section provides a summary of restricted functional abilities and their likely impact on Web interaction.

Implications of Restricted Functional Abilities on Web Interaction

Although many elderly users experience perceptual, cognitive, and mobility difficulties as part of the ageing process, this has not discouraged them from enthusiastically endeavouring to use computer technology; statistics have shown dramatic increases in computer use among the elderly population in recent years (Czaja & Lee, 2003). However, problems with vision and memory have greatly restricted the ability of the elderly users to interact and perform numerous routine tasks including browsing the Web. Studies of AAMI show how disadvantaged elderly users are when using computer applications (Jacko & Vitense, 2001). It has been suggested that elderly users have a deficit in semantic information processing, so their memory representations will contain less associative and inferential information. Also, elderly users are thought not to form distinctive, contextually specific encodings of new information, but to encode events in the same old way from one occasion to the next (Light, Owens, Mahoney, & Voie, 1993). Elderly users have difficulty finding information on the Web as it usually employs a complicated interface and presents content using inefficient structures. Zaphiris, Kurniawan, and Ellis (2003) state that, in comparison with younger adults, elderly users are significantly less likely to complete tasks with long, optimal path lengths, and adopt less-efficient search strategies. Searching for information on the Internet is a complex cognitive task and involves cognitive skills such as memory, reasoning, attention, learning, and problem solving. Deteriorating visual acuity and colour discrimination abilities can make user interfaces difficult or impossible to see (Zajicek, 2002). Small fonts, certain difficult text and background colour combinations, background images, and blinking text are all potentially problematic. Declining visual abilities also affect an elderly user's capacity to operate a standard graphical user interface (GUI) successfully. Czaja and Lee (2003) state that visual decrements make it more difficult for elderly users to perceive small icons on toolbars or to locate information on complex screens or Web sites.

Other problems involve remembering which pages they have visited (and their content), and understanding Web terminology and technical jargon (such as "home" and "cookies"). This may cause an elderly user to retreat from using the Internet as a source of information. A Web site with inaccurate links may result in disorientation, and cause an elderly user to be lost in hyperspace. Many Web activities require the user to scroll in order for them to read the contents of Web sites; scrolling is particularly difficult for elderly users for a number of reasons related to a combination of visual and motor factors. In terms of visual impairments, the small size of the scroll bar, particularly the target box, can be problematic. In terms of motor skills, scrolling requires the complex sequence of moving the mouse to the small target box, holding down the mouse button, and continuing to hold down the button while moving the mouse in the direction needed for scrolling (i.e., *dragging*) (Hanson, 2001). Most Web activities require hand movements and various aspects of mouse control, such as moving, clicking, fine-positioning, and dragging, that are obviously difficult for elderly people who have disabilities that affect their hand movement. Input devices such as mice and trackballs might not be appropriate for elderly users (Czaja & Lee, 2002). Although the performance of elderly users improves with practice, still they perform more slowly in many cases (Czaja & Lee, 2002). The literature generally suggests that elderly users are receptive to using new technology, even if they have to make great effort to adapt to the computer activities. Their sheer determination and commitment to use the Internet has created special bonding between the computer and elderly people. The following section shows how the Internet and elderly users become ideal partners.

Why are the Internet and Elderly Users Ideal Partners?

Decreasing physical, psychological, and social abilities can significantly reduce elderly people's participation in society. Changes in family structures have also affected elderly needs for social inclusion. For instance, many younger people choose to pursue career or studies   in other cities distant from their parents. A strong need to communicate with family members, especially with grandchildren, has encouraged elderly people to use the Internet. Older people in some particular ethnic communities place greater emphasis on closeness to family members. Other social factors include:

- the desire to participate in the community;
- building support groups among peers;
- the desire to acquire new skills as an activity of lifelong learning.

In the UK, elderly people tend to need easier access to facilities, such as post offices and doctors' surgeries, than the general community. Easy access to social and leisure facilities is likely to enhance independent, active living and to combat loneliness. At the same time, the Internet offers new opportunities for employment, including among older people. Having some knowledge of the Internet and computer skills is potentially an employable asset. Some older people are retired with good pensions and the security of ownership of valuable property, but even they may appreciate the opportunity to continue to take part in a work culture, possibly through freelance Internet work. At the same time, there are people who find the increasing cost of living, and the faster-increasing cost of health, a burden. For them, computers and the Internet may provide an invaluable opportunity for reemployment. We consider these opportunities in the following section.

Web and Internet Use by Elderly

The term *Cyberseniors* (Zajicek, 2002) refers to two distinct groups that are:

- the *technology lovers*, indulging a lifelong fascination with technology, and
- the *technology users* who are pragmatic and see computers as another tool to achieve what they require.

Cyberseniors use the Internet for a variety of purposes. They communicate with family members and friends, access information and services, and undertake continuing, lifelong education. One survey (Becker, 2004) has shown that one of the most popular online activities by elderly users in the U.S. is to access health information. At the same time, many cyberseniors feel that using the Internet gives them a closer connection with the present and the future, expanding their world by forming new friendships, and keeping them more active intellectually. They may access the Internet at senior centres, public libraries, and public organisations, as well as possibly having a PC at home. Such usage can only grow with current demographic changes. The current younger generation is becoming increasingly dependent on the Internet for activities such as shopping, entertainment, and education. In 20–30 years, they will form the bulk of the elderly population, who will take such access and facilities for granted. The size of this segment of the population is growing. Stroud (2004) states that the proportion of elderly Web users represents 25% of the UK online population, whilst in Scandinavia the figure is closer to 40%. In the U.S., there are 4.2 million Internet users over the age of 65 (Chadwick-Dias, McNulty, & Tullis, 2003). Zaphiris et al. (2003) suggest that the trends are similar in other countries too.

As noted previously, an important use of the Internet by elderly users is for communication with friends and family. This can be particularly important during special occasions, such as Eid Mubarak, Christmas, birthdays, and weddings. Electronic communication is both more convenient and cheaper than conventional communication. It also offers new forms of communication. For instance, modules in the *Warga Emas Networks* and *Eagle Nest* programmes introduced free instant messaging, using Yahoo Messenger and Windows Messenger. These may be supplemented with voice and video via Web cameras. In addition to communication with established friends and family, new communities are being created via Web sites that cater to elderly users, including http://www.seniornet.org, http://www.counselandcare.org.uk, and http://www.elderly.com. The Internet provides opportunities for international communication. Forums and mailing lists allow the possibility of sharing interests and life stories. Online services, such as shopping and financial services, are also attractive to many elderly users. It has been found in the U.S. and UK that Web services, including bank transactions, paying bills, and buying groceries, are popular among elderly users who have visual and/or mobility impairments that make conventional transactions difficult. However, in Malaysia, online transactions are less popular with elderly users, partly because they are unaware of their availability and also because of doubts regarding the security of online financial services. Interviews in Malaysia showed a marked difference between the attitudes of novice and more experienced Internet users. Novices agreed that they found the use of the Internet enjoyable, but did not consider it to be very important to them. On the other hand, experienced users (who had been using the Internet 1 and 3 years) stated that the Internet is part of their daily routines.

Although the Web is accessed in a stereotypical manner and is not fully utilised by the elderly, the increasing number of users, both in developed and developing countries, indicate that the technology is being positively accepted. Encouragement by family and social networks can generate interest among the elderly in using the Internet. Although still many elderly people are not connected to the Internet due to various reasons (e.g., personal reasons, accessibility, and affordability constraints), many of them are aware of what the technology offers for the future. The limited access may be due to certain key problems needing attention from all entities: Web technologists, academic researchers, social workers, and policy makers working together. With thorough planning and strategic implementation, issues pertaining to availability, affordability, and accessibility of the technology can be solved.

Why is the Internet Difficult for Elderly Users?

In order to use the Internet, older people must have knowledge and skill in computer use, including the ability to use the keyboard and mouse. Yet, as well as these real skills, people's perceptions of computers and their competence can be crucial in giving them the confidence to overcome any interaction problems. Czaja and Lee (2003) have found that the attitude towards technology is largely influenced by previous experiences with the technology. Collating a number of studies (Dickinson, Eisma, & Gregor, 2003; Goodman, Syme, & Eisma, 2003; Hanson, 2001; Hawthorn, 2003), it is possible to identify three different categories of barrier to computer use by older people:

- Personal barriers, including levels of confidence and awareness, literacy, and education
- Visual, cognitive, and physical impairments
- Technological barriers, comprising poor user interface design, poor content layout, unreliable content and resources, inefficient information architectures, poorly designed applications, and inaccessible functionality

In spite of all these barriers, through proper training and incentives to become ICT literate, elderly users can develop skills to compensate for the age-related impairments that have became an obstacle for their computer and Web interaction. In comparison with younger adults, elderly users had more positive attitudes toward the computer, though they expressed less computer confidence. A study indicated that people who had experience with computers had a more positive attitude, and greater computer confidence (Czaja & Lee, 2002). The concept of technology may be based on precomputer technology, which can affect the elderly people's attitude to computers and their expectations of interfaces. They may experience more computer anxiety and less computer efficacy. In many cases, elderly users are afraid of breaking the computer the first time they use it. With that in mind, they usually rely on the younger family members (e.g., sons, daughters, and grandchildren) or caretaker to assist them with using the Internet. From the interviews with the *Warga Emas Networks* participants, many elderly users refrained from using a computer and the Internet because of their concern that they might annoy their family members to do a simple task on the computer (e.g., restart the PC) that was too risky for them to fix themselves. This evidence shows the elderly people's perception of the technology and how it has affected their confidence level when interacting with computers. As a result, many elderly users would prefer to be assisted by an experienced Internet user within their peer group. They are likely to have a better understanding of each other's difficulties and needs (particularly regarding Web interaction) and lack of information that may be taken for granted by the younger assistant.

Statistics show that Web users over the age of 65 took 66% more time completing tasks than those in the age 21 to 55-years-old range. The U.S. financial services industry found that Web users over 55 took 40% longer and made 20% more errors than their juniors (Stroud, 2004). Language is an example of an illiteracy problem that inhibits elderly users' use of the Internet as a source of communication and information. According to an elderly user who joined the *Warga Emas Networks*, her task of learning to use the Internet has been difficult because the applications used are in English, whilst she could only speak Mandarin. Therefore, she has requested extra classes and made notes that have to be more detailed, as she could not read English. Learning to use the Internet represents a considerable investment of time and energy (Zajicek & Morrisey, 2003). The amount of skills and knowledge is also an important factor. Results of a survey in the UK have found out that the most common method of learning to use the computer was a course followed by work, whilst surveys in the U.S. have discovered that self-teaching was the most common method for elderly users (Goodman et al., 2003). Regardless of their learning method, researchers have noted that elderly users are more interested in application rather than the technology. Their interest is in how to get the machine to do what they want to be done (Hunt, 1993).

Assistive Devices and Software Aids

Access for elderly users can be enhanced through the use of assistive devices and software. However, there are a number of problems in using such aids for elderly people in developing countries. Firstly, there is cost. Buying a PC in the first place can be very expensive (i.e., in Malaysia, the cost of a desktop PC is equivalent to one month's salary for a graduate employee). To buy additional access equipment may be a prohibitive further cost. Assistive devices are not always appropriate for older users either. The devices tend to be aimed at people with specific, single disabilities, whereas (as already noted) older people tend to have a set of minor disabilities. People often prefer not to use assistive devices too because of the stigma attached to them; they would generally prefer to use equipment that is as standard as possible. New developments are happening all the time in assistive devices, and so it can be difficult for users to keep track of the latest developments and upgrades (Hanson, 2001).

Software solutions have the advantage that they do not require the purchase of additional hardware. Modern systems often have access software features built in, such as screen magnifiers, mouse alternatives, and formatting modification. There can be a conflict, though, between having features available and the user being able to find and activate them. To access such modifications, the user often has to go through a series of dialog boxes, selecting options in a manner that is confusing for the novice user, and it is a common complaint of elderly users that software interfaces are too complex (Syme, Dickinson, Eisma, & Gregor, 2003). There is a basic tension in human-computer interface design between providing a rich set of alternatives to as wide a range of users as possible, and making the interaction so complicated that almost no one can use it. As soon as the design includes anything more than the most basic features, the application can become overloaded with features, leading to a complicated interface with unstructured layout and menus, and inappropriate and redundant features. The result is that many features are not used by elderly users, either because they are not aware of their existence, or because they are more comfortable with familiar, basic features. It has been found to be more appropriate to allow users access to an e-mail system with reduced, basic functionality and then to add extra features later, once the users have mastered the basic system (Zajicek & Morrisey, 2003). Hawthorn (2003) has identified a number of e-mail tasks that elderly people find difficult, namely: managing attachments, navigating hierarchical directory trees, organizing and finding e-mails, creating new folders and maintaining them, dragging and dropping, managing windows, and visually searching complex displays.

With respect to the Web, a study by Chadwick-Dias et al. (2003) noted a number of characteristics in elderly people's interaction:

- **Cautious clicking:** Elderly users spend more time reading information before clicking, and even pondering the pros and cons of clicking before attempting to click a link.
- **Clicking nonlinks:** Elderly users clicked on items that were not links (table headings, bullets, icons, and plain text). The idea is to click on any items that seem to meet their expectations for whatever target they were seeking.

Figure 2. Mozilla Firefox version 1.0.4 (Web browser)

- **Spending more time reading text and instructions:** Especially when they were required to fill in information.

Despite the fact elderly users take extra time to complete their computer tasks, they were found to be more accurate because of their conscientiousness (Chadwick-Dias et al., 2003).

The differences in user interaction can be illustrated with reference to Figure 2, which is a screenshot of the Mozilla Firefox version 1.0.4 browser with the Google Web site displayed on it. The complexity of the interface is not always apparent to many users, but in practice, this picture shows no fewer than 74 interactive items, counting both icons and menu entries. Many menus have submenus, so that there are a total of 65 menu items in total (e.g., **View** → Toolbars → Navigation Toolbar, **View** → Text Size → Increase). The obvious question is of those 74 items, how many would be used by the average elderly user? Furthermore, suppose they did want to use some of the available features (e.g., to modify the default fonts and/or colours), how many elderly users would find their way through all the necessary steps? Would they be able to work out where to start: the Edit or Tools menu, for instance? While computer systems are complex, it is even more important to understand the human side of the interaction (Hunt, 1993). There are many examples of interaction design that are important for all users, but even more critical for elderly people. A poorly designed interface can lead to frustration and tiredness for any inexperienced user. Elderly users have limited computer experience, and do not have the same adventurous, exploratory approach to computer use as younger people. Bad design can cause errors that will then discourage them from risking further use.

Malaysia: Where Do We Go From Here?

The main pressure for ICT adoption by elderly people in Malaysia comes from the government's emphasis on developing an ICT culture, and encouragement of the development of knowledge workers to meet the challenges of globalization. It is never forgotten that the country has got to where it is thanks to the efforts of those who are now among the elderly population. The government has been inspired by the increasing use of the Internet by elderly people in the UK, U.S., and other developed countries, which has inspired them to implement a top-down approach to improving ICT literacy among elderly Malaysians. At present, 3.8% of Malaysians are aged 65 or above. As life expectancy continues to improve, access to ICT will become even more important for this growing group. A pilot programme for elderly ICT users in Malaysia ran from August 2003 to July 2004. Despite the end of funding from this source, some of the programmes run by organizations in Kuala Lumpur, Klang, and Kajang have continued and are still running. The objective to the *Warga Emas Networks* (which involves 100 participants at three different locations) is to promote the inclusion of elderly people in society. The programme's module on *Computing and the Internet* uses materials from SeniorNet.org, covering such topics as how to boot the PC, use of the mouse, drag and drop, word processing, the Internet, and the use of chat programs. By contrast, the *Eagle Nest* programme aims at promoting freelance employment for elderly people. The programme consists of eight modules from which participants must take at least five. These include advanced modules such as Web Master and technician training. One of the first graduates of the *Eagle Nest* programme is now working within the programme as a trainer. His first-hand experience of being a trainee is invaluable in teaching and inspiring the others coming along behind him.

ICT programme for the elderly in Malaysia was started in August 2003 and ended in July 2004. Though funding for the pilot project has stopped, the programmes are continuing with some initiatives by the elderly organisations in Kuala Lumpur, Klang, and Kajang, and expanding until today. ICT awareness has, thus, undoubtedly increased among elderly people in Malaysia, but there are still limitations, mainly due to the cost of PC ownership and Internet charges. While demand for organized training programmes has increased, it should be remembered that there will also be elderly users who receive informal training from family and friends, and by independent personal exploration. Principal lessons learned from these two projects are:

- There are access and equality gaps between racial groups. It has been found that Chinese elderly people are more likely to join ICT courses compared to Malays and Indians. It is thought that this is due to differences in lifestyle, whereby Chinese people are more likely to join clubs for senior citizens and to live in urban areas. There is a need, therefore, to encourage more Malays and Indians to get involved in ICT in both rural and urban areas.

- PC ownership. The cost of PC ownership and Internet access can be significant in households with low income. This has been overcome, to some extent, by donation of PCs from public and private organizations including IBM and MIMOS, which have helped to sustain the *Warga Emas* and *Eagle Nest* programmes. With more similar support, such programmes could be extended to other states in Malaysia.

- Content/application development. English is the dominant language in ICT, both in Web content and in applications. This is a barrier to elderly users who cannot read English. Microsoft Malaysia has launched the *Malays Interface Pack for Windows XP and Office 2003*, which is targeted at the Malays community—of all ages—especially in rural areas. However, as yet, the acceptance of these localized versions is minimal, most users preferring to continue to use the English versions.

- Accessibility features. The usefulness of accessibility features on local Web sites (e.g., enlarged text and text-only pages) is limited, causing barriers to access. Web designers and content providers need to be more aware of the needs of elderly users.

The Malaysian elderly and computer partnership programme is yet young, but the positive feedback from the elderly participants is strongly motivating expansion of the programme to encompass elderly Malaysians in rural areas. The programme has already led to new Web experiences for elderly users and, with Malaysian cultural and demographic divergence, should create new opportunities for research and development of truly universal design.

Conclusion

The population is continuing to age. During the 20th century, the proportion of the elderly population has continued to rise, and there is no reason not to expect this to continue in the twenty-first century. This ageing process is even more marked in less developed regions than in the developed regions. Thus, in this century, the less developed regions are continuing to attempt to bridge the socioeconomic gap at the same time as addressing this ageing issue. The Internet has played its part in the globalization process over recent decades, presenting both opportunities and threats to the ageing population in both developed and developing countries. As shown in this chapter, positive acceptance by elderly people has shown that the Internet can contribute to an improved quality of life. It has been observed that elderly people need not be technophobic, and can be most willing to use computers. In the ideal situation, elderly people can overcome their lack of experience of computer technology to benefit from the availability of social and educational opportunities, at the same time as accessing Web services, such as shopping. Web access can become more difficult as people's abilities in sight, memory, and mobility deteriorate. Nevertheless, elderly people can be accommodated if sites are designed with their needs in mind (e.g., fast-loading, simple, and uncluttered pages). At the same time, assistive aids are continuing to be developed that will tailor access better to individual needs. These aids will only be useful if the additional cost can be minimized.

The effect of culture and demographic differences has, as yet, received little attention in both developed and developing countries. Success in the adoption of the technology in developed countries is encouraging, and it is to be hoped that it will be possible to transfer these ideas into other cultural contexts. The objective is not to develop a generic global interface, suited to all cultures, but to suggest that cultural markers can be manipulated to facilitate international interaction. Cultural markers tagged according to region, country, genre, and language can be used to establish a set of guidelines. Such guidelines will offer Web and software designers specific information about the region and country for which they are developing an interface. Localization has not received a lot of attention in recent years, and localization anomalies have created additional barriers for elderly users. Research on intercultural accommodation of elderly people is likely to feed in to the development of better localization. Better access may be achieved for elderly people in less developed regions through understanding of cultural differences and the effects of demographics. This should, in turn, lead to a much greater take up of the Internet.

References

Barber, W., & Badre, A. (1998). *Culturability: The merging of culture and usability.* Retrieved May 9, 2005, from http://research.att.com/conf/hfweb/proceedings/barber/

Becker, A. S. (2004). A study of Web usability for older adults seeking online health resources [Electronic version]. *ACM Transaction on Computer-Human Interaction 11*(4), 387-404.

Chadwick-Dias, A., McNulty, M., & Tullis, T. (2003, November 10-11). Web usability and age: How design changes can improve performance [Electronic version]. In *Proceedings of the 2003 ACM Conference on Universal Usability (CUU'03)*, Vancouver, British Columbia, Canada (pp. 30-37). New York: ACM Press.

Czaja, S. J., & Lee, C. C. (2003). Designing computer systems for older adults. In J. A. Jacko & A. Sears (Eds.), *The HCI handbook: Fundamentals, evolving technologies and emerging application* (pp. 413-425). NJ: Lawrence Erlbaum Associates.

Dickinson, A., Eisma, R., & Gregor, P. (2003, November 10-11). Challenging interfaces/redesigning users [Electronic version]. In *Proceedings of the 2003 ACM Conference on Universal Usability (CUU'03)*, Vancouver, British Columbia, Canada (pp. 61-68). New York: ACM Press.

Goodman, J., Syme, A., & Eisma, R. (2003). *Older adult's use of computers: A survey*. Retrieved June 17, 2005, from http://www.computing.dundee.ac.uk/projects/utopia/Publications.asp

Gregor, P., Newell, A. F., & Zajicek, M. (2002, July 8-10). Designing for dynamic diversityInterfaces for older people [Electronic version]. In *Proceedings of the Fifth International ACM Conference on Assistive Technologies (ASSETS'02)*, Edinburgh, Scotland (pp. 151-156). New York: ACM Press.

Hanson, V. K. (2001, May 22-25). Web access for elderly citizens [Electronic version]. In *Proceedings of the 2001 EC/NSF Workshop on Universal Accessibility of Ubiquitous Computing (WUAUC'01)*, Alcácer do Sal, Portugal (pp. 14-18). New York: ACM Press.

Hawthorn, D. (2003, November 10-11). How universal is good design for older users? [Electronic version]. In *Proceedings of the 2003 Conference on Universal Usability (CUU'03)*, Vancouver, British Coloumbia, Canada (pp. 38-45). New York: ACM Press.

Hunt, E. (1993). What do we need to know about aging? In J. Cerella, J. Rybash, W. Hoyer, & M. Commons (Eds.), *Adult information processing: Limits on loss* (pp. 587-598). CA: Academic Press.

Jacko, J. A., & Vitense, H. S. (2001). A review and reappraisal of information technologies within a conceptual frame. *Universal Access in the Information Society, 1*(1), 56-76.

Light, L. L., Owens, S. A., Mahoney, P. G., & Voie, D. L. (1993). Comprehension of metaphors by young and older adults. In J. Cerella, J. Rybash, W. Hoyer, & M. Commons (Eds.), *Adult information processing: Limits on loss* (pp. 459-483). CA: Academic Press.

Preece, J., Rogers, Y., & Sharp, H. (2002). *Interaction design: Beyond human computer interaction* (pp. 74-102). NY: John Wiley.

Stroud, D. (2004). *Make the Web "50+ friendly."* Retrieved October 24, 2005, from http://www.academyinternet.com/consulting/Making%20The %20Web%2050+%Friendly.pdf

Syme, A., Dickinson, A., Eisma, R., & Gregor, P. (2003). Looking for help? Supporting older adults' use of computer system. In M. Rauterberg, M. Menozzi, & J. Wesson (Eds.), *Human-computer interaction INTERACT'03* (pp. 924-931).

United Nations. (2002). *World population ageing: 1950-2050.* NY: United Nations Publication.

Wolfe, G. (1994). *The (second phase of the) revolution has begun.* Retrieved August 14, 2003, from http://www.wired.com/wired/archive/2.10/mosaic_pr.html

Zajicek, M. (2002). *Supporting older adults at the interfaces.* Retrieved August 14, 2003, from http://www.brookes.ac.uk/speech/publications/95_ING~1.pdf

Zajicek, M., & Hall, S. (2000). *Solutions for elderly visually impaired people using the Internet.* Retrieved July 15, 2003, from http://www.brookes.ac.uk/speech/ publications/81_HCI2000.pdf

Zaphiris, P., Kurniawan, S. H., & Ellis, R. D. (2003). Age-related differences and depth vs. breadth tradeoff in hierarchical online information systems. In N. Carbonell & C. Stephanodis (Eds.), *User interface for all* (pp. 23-24).

Zajicek, M., & Morrisey, W. (2003). Multimodality and interactional differences in older adults. *Universal Access in the Information Society, 2*(2), 1-9.

Section III

Gender Issues

Chapter VI

Gender Issues in HCI Design for Web Access

Stefania Boiano, InvisibleStudio, Italy

Ann Borda, London South Bank University, UK

Jonathan P. Bowen, Museophile Limited, UK

Xristine Faulkner, London South Bank University, UK

Giuliano Gaia, InvisibleStudio, Italy

Sarah McDaid, London South Bank University, UK

Abstract

We consider the design and provision of Web sites, with respect to gender issues, from various perspectives. A general view of the field is given, and educational issues are specifically considered in relation to gender differences in the use of IT as an effective educational aid, especially by children. Human-computer interaction (HCI) models at different levels of abstraction are presented, together with how gender issues could impinge at each of these levels. A number of examples, both from the commercial and cultural fields, are discussed as design case studies of home pages for Web sites that exhibit gender-related orientation. Finally, look-

ing to the future, online gaming is discussed in the context of usage. It is hoped that the guidance provided here will help minimize any gender discrimination on Web sites with respect to their interfaces, increasing general accessibility in the process.

Introduction

Everyone has his style when designing a site. There is no such a thing as a 'feminine design' or a 'male design.' The most important thing here is to seek inspiration to create something different each time. (Mark, male Web designer, http://www. redpolka.org)

Even if half the potential users of the Web are female, it is still a rather male-oriented environment. A study of UK university Web sites has shown 94% of them to have a masculine orientation, compared with only 2% having a female bias, with 74% of them designed by male-dominated teams and only 7% by female teams (Harden, 2005; Moss & Gunn, 2005; Tysome, 2005). This is despite the fact that there are more female than male students. It was found that men preferred regular, unfussy, formal content and layout in straight lines, whereas women preferred more colour and rounded forms with less conventional design, formality, and linearity. Both men and women seem to prefer Web sites produced by designers of the same sex. In general, the specific area of human-computer interaction (HCI) and gender issues is not well studied in the research literature. However, Balka (1996) briefly discusses HCI skills with respect to gender and Cassell (2002) discusses HCI for video games, commenting on how it is often gender biased.

In this chapter we first consider the background to Web interface design with respect to gender issues. In particular, we look at some educational differences. We then consider some HCI models at different levels of abstraction, and how consideration of gender preferences could impact on these. A number of Web sites, both commercial and, by way of contrast, cultural as well (Baiget, Bernal, Black, Blinova, Boiano, Borda, et al., 2005; Gunn et al., 2006), are used to consider various design issues with respect to gender differences. Looking to the future as the Web becomes more interactive, we also consider the issues in online gaming design. In conclusion, we briefly summarize the current situation, and what could be done to help rectify it.

Background

If you are design-minded you can really do whatever you want (masculine or feminine design). (Makiko Itoh, http://www.makikoitoh.com)

The question over women and their attitude to technology continues to be an interesting one. On the one hand, they appear to be very enthusiastic users of mobile phones (especially text messaging) despite the problems there are in the use of these devices (Faulkner & Culwin, 2005), while on the other hand, their less enthusiastic take up of computers still continues to be a cause for concern. There have been several attempts to look at gender issues in relationship to design, with technologists attempting to create designs that will particularly appeal to women. This section looks at the major aspects of HCI that need to be considered on the Web, and how design might be slanted towards creating systems that will support and encourage women in their use of the Web.

Harding (1986) argues that "women have been more systematically excluded from doing serious science than from performing any other social activity, except, perhaps frontline warfare." She says that a concentration on the hard sciences means that gender is thus viewed as a variable that affects individuals and their behaviour, rather than as an aspect of society and its structures. This inevitably affects the way in which technology is designed. As use of technology increases in the workplace and the home, so it becomes more urgent for designs to be inclusive of everyone. This might mean investigating and addressing the differences, be they due to age, ability, gender, and so forth, that may exist between various sections of society. The best way to ensure that people can use a system is to involve them in the design and development process by way of user groups, focus groups, and iterative evaluation exercises (Faulkner, 2000).

The research that has taken place on differences between men and women, and their acceptance of technology, would suggest that women are more influenced, at first, by usability—how easy it is to use a system—and by the responses of others. However, future encounters with the system mean they tend, gradually, to discount social norms and to concentrate on aspects of usability and usefulness. Males, however, are initially attracted to systems on the basis of their usefulness, and that opinion does not change over time (Venkatesh & Morris, 2000). There is the additional problem that women tend to exhibit low self-confidence, and that can affect their attitude towards new systems. Women tend to assume that if they cannot perform a task with software then it is down to their lack of ability. Men, on the other hand, blame the system rather than themselves (Beckwith & Burnett, 2004). It would thus appear that Web-based systems need to be usable and useful if they are to be effective for both men and women. Systems that appear complex, at first sight, might deter women or decrease their effectiveness.

Designing Web-based applications or Web pages is a challenge since the audience might be anyone, in any place, and using the product at any time. Through the work of people like Jakob Nielsen, the design of Web pages is now quite well understood. Designers are encouraged to create designs that facilitate easy access and navigation, avoiding clutter. Reading from the screen is still far from pleasant, and users typically prefer to scan rather than to read pages completely (Morkes & Nielsen, 1997). In fact, there is a gender difference over this aspect of design, with girls typically being more tolerant of reading on a screen than boys, though this could simply be an extension of the fact that girls develop language skills sooner than boys. However, the basic guideline, that less is more where text is concerned, certainly applies to Web pages.

Web Design Issues: Fonts

Font use has been examined in some detail. Nielsen carried out some work with older users and discovered that the most sensible decision for readability was to use at least a 12 point size of font if possible (Nielsen, 2002b). The very young need large fonts in order to facilitate reading. Although youngsters and young adults can read smaller text sizes, they express a preference for a larger size (Nielsen, 2005). The problem is that 12- or 14-point fonts do not look particularly attractive on the page, and they also limit the amount of information that can be presented, so Web designers tend to choose smaller sizes for aesthetic reasons. However, taking this approach does not help with readability.

Those who experience extreme difficulties reading from the screen may be forced to resize pages, but other users will undoubtedly soldier on or abandon the site. In designing a Web site, it is wise to consider what will happen if the font size is increased or even decreased, since sites should honour user preferences set by a browser. Users do not like their preferences to be ignored or overruled, although some graphic designers try to do this to control the display of the page. Web users need to feel in control of the system, and this need is quite deep-rooted (Faulkner, 2000).

Font type has likewise been the subject of much research, with arguments for and against sans serif fonts on the screen. Although there is evidence to show that serif fonts are more readable on paper, the evidence to support this on-screen is less conclusive, though arguments have raged (Faulkner, 1998). It could be that the on-screen experience is different because of the angle of viewing, or it could be that screens are still not as easy to read from as good quality print because the resolution is significantly worse. However, sans serif fonts are still the preference of many designers, with Verdana or Arial being the typical font of choice. This is probably still due to screen quality.

Fonts do seem to be a matter of personal preference; however, it needs to be remembered that an attractive font might attract attention, but it still has to be readable if it is presenting information. Women may prefer more curvy "scripty" fonts, although these can be less readable, especially on a screen, unless a large font size is used. A font that does not really need to be read quickly (e.g., within a logo) can concentrate on looking eye-catching. Designers must not assume that users will struggle to read large amounts of text in a difficult-to-read font. It is faster for them to move to another site.

Web Design Issues: Colours

As far as colour is concerned, it is best to limit its use on screen. An exception can be made for children, who appear to enjoy bright colours. It is argued that they find bright colours visually exciting, and that adults find the same colour schemes distracting. However, women also tend to prefer brighter and warmer colours than men. Background colours are a matter of preference, but if there needs to be a lot of reading to be done on the screen, then it is best to adopt a white background and black print, or if that is not acceptable, then pale colours: blue, yellow, and green work particularly well.

Warm colours like red are particularly troublesome as background as they are viewed as moving towards the user, and if they are supposed to act as a background, then this is obviously problematic. Red and green should be avoided on screen where possible, and should not be used to indicate states without the presence of a secondary cue. This is because the most common form of colour blindness is red-green, and anyone thus affected may have problems differentiating between the colours. If it is necessary to use these combinations as indicators, then ensure that there is a secondary cue. For example, traffic lights do not pose a problem for the colour blind because they also offer a positional cue for the driver.

On screen, either positional cues or sound cues could be used as a secondary indicator. Incidentally, there are fewer colour-blind women than men. This is because in order for a woman to be colour blind, both her parents need to be colour blind. For a man, colour blindness is inherited via the mother.

Latency

The last issue considered here is that of latency. Sites need to be fast. Users of a hypertext system need a response time of less than 1 second when swapping between pages if they are to experience a good sense of continuity. A delay of more than this will be noted by the user as a pause. A 1-second delay is probably the maximum users can tolerate without having their train of thought interrupted.

This means that Web pages need to be delivered as quickly as possible (Culwin & Faulkner, 2001). This does create a problem on the Web since the delivery of Web pages is partly down to technical issues and network access speeds that are often beyond the remit and control of the designer. However, there are design decisions that can be made that will cause the slowing down of entry to a site or the loading of a page. For example, forcing users to log on, or to watch animated introductions, or to read acceptance pages, will all slow down entry to a site. Large images also cause slow downloading.

Women and Technology

In designing a site, it is necessary to consider what the user is doing, what sort of delays they can tolerate, and how these delays can be conveyed to the user before-hand. Delays that are known and can be planned for are much better tolerated than delays that are unexpected. It is possible that women are more patient than men in the case of delays, but often this depends more on the interest in the material that has been requested.

It would appear from an examination of women's use of technology that when they see an advantage of a technology, they are willing to invest the time to use it. Women are not technophobes *per se*. The uptake of the mobile phone and the enthusiastic use of text messaging by women and girls demonstrate that they have no great problem in gaining expertise in a technology that they find useful (Faulkner & Culwin, 2005). Women typically use all manner of household and personal technologies. They have, in the past, used new technologies, even though these have been difficult and time consuming to learn; for example, early sewing machines were far from easy to use before the technology matured (Forty, 1986).

The slow uptake of computers does not appear to be due to a dislike of the technology, but rather a lack of interest in anything it has to offer. Norman (1998) thinks that if technology confers benefits it will be used:

In the early days of a technology, it doesn't matter if it is hard to use, expensive or ungainly. It doesn't matter as long as the benefits are sufficiently great: if the task is important, valuable, and can't be done in any other way.

His beliefs are certainly borne out by the success of other technologies that have conferred benefits.

The Web needs to address women's needs if it is to capture their hearts and minds; it must ensure that it offers advantages and solutions with minimal learning investment. Women are currently enthusiastic users of online communities (Beler, Borda, Bowen, & Filippini-Fantoni, 2004), with some dominated by them or used exclusively by them. An examination of these communities will show that women are taking part effectively and learning how to use the technologies, posting messages and replies, downloading and uploading images and programs. Indeed, a report from Stanford University has found that, by far, the biggest block to Internet use is not gender, ethnicity, or even income, but age (Nie & Erbring, 2002).

Design for the Web needs, therefore, to aim to be usable by everyone without any extensive learning requirements. It is always easy to find a new site, and users are fickle. If designers want people to use their sites, then they must make those sites accessible for everyone. That means catering to men, women, girls, boys, old, young, and those with special needs. Many of the design decisions made for accessibility by those with special needs, or the young or elderly, will often make the site easier to use for everybody (Bowen, 2005). Good design is inclusive not exclusive (Clarkson, 2003): that is, it is designed to consider everyone rather than the few. In many cases, designs aimed at those with reduced motor ability or visual acuity, for example, are preferred by all users simply because they are easier to use.

The way to assess user needs is by ensuring that they are involved in the process of design, and that applications are evaluated with a representative group, including women as appropriate, throughout the developmental process (Faulkner, 2000). This might mean that we must design a Web site for specific users (sometimes women or girls, for example), but we need to design sites that will cater for all users. Good designs do just that; bad designs inevitably make sites difficult to use so that those who have special needs or require encouragement to use the Web will give up or be diverted elsewhere.

Education Issues

Masculine design is Bauhaus, emphasizing form and function. Except the function is the Web site itself, not its content. Feminine design is Dada, emphasizing expression and the destruction of form. (http://www.redpolka.org)

Gender issues are an important consideration for online information access in general, especially with respect to educational matters (Inkpen, 1997). Different attitudes and approaches to learning influence the effectiveness of educational material, both within a real educational institution and on its associated Web site. The use of computers and networks for learning is increasingly prevalent as an educational aid. The interface to the information is very important in minimizing the barrier to the information that is being made available.

A study of 11-year-old children in the context of Web-based science lessons (Leong, & Hawamdeh, 1999) found that boys used computers more regularly than girls (e.g., for games), and also used the World Wide Web more. However, it also showed that girls preferred Web-based lessons to traditional class-based lessons, compared to boys, and that they favoured working in pairs more that singly. Compared to girls, boys disliked reading from the screen, since they had more difficulty with longer pieces of text.

Nachmias et al. (Nachmias, Mioduser, & Shemla, 2001) found significant gender differences in a study of 384 junior-high and high-school students in Israel. Boys were more extensive information and communication technology (ICT) users than girls, in general. They spent about 9.4 hours per week using computers, compared to around 5.6 hours for girls. The difference was most dramatic at home (6.7 vs. 3.5 hours), whereas school usage was more similar (1.4 vs. 1.3 hours), presumably because this was largely directed use. On the other hand, a study of 110 eighth and ninth graders (14-15 year olds) on a 3-month virtual classroom course by Shany & Nachmias (2001), also based in Israel, did not find any particular correlation between gender and various uses of ICT (e.g., bulletin boards, forums, e-mail, Web searches, etc.) with respect to thinking styles in an educational context.

Nielsen (2002a) reports that there are bigger differences between boys and girls with respect to Web site usability than for men and women, in general. In his study, he found that 40% of boys complained about verbose Web pages, compared to 8% of girls. On the other hand, girls criticized the lack of instructions much more (76% vs. 33% for boys). Boys spent more time alone on the computer, whereas girls spent more time with a parent. However, Nielsen notes that age differences are more important than gender difference when considering Web design usability. When it comes to the digital divide, age, education, and income are the key factors, compared with race/ethnicity/gender, which are statistically insignificant with less than 5% effect on the rate of access (Nie & Erbring, 2000). Males used the Internet around 1.2 additional hours per week compared to females, that is, not a huge difference. Gender differences were found to be more significant for those based or working at home.

Traditionally, men are more attracted to direct use of computers, but for more indirect use through other media, the gender balance is more even (Dierking & Falk, 1998). However, the subject matter being presented also has a bearing, with evidence that in the case of fine art, females are more prevalent users, even when technology is used. In the area of online museums, Bowen et al. (1998) noted that an early survey of virtual visitors recorded 46% as being women, compared to only 22% of high-use Internet/Web users being female in a more general survey at around the same time. Thus, the gender balance of those with an interest in culture may be better than the general case (Bernier, 2002). There is also a bias towards older users visiting cultural Web sites, compared to the norm on the Internet.

Chadwick and Boverie (1999) considered the gender gap in the number of men vs. women who completed a museum Web site visitor survey to be worthy of further study. Around 62% of those who completed the questionnaire were male, and only

38% were female. However, they questioned whether men are more likely to complete an online survey.

A more recent survey of online discussion forum usage (e.g., electronic mailing lists, Web forums, newsgroups, etc.), specifically by museum professionals, has been undertaken by Bernier & Bowen (2004). This reports that 65% of the 153 respondents were female, not so surprising given the predominance of women in museum-related jobs. There are more male museum managers and IT workers, but education-related posts are largely occupied by women. Collections managers and researchers are more evenly divided by gender. Fifty-five percent of ICOM (International Council of Museums) members in the UK are female; in Canada, 79% of heritage workers are women, and in the U.S., 84% of archivists and librarians are female. The typical first-time online discussion forum user was a U.S. 25–44-year-old female, mainly from education-related areas, wishing to obtain information. Women over 60 were more likely to be using online forums to ask a question in their area of expertise. Men were most likely to be 45-59 years old, seeking information and sharing knowledge. Daily users were typically 25-34-year -old females.

Overall, there are some interesting and notable differences in the educational and cultural fields online, and these are worthy of consideration by Web designers when producing education subject matter and related resources. This will help to avoid any prejudicial bias in the material on offer.

HCI Models

Interaction between a person (female or male) and a computer-based information system can be viewed as a dialogue or conversation. Modelling this dialogue is an important aspect of human-computer interaction (HCI). Such models provide a useful framework for the design and evaluation of user interfaces and the interaction process.

There are a number of ways to model interaction in HCI. However, the majority of these approaches concentrate on modelling the task, often in an office or business context. Some models also provide a simplistic definition of the user in terms such as naïve, novice, or expert. Nevertheless, there is significantly more to human interaction than can be described through task modelling. Increasingly, people interact with computers to realize social goals such as enabling social interaction, or to gain an experience (Hsu & Lu, 2004). Also, the number of information systems with which people interact is increasing, as is the scope of such systems with respect to everyday aspects of life. These changes, and the need to minimize social exclusion on the basis of individual difference, are leading to new frameworks for the study of HCI.

An important goal in interface design is to support user individuality. Current approaches include user preferences and personalization in information systems; for example, see Filippini-Fantoni et al. (2005). However, these strategies try to accommodate individual differences once the interface has been completed, rather than take account of such aspects during the design process.

The next two sections introduce the main HCI modelling techniques that have been developed, and a number of models from the realms of sociology and social psychology, with special consideration to gender issues. This part goes on to describe, in greater detail, a more holistic modelling approach that takes account of the social and personal context.

Modelling HCI

Many models of human-computer interaction have been influenced by cognitive psychology. For example, the model human processor (MHP), described in Card, Moran, and Newell (1983), draws an analogy between computer processing and the way in which people perceive, process, and output information. It defines the human perceptual, motor, and cognitive systems in terms of the storage capacity and decay times of memory and processor cycle times.

A number of modelling techniques have been based on the MHP including the goals, objects, methods and selection (GOMS) model—which includes the keystroke model (Card et al., 1983)—and cognitive complexity theory (CCT) (Kieras & Polson, 1999). A more recent model of the human mind, using a distributed architecture of human cognition, has led to the definition of the interacting cognitive subsystems (ICS) model (Barnard, 1986).

Other HCI models use grammars to describe the cognitive and physical actions a user must know/perform in order to use a system. For example, the command language grammar (CLG) (Moran, 1981) describes a system in terms of three components: the conceptual component (task and semantic levels); the communication component (syntactic and interaction levels); and the physical component (input/output devices).

A series of related modelling techniques including task action language (TAL) (Reisner, 1982), task action grammar (TAG) (Payne & Green, 1986), and extended task action grammar (ETAG) (Tauber, 1990) use Backus-Naur Form (BNF) to describe the sequence of physical, observable, and cognitive actions required to complete a task (the user task language). By analyzing the features of the resultant grammar (symbols, strings, rules), the relative complexity of different interaction designs can be compared.

External-internal task mapping (ETIT) (Moran, 1983) analyzes the relations between the real-world tasks that a user wishes to complete (the external task domain), and how those tasks are mapped on to the computer system (internal task domain). This method allows both the complexity of the system and the possible knowledge transfer from one system to another to be determined.

A primary goal of HCI modelling techniques is to design, compare, and evaluate interactive systems. Analysis of the models can predict a variety of system interaction properties. These include the speed at which a user can complete a task; how easy it is to learn and remember the system; how easy it is to use without making errors; and whether skills can be transferred from one system to another. The emphasis of these techniques is task decomposition. While some of these approaches consider other aspects of interaction, such as motor skills or environmental context, individual user differences, such as those related to gender, are not the main focus of the analysis.

Other Models of Interaction

In research areas such as sociology and social psychology, models of interaction have been developed that consider how people interact naturally and in social situations. In particular, HCI researchers have looked at the work of conversation analysts to give them insight into how interaction takes place. This microanalysis of everyday conversation *in situ* has identified naturally occurring structures, protocols, and patterns of dialogue in human-human communication. These "rules of conversational sequence" are independent of the participants involved and the setting in which they take place (Sacks, 2001). Common structures in natural conversation include adjacency pairs, patterns of turn taking, and repair of failed sequences.

The potential for using findings from conversation analysis as a means of formulating HCI design guidelines that result in more natural interaction has already been recognized (Norman & Thomas, 1990). Frohlich and Luff (1990) successfully incorporated these elements into an online benefits system that allowed mixed initiative, multiutterance turn-taking, and the repair of previous invalid statements. They also provided preclosing sequences, allowing the system to volunteer additional information to the user.

An influential model from the area of social psychology is the social skills model (Argyle, 1969; Hargie, 1997) that draws an analogy between the motor skills used, for example, while driving a car and those social skills used in effective social interaction. As with the HCI task analysis models, the participants come together in order to attain a primary goal. Clark (1996) suggests that there are, in fact, a set of three goals supported by the interaction. In addition to the primary or domain goal, the participants also have interpersonal goals that establish and maintain their relationship and the procedural goals that support the process of communication.

The social skills model places interaction in a person-situation context that determines the particular set of social constraints (many of these gender related) in play.

These take the form of social norms, roles, relationships, and rules, and provide a system that supports the development of cooperating societies and the attainment of shared goals. Within a relationship, individuals take on roles that prescribe their status, responsibilities, and rules regarding their behaviour towards each other. Rules ensure the smooth operation of relationships by coordinating behaviour, regulating levels of intimacy, and avoiding relation-specific sources of conflict (Argyle, Henderson, & Furnham, 1985).

Modelling Gender Issues in HCI

Figure 1 shows a layered model for HCI that is based on natural human-human communication (McDaid, 2005). This model is a synthesis of social and HCI models, and recognizes that communication takes place on many different levels, and that multiple goals are in play concurrently. Its purpose is to create a richer, more satisfactory human-computer interaction.

The model is intended as a framework for the design of human-computer interaction in a social context. The following section highlights aspects of relevance to gender issues that could be considered at each layer when designing or evaluating computer-based information systems.

Figure 1. A model of human-human communication (© 2006, Sarah McDaid. Used with permission.)

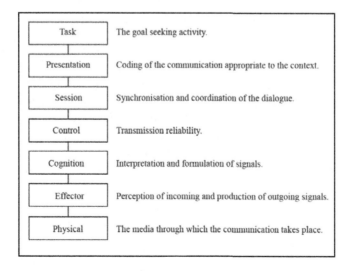

Physical Layer

The physical layer represents the media over which the communication takes place: that is, the real physical world through which, for example, sound waves, light waves and even smells travel. The behaviour and characteristics of these phenomena are governed by the natural laws of physics. As part of this real world, human-human communication takes place using those physical phenomena that human beings are able to generate and detect. This layer determines the possible modes or channels of communication that are available for human-human communication.

While we all live in the same world, are there some channels of communication more useful for a particular gender? The evidence that women generally possess better verbal memory skills (Kimura, 2000) might suggest that the use of speech interfaces on the Web, in the future, would benefit females in particular. While greater male visual spatial ability, seen for example in 3-D image rotation, might suggest that virtual reality interfaces would be more usable by men (Vila, Beccue, & Anandikar, 2003).

Effector Layer

This layer represents the point at which humans interact with the external physical world. It includes the human input and output systems. Information is packaged, and sent or received as a coordinated set of verbal and/or nonverbal signals. An individual's ability to send and perceive signals and stimuli will determine the available channels for communication and their specification. For example, a visually impaired Web user would rely on speech output generated by text to speech software to interact with a Web site, rather than the text and images themselves.

Design considerations, at this layer in general, relate to the physical characteristics of the user. Research suggests that differences exist between the sexes in motor skills, spatial ability, and perceptual acuity (Kimura, 2000). Gender specific differences significant to Web page design at this level could relate to issues such as the higher occurrence of colour blindness in men, or that men excel at targeting skills while women generally exhibit superior fine-motor skills. However, investigation of gender differences can lead to interfaces that overcome previously perceived inabilities of one gender and improve interaction for all users, for example, providing more visual cues in 3-D navigation systems (Tan, Czerwinski, & Robertson, 2003), which may become more prevalent on the Web in the future as technology improves.

Cognition Layer

This layer is concerned with recognizing or generating the communication event, and interpreting or formulating its associated meaning. At this layer, information may be added to the signal or filtered out, thereby changing its content. The transformation that takes place at this layer is determined by a number of factors that are personal to the individual participants, such as their personality, emotional state, mental schema of the world, and so forth. Errors in perception and transmission can occur when too much or not enough attention is paid to a particular piece of information. These errors can result in overly positive or negative interpretations.

Research indicates that women have superior social cognitive skills due, in part, to greater verbal ability and differential socialization (Bennett et al., 2005). A specific example would be that, generally, females are better encoders and interpreters of nonverbal communications than males. As interface designers design social agents that interact with the user using facial expression, and so forth, these differences may impact on the usability of the interfaces for different genders.

The layers described previously are responsible for the actual, physical end-to-end transmission of communication events. The following layers relate to further cognitive processes that form the basis for conscious goal-seeking communication in humans. The form and content of the control, session, and presentation layers are, in particular, influenced by the environmental, cultural, and institutional context in which they occur.

Control Layer

The purpose of this layer is to ensure the reliability of the data that is transmitted, and the smooth running of the communication. The processes on this layer are responsible for successfully opening and closing the communication, monitoring quality control, requesting repair of any failure in transmission, and acknowledging successful transmission by generating feedback to support continuation of the conversation.

At this level, different types of communication feedback with respect to the two genders could be investigated. For example, are there specific forms that opening and closing sequences should take to cater more specifically for males and females?

Session Layer

The role of this layer is to synchronize and coordinate the main dialogue. This synchronization of the communication is supported by the elements identified by conversation analysis such as adjacency pairs, rules of turn taking, insertion sequences, and so forth. The protocols of natural speech mean that, for example, it is uncommon for participants to talk over each other or for there to be long gaps between alternating speakers. Where a situational influence applies, it will constrain the protocols in use to a subset of those used in everyday conversation, for example, the rules of turn allocation are more limited during an interview, in a schoolroom, or at a court of law.

Again the question to ask is: are there any gender specific issues that would constrain the form that, for example, turn taking would take? It is generally accepted that men and women communicate for different purposes. In both face-to-face and in virtual communities, men communicate to gain social standing and women with underlying compassion and empathy (Gefen & Ridings, 2005). As the Web becomes, increasingly, a medium for human–human communication, this may become a more important design consideration.

The control and session layers primarily support the procedural goals of the interaction.

Presentation Layer

The presentation layer deals with those elements and coding that constrain the communication as determined by the social context in which it takes place. Communication takes place against a backdrop of social roles, social responsibilities, as well as social norms and rules. These may include special codes or language sets recognized by different subgroups such as rules of address (based on gender, culture, class, organization, profession, etc.). The environmental context will determine the particular roles, relationships, rules, and norms that are available for use. This layer supports the interpersonal goals, and can also have a constraining effect on the form of the control and session layers.

The two genders take on diverse roles within society. At this layer, consideration should be made regarding both roles that make up the relationship, as well as the rules associated with their interaction. For example, for every student there is a teacher. If the teaching role is taken by a computer system, how should the interaction be designed to reflect the different preferences for learning styles of males and females?

Task Layer

This layer represents the shared domain of the participants involved in the communication. The task layer supports and defines the domain goals (public and private) of the activity. To participate successfully in a goal seeking activity, the participants must wish to attain the same or compatible goals. They must also share common knowledge and experience of the domain.

Evidence suggests that males and females have different ways of solving problems (Beckwith & Burnett, 2004). Ultimately, all users of the Web are trying to perform some task. Understanding how different people (perhaps of different genders) might approach the task could help to ensure that it can be completed efficiently by most people.

Summary

Models provide a useful tool for supporting the design and evaluation of user interfaces. In particular, task analysis has been the mainstream HCI modelling technique for a number of years. While still useful, this was developed in an era when computer use was predominantly office based. Technology has changed dramatically in recent years, and much computer use has moved into a social context at home and elsewhere. HCI modelling has been extended to accommodate such changes through the study of human-to-human communication in a social context. The user model presented represents a useful framework for exploring user differences (including gender) in interaction. We believe that more consideration should be given of these aspects in future Web design.

Design Issues

I do Web design and I'm a girl. And I hate pink. A lot. You may find this interesting—We recently went through a major hiring phase at my job. I'm a Web programmer, and the majority of the applicants for my job were female. The majority of the applicants for the graphic designer positions were male. How's that for breaking stereotypes? (Theresa, http://www.dandelionwine.org quote on http://wisdump.com/)

Web design crosses many of the layers previously analyzed. In this section, we will focus on how Web design and interface design is related to gender issues. In fact, Web design is strictly related to the audience. In particular, audience gender is, or should be, an important issue for designers. A designer should know the different reactions of the genders to graphic elements in order to design effective Web sites and avoid communication mistakes.

From studies conducted by http://www.women.com and the University of Chicago, it is possible to list some of the communication aspects that women like most (see Table 1).

Table 1. Layout composition

IMAGES	COLOUR	LAYOUT	MOOD	TONE
Babies	Pastels	Flowing	Light	Caring
Butterflies	Neutral Tones	Asymmetrical	Airy	Sharing
Flowers	Soft Colours	Curves	Bright	Sincere
Plants	Sky Blue	Smooth	Upbeat	Committed

Layout Composition

With these issues in mind, before starting to design a Web site, the Web designer should always consider the following:

1. What is the Web site's audience? Age, sex, culture, nationality, and so forth.
2. How should the Web site be designed to attract the right audience?
3. Should the Web site cater to a particular gender?
4. Which elements appeal to males and which to females? (Shapes, colour palette, fonts, sounds, etc.)
5. Should the Web site attract a specific gender? Why?
6. If yes, how should a specific gender be attracted to the Web site?
7. Is the Web site better off with gender neutrality?
8. Which kind of reaction does a particular gender have to the colour used?
9. And what reaction might each gender from different countries/cultures have to the colour used?

In this section of the chapter, we will also refer to the concept of "feminine," "masculine," and "neutral" Web design. We intend, with the first two terms, to mean a design that seems to be openly intended to attract users of a specific gender, and with the term "neutral" to indicate a design that does not explicitly address a single gender.

To define the design for a number of Web sites, we have combined our personal observations with a test using a focus group of 20 people (10 male and 10 female) of different ages (from 10 to 64); volunteers were interviewed about how they felt about the design. After having them navigate the Web site, we posed the following questions to them:

1. How do you feel about the Web site? Is it intended for men, women or both?
2. Why?
3. Define the Web site with three adjectives
4. How would you describe the "atmosphere" of the Web site and the sensations that you are experiencing using it?
5. Do you desire to navigate the Web site further?
6. Which colour do you feel is dominating the Web site design?
7. Which shape do you feel is dominating the Web site design?
8. Do you find the Web site easy to navigate and use?

We found our test results confirmed the research that we will illustrate further in the rest of this section.

Commercial Examples

We will now analyze four commercial Web sites, each one very gender targeted:

*   *Surf*, aimed at adult women;
*   *Gillette Complete Skincare*, for adult men;
*   *Barbie*, for young girls;
*   *Action Man*, for boys.

All of these Web sites show clearly how the design tries to focus on a specific gender.

Surf: http://www.surf.co.uk

*   **Overall description:** *Surf* is a washing brand. As for the interface and the text, its Web site is aimed at women and made by women. The design is characterized by naïve illustrations and a colourful palette. This gentle and emotional style explicitly tries to appeal to and please a feminine audience.
*   **Colours:** The colour palette is based on fuchsia, hot pink. Pink is usually considered a "feminine" colour and is commonly associated with the feminine stereotype. The Surf Web designers have accepted this stereotype and used it to create a humorous and emotionally involving Web site. The use of bright colours adds to this sensation and appeals to a positive audience.

- **Shapes:** As pointed out in the introduction, men prefer regular, unfussy, formal content and layout in straight lines, whereas women prefer more colour and rounded forms with less conventional design, formality, and linearity. This is confirmed by the Surf interface: circles and free-form shapes express emotion, warmth, fun, movement, energy, and forms that can be attributed to the "irrational" feminine world. It is a well-known fact that the circle is often associated with women. Actually, the Surf interface is based on circles: curved graphic elements, "bubbles," rounded photographs, birds, flowers, clouds. Besides circles, the naturalistic elements (such as birds and flowers) refer to nature in a typically feminine way. The overall layout is slightly asymmetrical, and this has been recognized as a feminine characteristic as well.

- **Font:** In an emotional site, the Web designer can be a little more daring in the use of decorative fonts. In this case, the designers chose to use only graphics fonts in order to use more swishy fonts and not to be limited to the default ones, even though this gives worse accessibility and poor legibility. Quoting from RedPolka.org (n.d.), we can reiterate by saying:

There are aspects of "feminine" design, then, that diminish usability on the Web. Our eyes read certain fonts better, for instance, and scripty fonts are not among them. Colour, used in excess, can become a distraction for the eyes (not to mention issues of colour-blindness and contrast for various folk). The same is true of graphics.

- **Sound:** Instead of background music, the designers chose natural sounds, such as birds singing. The result is a soft, not disturbing soundtrack that adds significantly to the naturalistic sensation of the Web site.

- **Mood and tone:** The Surf Web site seems to be both "light" and with a caring tone, trying to express optimism and an "upbeat" overall feeling, reinforced by the pictures.

Gillette: http://www.gillettecomplete.com

- **Overall description:** *Gillette Complete Skincare* is a Web site aimed at a male audience and willing to convey a masculine message. For example, it includes the phrase "It's time to face skincare like a man." The design is oriented towards this overtly masculine mission, and it is based on male stereotypes.

- **Colours:** The colour palette is based mostly on black and grey, with inserts of light blue and electronic green. Black and dark grey, in this context, are associated with power, sexuality, and sophistication. Blue reminds one of cleanliness, technology, and freshness. Bright green is associated with technology and computers. Moreover, according to Morton (1998, 2004), blue is one of men's favourite colours. Quoting from Khouw (n.d.):

A review of color studies done by Eysenck in early 1940's notes the following results to the relationship between gender and color. Dorcus (1926) found yellow had a higher affective value for the men than women and St. George (1938) maintained that blue for men stands out far more than for women. An even earlier study by Jastrow (1897) found men preferred blue to red and women red to blue.

- **Shapes:** Rectangles and sharp shapes express solidity, order, security, logic, and science; forms that can be attributed to the rational masculine world. Combining a rectangle and a triangle can communicate security and dynamism. In fact, the Gillette Complete Skincare design is based on rectangles and triangles. The page layout tends to be more symmetrical than Surf, a feature that reflects the male attitude towards rationality and order.

- **Font:** Fonts are made using graphics. Many of the fonts are in italics, with inclining lettering to express dynamism. The menu in the main box "Products—Face facts—3 easy steps for skincare" uses a font in capital letters that emphasizes technology and toughness.

- **Sound:** The Web site has no background music, in general. In some sections, there are limited sound effects, usually "technological" sounds.

- **Mood and tone:** The Gillette Web site conveys energy, toughness, technology, and modernity, with an overall mood and tone that tries to appeal to the traditional "masculine" image. This was definitely confirmed by our user tests.

Barbie: http://www.barbie.com

- **Overall description:** *Barbie* dolls are the ultimate in feminine stereotypes, and the Web site conforms with this image. The target audience is young preteenage girls, and the Web site can be overly feminine without fear of being seen as ridiculous. Quoting from RedPolka.org (n.d.):

But what is "feminine" in Web design? We could say that "feminine" is frequently ornamented, not necessarily floral (though there are many extreme examples of that), and is rarely spare and minimal. It favors the figural and human over the abstract. Pastels are definitely a theme, but dramatic or extensive use of any colors might be construed as feminine.

Barbie is very ornamented, colourful, figural, and pictorial.

- **Colours:** Barbie.com is full of different colours, but pink, in its different nuances, is the main feature. As Bear (n.d.) reminds us:

in some cultures, such as the U.S., pink is the color of little girls. It represents sugar and spice and everything nice. *Pink for men goes in and out of style. Most people still think of pink as a feminine, delicate color." Bear also suggests to "use pink to convey playfulness (hot pink flamingos) and tenderness (pastel pinks). Multiple shades of pink and light purple or other pastels used together maintain the soft, delicate, and playful nature of pink.*

In Barbie.com, pastels are mixed with bright shades, and the overall effect is "full," but with harmony. Even if, as noted in the *Background* section earlier, warm colours are particularly troublesome as a background to Web pages, Barbie.com often uses them because the overall emotional impact of the Web site seems to be more important than specific readability or usability.

- **Shapes:** Curved shapes are dominant in the whole Web site, together with illustrations and photographs. Straight lines are usually avoided; every corner is rounded or softened.

The home page is heavily animated: most of the objects move either alone or when the mouse-controlled cursor rolls over them. This is to fulfil the desire of playful interaction that children exhibit when using a computer. Also notable is the lack of symmetry in the home page: Barbie is not exactly in the middle of the page, and the objects are spread around in an asymmetrical and seemingly haphazard way.

- **Font:** On the Barbie Web site, there are many different kind of fonts: some swishy, some not. As we have seen above, there are aspects of feminine design that go against usability principles, such as *scripty* fonts or excessive use of colours. Barbie is probably not a very usable Web site, even if it is funny and playful. The effect of this lack of usability on its audience would be an interesting subject to study.

- **Sound:** Like colours and figures, sounds are very important to engage children. Barbie has a wide variety of sounds, from the background music to the sound effects that are triggered by clicking on an object or just by rollover, sometimes overlapping, which adds extra complexity. All the voices are feminine, reinforcing the gender orientation of the Web site.

- **Mood and tone:** The design is colourful and the feminine character is fashionable and young; all these elements converge in an overall sunny and cheerful atmosphere. Therefore, Barbie.com is definitely bright and upbeat, emanating a sharing tone to its users.

Action Man: http://www.actionman.com

- **Overall description:** *Action Man* is a cartoon targeted at young boys. Its masculine features are exaggerated in the same way Barbie's feminine stance is emphasized. The Web site aims to express the idea of energy, fighting, muscles, and dynamism. As with Barbie, in this Web site, we can clearly distinguish the gender stereotypes that are used to maximum effect.

- **Colours:** All the colours tend to be "metallic" and with strong contrasts between each other. Orange is the framing colour. It is also one of the shades favoured by males. Morton (1998, 2004) reports that:

  Eysenck's study, however, found only one gender difference with yellow being preferred to orange by women and orange to yellow by men. This finding was reinforced later by Birren (1952) who found men preferred orange to yellow; while women placed orange at the bottom of the list. (Khouw, n.d.)

- **Shapes:** The triangle is the strongest shape in this Web site; it is so important that it overlaps content and frames it. The triangle, opposite to the circle, is a typical male shape with sharp corners expressing force, aggression, and dynamic movement. In this case, the triangles also emphasize the central content of the page by directing the eyes towards it. The page tends to be symmetrical, a typical masculine feature.

- **Font:** Fonts are large and often in capital letters and italic, all to convey dynamism, although this results in a loss of legibility. This could be a problem also because, as reported in the *Educational Issues* section, usually boys tend to have worse linguistic skills than girls, and have more problems in reading from a screen.

- **Sound:** Sounds recall the graphic style of the Web site. The background music is aggressive and energetic, while sound effects are metallic and technological.

- **Mood and tone:** The overall mood of this Web site is definitely aggressive, energetic, and somewhat violent. Reactions to the atmosphere vary significantly between sex and ages, with a preference by young boys, the main target audience.

Cultural Examples

In the cultural field, specific audiences are important, but accessibility by all is a core value. This implies that gender-specific Web sites should try not to make the other gender feel set apart. In the two following examples, we will show how some elements of a feminine design can be combined with an overall neutrality.

National Museum of Women in the Arts: http://www.nmwa.org

- **Overall description:** The content, both of the museum and of the Web site (Figure 2), is explicitly gender-related. On the other hand, the audience is not only feminine, but the most general possible. According to this, the design is neutral and does not use any of the feminine stereotypes, as previously discussed.

- **Colours:** The dominant colours are blue, white, and sand. Blue, as we have already seen, is appreciated by males and conveys the idea of trust, conservation, cleanliness, and order. It is suitable for international audiences.

  Morton (1998, 2004) states that if you are designing for a worldwide audience, blue is the most globally accessible colour. As a result, you can use blue for just about any kind of site, regardless of its audience, goal, or location. Blue happens to be one of the colours that is safe in almost every culture. But why is blue so globally attractive? Morton (1998, 2004) speculates that "there's nothing on the planet that exists in isolation except the sky—that stands alone."

- **Shapes:** The Web site does not make an extensive use of shapes; anyway, straight lines are common to frame navigation areas.

- **Font:** All the graphic fonts are sans-serif; the default font is Arial. This choice is very neutral.

Figure 2. National Museum of Women in the Arts Web site

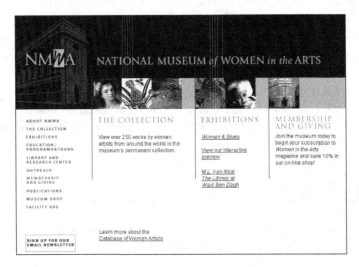

- **Sound:** The Web site also respects neutrality by not using any sounds.
- **Mood and tone:** The mood is not particularly light or upbeat, but it is felt by the users to be serious and credible, partly due to its institutional colours and design.

Fashion and Textile Museum: http://www.ftmlondon.org

- **Overall description:** The content of the museum is of interest to women, even if not exclusively so. The museum was founded by a woman, and the physical building is pink and orange. This choice could have led to a very feminine design, but in this case, only some elements are feminine, while others are masculine or neutral.
- **Colours:** Orange, fuchsia and white dominate the layout. They refer to the logo and to the building more than to a specific feminine taste.
- **Shapes:** The layout is based on rectangles, which are mainly masculine. Moreover, symmetry is important, another feature of more rationalistic designers.
- **Font:** All fonts are sans-serif and neutral.
- **Sound:** As in the previous Web site, this too does not use any background music or sound effects.
- **Mood and tone:** The colours used in the home page tend to create a bright atmosphere, friendly and welcoming like the museum building. Users expressed that the geometrical layout gives the impression that the site is simple and easy to use, even beyond its real usability.

Summary

In this section, we have considered a number of Web sites with strong gender bias of some sort, whether through the content, design, or both. We have presented brief descriptions of the overall design, colours, shapes, fonts, and sounds (if any) used, together with brief comments on the overall mode and tone of the site. Readers can draw their own conclusions, but may like to try a similar exercise on a small selection of Web sites of their own choosing.

In the next section, we consider the strongly commercial development of online gaming from the video game market, giving the potential of a community of games players. For females, this may encourage a collaborative response; in males, an adversarial and competitive attitude, if stereotypical lines are followed.

Online Gaming

Despite growing evidence that more and more girls and women play games online and in the home, the public image of the gamer... has remained fairly resistant to change. (Here come the game grrls. H. W. Kennedy, 2004, http://www.hero.ac.uk/)

In this section, we focus on how women gamer Web sites use different strategies of inclusion for their communities of gamers, often reflecting social features common in online game play, and supporting HCI models of social interaction (Argyle et al., 1985).

Not surprisingly, these community-building strategies have evolved from a history linked to the video game market and, latterly, to the rise of online gaming and online-enabled consoles. Recent surveys show a marked take-up by women in what has been perceived as a male-dominated domain, namely the playing of online and computer games. For instance, the Entertainment Software Association (2003) in the U.S. tallied that half of all Americans play computer and video games, with women making up the second largest group of gamers. A U.S. survey by Peter D. Hart Research Associates on behalf of the Entertainment Software Association reported on a random 1,048 computer or video-game players, with ±3.5% error. The summary findings are as follows (Ramirez, 2003):

- Men aged 18 and older: 38%
- Women aged 18 and older: 26%
- Boys aged 6-17:   21%
- Girls aged 6-17:   12%

Outside the U.S., statistics reveal comparable findings: "According to Screen Digest's ISFE 2003 yearbook, across Western Europe female gamers make up 25.1% of the region's total active gamers" (ELSPA, 2004). Of UK gamers, 27.2% are women, the second largest game playing population in Western Europe. Japan leads the international statistics in that 69.2% of women have at least one games console in the home, and game play on mobile phones is particularly pervasive (ELSPA, 2004).

Rise of the Girls' Game Movement

Before the development of gaming communities on the Internet, the "traditional" market of video and console games was clearly male dominated in terms of players and designers (Cherney & Weise, 1996). The development of girls-only video games did not appear prominently on the market until the early 1990s, although in the 1980s, Roberta and Ken Williams developed a series of adventure games (e.g., Mystery House) and the arcade classic Frogger (1983), which were popular with boys and girls.

In 1994, the first game specifically targeted towards girls was called "Hawaii High: The Mystery of the Tiki," designed by Trina Roberts, a writer for Barbie Comics and designer of Wonder Woman. This game was not a success, but used features that would influence the girls' games movement, namely, more character-centred plots, friendship, and social relationship activities, as well as incorporation of bright graphics (Cassell, 1998). Concurrently, Patricia Flanegan, co-owner of American Laser Games, and Sheri Graner Ray, an established games designer, set up HerInteractive in 1995 to create games that particularly appealed to girls (Krotoski, 2004).

However, the scene was dominated with the launch of "Barbie Fashion Designer," which sold significant numbers of copies (600,000 in the first year) and was the benchmark for so-called "pink games." Interestingly, Core Design's *Tomb Raider,* with its strong female protagonist Lara Croft, came onto the market around the same time and provided further thought to assumptions about gender (e.g., postfeminist equality) and, contrastingly, a stereotypical rendering of the female form. Lara Croft has adapte d to be more female-friendly as the games have developed subsequently, with a change in dimensions of Lara herself!

Among the challengers to both gender assumptions and the girls' game movement itself arose organizations of female gamers, such as *Grrlgamer* (http://www.grrl-gamer.com/), who sought to confront fixed identities and take on traditional combat games as a space where they could tackle male gamers on their own terrain (Cassell, & Jenkins, 1998; Groppe, 2001).

They addressed concerns around sexism and exclusion from the games playing community itself. They did this through active participation in games seen as "hard core," and they directly took on the assumption that first-person shooter games were only intended for boys and men. As Funk and Buchman (1996) and Funk (2001) observe, games that simply focus on friendship and sociality may overlook the fact that "girls are looking for games which also push them to take risks and where there is a chance to be absolutely and unequivocally dominant."

In a parallel development, more games became available from the late 1990s that could be played on home computers and on the Internet via the Web. This enabled female gamers to gain greater private access to gaming spaces and technologies. It allowed greater liberty for female gamers to become proficient in their own right and to play more anonymously, and with less sanction in playing what may be seen as games for boys (Griffiths, Davies, & Chappell, 2003; Groppe, 2001).

Within this climate, and on the heels of the underground success of *Grrlgamer*, sites like *GameGirlAdvance.com* and *WomenGamers.com* were established by women for female players. *GameGirlAdvance* is a Web log and online journal that brings alternative perspectives to videogame culture with a focus on girls and women. *WomenGamers.com* has positioned itself as one of the largest women's gaming portals on the Internet.

Female Gaming Sites and Social Interaction

Both *GameGirlAdvance* and *WomenGamers* have striking similarities in approaches to their communities that underpin those of other women-led online gaming sites (e.g., *GameGal*). A key feature is their emphasis on the social role they offer users and female gamers who do not easily fit into contemporary models of play preferences.

In terms of social roles, for instance, the sites are critically aware that virtual and gaming worlds are habitually regarded as replacements of an individual's world. In this world, individuals can undertake an alias to align their membership to certain groups. Online gaming worlds such as multiuser dungeons (MUDs) and massive multiplayer online games (MMOGs), for example, *Asheron's Call*, *Ultima Online*, and *EverQuest,* have paved the way toward a wider space for exploring identity and community through membership and participation (Manninen, 2001; Vogiazou & Eisenstadt, 2005).

In general, a more participatory approach in online gaming development follows an increased awareness and application of HCI models of social interaction (see the Modelling HCI Interaction section) in which social or person-situation contexts incorporate social norms, roles, relationships, and rules. Together, these provide a framework that supports the development of cooperating communities and the attainment of shared goals—a "natural fit" to the multiple player relationships within gaming worlds—regardless of gender or "real" world identity.

Likewise, game designers themselves have been innovating new forms of interaction and creating paradigms for HCI. The availability of dynamic user modelling and alternative input modalities driven by gaming applications, and the trend toward large, online communities of players have created opportunities for researchers to test theories and form new models of interaction strategies.

For instance, game designer and researcher, Manninen (2001, 2003), provides an insight into categories of perceivable interaction forms available in multiplayer games by analysing the communicative and social aspects of computer-mediated gaming. These categories effectively go across, and intersect with, the layered framework (Figure 1) of human-human interaction. Manninen (2003) defines interaction forms as actions that can potentially be perceived by players. They can act as manifestations of interaction occurring between players, or between players and the game world, and are used to convey the actions of the player to oneself, as well as to others. Interaction forms further enable awareness of actions by offering mutually perceivable visualizations and auralizations within the game world.

In Taylor (2003), the offerings of social interaction, mastery and status, team participation, and exploration provided by MMOGs are shown, particularly, to support the types of activities that appeal to female gamers in online environments (Krotoski, 2004). This is not least because of the ability of the player to create and deploy an alias with relative anonymity, and their subsequent alignment of this alias to a community. In MMOGs, players are also free to present themselves according to their imagination. When entering an MMOG, players choose a character and personalize it.

In an analogous manner, Web sites, like *WomenGamers,* incorporate personalization features and a member log in that extend the deployment of aliases, as well as the content itself, and encourages and facilitates the use of gaming nicknames for contributors to articles and blogs, for example.

Related to this, the design of a site for female gamers reflects the composition of gaming communities, often representing a virtual diaspora, who bear different markers and names that are used to support their claim to a certain identity and assertion of a virtual self. These can involve more elaborate structures than those in more established groups.

What can tie together this community of diaspora is a common set of visual information. For instance, there may be a certain emphasis on open "fanzine" formats with incorporation of associative symbols of female empowerment, notably in the form of female avatars not unlike Joanna Dark from Perfect Dark/Nintendo and Jen from Primal/SCEE, and other gamers with "attitude." Although there is more evidence of targeting a young adult audience in *GameGirlAdvance* than *WomenGamers*, users have more fluid gender identities in games that are populated by both strong male and female characters.

Designing Identity

Female identity in both image and content seems to be constantly reinforced across the sites. This raises the wider question of gender association that the sites promote and on which the community is largely built. Interestingly, gender is a commonly manipulated element by gamers in gaming environments, in terms of avatars and game characters.

Taylor (2004) notes that while there is a fair amount of diversity among female gamers about what style of avatars are preferable, there seems to be a consistent message that they want a choice in how they look online. It is indeed possible for women to hold complicated relationships to even stereotypically gendered characters (like Lara Croft). It can be said that the relationship between an avatar and its user or agent is one of the most active areas of play and interaction among women gamers. The importance of identifying with a character is borne out by interviews with a selection of women gamers who indicated that favourite titles include "role playing" games like the *Final Fantasy series/Square Enix*, narrative adventures like *Legend of Zelda/Nintendo*, and life simulations like *The Sims/EA/Maxis* (Krotoski, 2004).

Female gaming Web sites provide an additional channel for this interaction to be translated with the submission of gamers' own created and customized avatar images, articles, online discussions, and Web logs. In the August 2005 edition of *WomenGamers*, for example, gamers were invited to rank the top female avatars in online and computer games on the market, and for the same month in *GameGirlAdvance*, there was a debate on types of combat that may or may not be acceptable to young adult gamers.

Such communication tools assist further in the development of strong female identity through community dialogue, and can substitute for the absence, in real game play, of equivalent, strong, female models or roles. Similarly, they permit users to take on an avatar (their own or others) and make sense of it through a variety of social and personal "stories" beyond the gaming environment. Again, the option for anonymity and the nature of interactive Web facilities (e.g., chat rooms) allow users to meet relatively independently, and to retain a given social identity in the process.

An elementary design principle shared in both *GameGirlAdvance* (Pinckard, 2003) and *WomenGamers* is the importance of identifying and defining the target audience and their interests, capabilities, and contexts of use of the Web site, and not least, the incorporation of appropriate tools to support this (Sørensen, 2004). Here, of course, it must be remembered that the female gamer audience is not a fixed or universal category, but can be highly variable with respect to its genres of play and/or technical interests or capabilities (Cherney & Weise, 1996; Groppe, 2001; Taylor, 2004).

Therefore, the presentation layer should equally identify, and take account of, the issues of relevance and interest of its target audiences (Culp & Honey, 2002). The range (genres) of content or sets of functions/applications must be designed to appeal to the spectrum of interests of the female gamers being targeted (Ray, 2003). The use of up-to-date news columns, articles by a mix of well-known gamers and member contributors, and real-time communication tools on the Web sites would appear to fulfil some of these broad requirements.

With regard to the overall interface design, the principle of "less is more" has been adopted by the two women gaming sites in question, to a certain extent. The design of the entry points or interfaces immediately seeks to do two things to optimize social interaction and identity: (1) at the presentation layer, enable community identification by active use of associative images and text and (2) at the task layer, enable participation among the targeted groups through prominent discussion areas. There is also the inclusion of a platform approach to the access and use of other applications and functions, including online channels for exchanges between users (e.g., Web logs).

These communication features, in turn, can add substantially to the potential for the sites to play an informal educative role (Powazek, 2001). As elsewhere, participants in online communities potentially enjoy a far more strategic, precise, and focused type of support than is available off-line (Powazek, 2001; Rheingold, 2000). Suzie Cardwell, Director of 3RD Sense, notes that the importance of community-based content cannot be underestimated on a female gamer Web site (e.g., *Chickstop. com*), and cites that women's tendency to seek social contact with other like-minded women finds an outlet in the forum that cannot easily be found elsewhere (Krotoski, 2004).

Perhaps more important than the type of information that these communities can exchange is the emotional support they provide for community members (e.g., novice gamers or game developers). In a community that has been historically marginalized and has needed to resort to their own adaptation of habitually stereotyped approaches to game development (Cassell & Jenkins, 1998; Griffiths et al., 2003; Huff & Cooper, 1987; Ivory & Wilkerson, 2002), women gamer Web sites are particularly pivotal in the fostering and support of the female gamer.

It is not surprising, then, that the design and tools that make up women gamer sites put an emphasis on community-centric and collaborative activities (Sorensen, 2004). They are not only intended to stimulate loyalty, attract new audiences, and mobilize informal sharing and learning, but to contribute to women gamer identities (whatever form that may take), and simply to offer environments for women to communicate about computer gaming culture from their perspective. The latter is the real challenge and *raison d'être* of these Web sites. Designers of such sites must ensure that the interfaces presented to the users help in promoting their purpose, which will include serious consideration of more sociological gender issues.

Conclusion

I read recently that women had finally become more than 50% of online shoppers and that in a couple of years they would be 80%. So most Web sites will be designed for women. What do the women here think of that?

In conclusion, there are significant differences in the preferences of males and females with respect to Web sites and their interfaces. Recent survey research on Web sites reinforces this view (Moss & Gunn, in press; Moss, Gunn & Kubacki, in press). Content is very important too, with females using broadband connections favouring Web sites on pets (65% female users), and males much preferring automotive parts and accessories (80% male users), for example (Burmaster, 2005). Online habits increasingly reflect real-world interests of both genders, as the Web becomes less of a novelty and more an integral part of people's lives and daily activities.

The framework for modelling HCI, suggested in this chapter, is still an area of research that could be developed into a sophisticated way to evaluate HCI at a number of different levels of abstraction, with respect to gender or other issues. The framework for evaluating design is a more practical and pragmatic approach that can be applied immediately to Web sites in any desired field. It would be an interesting exercise to undertake a wider survey within this framework, perhaps evaluating Web sites covering topics with a high degree of gender bias, as presented in Burmaster (2005) for example.

For educational resources, in general, it is best to try to accommodate the needs of both genders as much as possible. Gender differences in online preferences can be even more marked for children than adults, as demonstrated in the targeted commercial Web sites for the youth market in the *Design Issues* section. The concern for wide accessibility is reflected in the gender-neutral designs of the cultural Web sites also presented in the same section. Provided this aspect is considered carefully, the content is likely to have more effect on usage than the user interface. Only in extreme examples, where the users are dominated by one gender, should a significant bias be introduced to accommodate the majority. Even then, catering for the minority gender could still be well worthwhile to attract more users.

Whether a gender-neutral design should be adopted or whether a specific gender should be targeted will always depend on the precise purpose of the Web site in question. However, there is currently, still, a very real gender bias towards male preferences online, perhaps partly because Web site designers and related decision makers are statistically dominated by males. On the other hand, the number of Web surfers is much more evenly matched with respect to gender balance. Thus, it is recommended that the issue is considered more seriously in the design of future Web interfaces.

The problem of accommodating gender preferences is also important for other HCI paradigms such as virtual reality for games, and so forth, that may become more significant as interactive/networking technology and speeds improve. If this chapter influences future Web interface designers even in a small way, and at least raises awareness of some of the issues, it will have been worthwhile.

Acknowledgments

The original inspiration for this chapter came from a Profession Forum presentation at the *Museums and the Web* 2005 Conference (Baiget et al., 2005). The anonymous reviewers, Gloria Moss of the University of Glamorgan and Yva Thakurdas of Museophile Limited, provided some useful feedback that improved this chapter.

References

Argyle, M. (1969). *Social interaction*. London: Methuen.

Argyle, M., Henderson, M., & Furnham, A. (1985). The rules of social relationships. *British Journal of Social Psychology, 24,* 125-139.

Baiget, C., Bernal, I., Black, S., Blinova, N., Boiano, S., Borda, A., Bowen, J. P., Grahn, W., Lisney, E., & Numerico, T. (2005, April 13-15). Gender issues and museum websites. In D. Bearman & J. Trant (Eds.), *MW2005: Museums and the Web 2005*, Vancouver, Canada. Retrieved from http://www.archimuse. com/mw2005/papers/bowen/bowen.html

Balka, E. (1996). Gender and skill in human computer interaction. *CHI 96 Electronic Proceedings*. ACM, Interactive Posters. Retrieved from http://sigchi. org/chi96/proceedings/intpost/Balka/be_txt.html

Barnard, P. J. (1986). Cognitive resources and the learning of human computer dialogs. In J. M. Carroll (Ed.), *Interfacing thought: Cognitive aspects of human-computer interaction* (pp. 112-158). Cambridge, MA: The MIT Press.

Bear, J. H. (n.d.). *Pink: Color profile*. Retrieved from http://desktoppub.about. com/cs/colorselection/p/pink.htm

Beckwith, L., & Burnett, M. (2004, September 26-29). Gender: An important factor in end-user programming environments? *Proceedings of IEEE Symposium on Visual Languages and Human-Centric Computing (VLHCC'04)*. IEEE Computer Society. Retrieved from http://doi.ieeecomputersociety.org/10.1109/ VLHCC.2004.28

Beler, A., Borda, A., Bowen, J. P., & Filippini-Fantoni, S. (2004, July 26-30). The building of online communities: An approach for learning organizations, with a particular focus on the museum sector, In J. R. Hemsley, V. Cappellini, & G. Stanke, G. (Eds.), *EVA 2004 London Conference Proceedings* (pp. 2.1-2.15). London.

Bennett, S., Farrington, D. P., & Huesmann, L. R. (2005). Explaining gender differences in crime and violence: The importance of social cognitive skills. *Aggression and Violent Behavior, 10*(3), 263-288.

Bernier, R. (2002). *The uses of virtual museums: The French viewpoint*. In Dr. Bearman & J. Trant (Eds.), Proceedings of the Museums and the Web Conference, Boston. Retrieved from http://www.archimuse.com/mw2002/papers/bernier/ bernier.html

Bernier, R., & Bowen, J. P. (2004). Web-based discussion groups at stake: The profile of museum professionals online. *Program: Electronic Library and Information Systems, 38*(2), 120-137. Retrieved from http://dx.doi.org/10.11 08/00330330410532832

Bowen, J. P. (2005). Web access to cultural heritage for the disabled. In J. R. Hemsley (Ed.), *Digital applications for cultural and heritage institutions: Selected papers from the EVA Conferences* (pp. 215-225). Ashgate Publishing Limited.

Bowen, J. P., Bennett, J., & Johnson, J. (1998). Visiteurs virtuels et musées virtuel. *Publics et Musées, 13*, 115-127, January–June. France: Presses universitaires de Lyon.

Bowen, J. P., Moss, G., Gunn, R., Bernal, I., Lisney, E. McDaid, S., et al. (2006, April 3-7). Encouraging gender balance: A survey of European art museum websites, In V. Cappellini & J. R. Hemsley (Eds.), *EVA 2006 Florence Conference Proceedings*, Florence, Italy (pp. 185-190). Pitagora Editrice Bologna.

Burmaster, A. (2005). Who's winning the broadband revolution? Nielsen//NetRatings, 18 October. Retrieved from http://www.netratings.com/pr/pr_051018_uk.pdf

Card, S. K., Moran, T. P., & Newell, A. (1983). *The psychology of human-computer interaction*. London: L. Erlbaum Associates.

Cassell, J. (2002). *Genderizing HCI*. MIT Media Lab, Cambridge, MA. Retrieved from http://www.media.mit.edu/gnl/pubs/gender.hci.just.pdf

Cassell, J., & Jenkins, H. (Eds.). (1998). *From Barbie to Mortal Kombat: Gender and computer games*. Cambridge, MA: MIT Press.

Chadwick, J., & Boverie, P. (1999, March 11-14). A survey of characteristics and patterns of behavior in visitors to a museum Web site. *Museums and the Web Conference*, Pittsburgh, PA. Archives & Museum Informatics. Retrieved from http://www.archimuse.com/mw99/papers/chadwick/chadwick.html

Cherney, L., & Weise, R. (Eds.). (1996). *Wired women: Gender and new realities in cyberspace*. Seattle: Seal Press.

Clark, H. H. (1996). *Using language*. Cambridge, UK: Cambridge University Press.

Clarkson, J. (2003). *Countering design exclusion: An introduction to inclusive design*. London: Springer.

Culp, K. M., & Honey, M. (2002). Imagining less-gendered game worlds. In N. Yelland, A. Rubin, & E. McWilliam (Eds.), *Ghosts in the machine: Women's voices in research with technology* (pp. 33-53). New York: Peter Lang Publishing.

Culwin, F., & Faulkner, X. (2001, January 3-6). Brewsing the Web: Delay, determination and satisfaction. *IEEE Proceedings of the 34th Annual Hawaii International Conference on System Sciences (HICSS-34)* (pp. 5018-5022).

Dierking, L. D., & Falk, J. H. (1998, April 22-25). Understanding free-choice learning: A review of the research and its application to museum Web sites. *Museums and the Web Conference*, Pittsburgh, PA: Archives & Museum Informatics. Retrieved from http://www.archimuse.com/mw98/papers/dierking/dierking_paper.html

ELSPA (2004). *Chicks and joysticks: An exploration of women and gaming.* White Paper, The Entertainment & Leisure Software Publishers Association, September. Retrieved from http://www.elspa.com/assets/files/chicksandjoysticksanexplorationofwomenandgaming_176.pdf

Entertainment Software Association. (2003). *Game players are a more diverse gender, age and socioeconomic group than ever, according to new poll.* Retrieved from http://www.theesa.com/archives/2003/08/game_players_ar.php

Faulkner, X. (1998). *Essence of HCI.* Hemel Hempstead: Prentice Hall.

Faulkner, X. (2000). *Usability engineering.* Basingstoke: Palgrave.

Faulkner, X., & Culwin, F. (2005). When fingers do the talking, interacting with computers. *BCS BHCI Journal, 7*(2), 167-185.

Filippini-Fantoni, S., Bowen, J. P., & Numerico, T. (2005). Personalization issues for science museum websites and e-learning, In L. T. W. Hin & L.T.W. R. Subramaniam (Eds.), *E-learning and virtual science centers* (pp. 272-291). Hershey, PA: Idea Group Publishing.

Forty, A. (1986). *Objects of desire.* New York: Pantheon Books.

Frohlich, D., & Luff, P. (1990). Applying the technology of conversation to the technology of conversation. In P. Luff, N. Gilbert, & D. Frohlich (Eds.), *Computers and conversation* (pp. 187-220). London: Academic Press.

Funk, J. B. (2001). Girls just want to have fun. *Playing by the Rules: The Cultural Policy Challenges of Video Games Conference,* University of Chicago, October. Retrieved from http://culturalpolicy.uchicago.edu/conf2001/papers/funk2.html

Funk, J. B., & Buchman, D. D. (1996). Children's perceptions of gender differences in social approval for playing electronic games. *Sex Roles, 35*(3/4), 219-231.

Gefen, D., & Ridings, C. M. (2005). If you spoke as she does, sir, instead of the way you do: A sociolinguistics perspective of gender differences in virtual communities. *SIGMIS Database, 36*(2), 78-92.

Griffiths, M. D, Davies, M. N,. & Chappell, D. (2003). Breaking the stereotype: The case of online gaming. *Cyberpsychology & Behavior, 6*(1), 81-91.

Groppe, L. (2001). Teen girl gaming: The new paradigm. *Playing by the Rules: The Cultural Policy Challenges of Video Games Conference.* University of ChicagoOctober. Retrieved from http://culturalpolicy.uchicago.edu/conf2001/papers/groppe.html

Gunn, R., Moss, G., Bowen, J. P., Bernal, I. Lisney, E., & McDaid, S. (2006, July 26-28). A comparison of gender bias in art and science museum Websites. In J. Hemsley, S. Keene, L. MacDonald, P. Bowen, V. Cappelini, & G. Stanke (Eds.), *EVA 2006 London Conference Proceedings,* London (pp. 5.1-5.7). London: EVA: Conferences Int.

Harden, A. (2005). *Key website research highlights gender bias.* University of Glamorgan, UK, August 2. Retrieved from http://www.glam.ac.uk/news/releases/003056.php

Harding, S. (1986). *The science question in feminism.* Ithaca: Cornell University Press.

Hargie, O. D. W. (1997). *The handbook of communication skills.* London: Routledge.

Hsu, C.-L., & Lu, H.-P. (2004). Why do people play online games? An extended TAM with social influences and flow experience. *Information & Management, 41*(7), 853-868.

Huff, C., & Cooper, J. (1987). Sex bias in educational software: The effect of designers' stereotypes on the software they design. *Journal of Applied Social Psychology, 17*(6), 519-532.

Inkpen, K. (1997). Three important research agendas for educational multimedia: Learning, children, and gender. *AACE ED-MEDIA '97: World Conference on Educational Multimedia and Hypermedia*, Calgary, Canada. Retrieved from http://www.edgelab.ca/publications/edmedia97.pdf

Ivory, J. D., & Wilkerson, H. (2002). Video games are from Mars, not Venus: Gender, electronic game play and attitudes toward the medium. *Commission on the Status of Women at the Annual Convention of the Association for Education in Journalism and Mass Communication.*

Khouw, N. (n.d.). *The meaning of color for gender.* Retrieved from http://www.colormatters.com/khouw.html

Kieras, D., & Polson, P. G. (1999). An approach to the formal analysis of user complexity. *International Journal of Human-Computer Studies, 51*, 405-434.

Kimura, D. (2000). *Sex and cognition.* Cambridge, MA: MIT Press.

Krotoski, A. (2004). *Chicks and joysticks: An exploration of women and gaming.* ELSPA White Paper, September.

Leong, S. C., & Hawamdeh, S. (1999). Gender and learning attitudes in using Web-based science lessons. *Information Research, 5*(1). Retrieved from http://informationr.net/ir/5-1/paper66.html

Manninen, T. (2001). Rich interaction in the context of networked virtual environments – experiments gained from the multi-player games domain. In A. Blandford, J. Vanderdonckt, & P. Gray (Eds.), *Joint Proceedings of HCI 2001 and IHM 2001 Conference* (pp. 383-398). Springer-Verlag.

Manninen, T. (2003). Interaction forms and communicative actions in multiplayer games. *International Journal of Computer Game Research, 3*(1). Retrieved from http://www.gamestudies.org/0301/manninen/

McDaid, S. (2005, September 5-9). A model of human-computer interaction based on human-human communication. In L. MacKinnon, O. Bertelsen, & N. Bryan-Kinns, N. (Eds.), *Proceedings of HCI2005: The Bigger Picture, Volume 2* (pp. 215-217). Edinburgh, UK.

Moran, T. P. (1981). The command language grammar: A representation for the user interface of interactive computer systems. *International Journal of Man-Machine Studies, 15,* 3-50.

Moran, T. P. (1983). Getting into a system: External-internal task mapping analysis. *Proceedings of the SIGCHI Conference on Human Factors in Computing Systems,* Boston. New York: ACM Press.

Morkes, J., & Nielsen, J. (1997). *Concise, SCANNABLE, and objective: How to write for the Web.* Retrieved from http://www.useit.com/papers/webwriting/writing.html

Morton, J. L. (1998). *Color logic.* Colorcom.

Morton, J. L. (2004). *Colors that sell: Tried and tested color schemes.* Colorcom.

Moss, G., & Gunn, R. (2005, July). Websites and services branding: Implications of Universities' websites for internal and external communication. *The 4th International Critical Management Studies Conference,* Cambridge, UK.

Moss, G., & Gunn, R. (n.d.). *Design psychology.* Weblog. Retrieved from http://designpsych.weblog.glam.ac.uk/

Moss, G., & Gunn, R. (2006). Some men like it black, some women like it pink: Consumer implications of differences in male and female website design. *Journal of Consumer Behaviour, 5*(4), 328-241. Retrieved from http://dx.doi.org/10.1002/cb.184

Moss, G., Gunn, R., & Kubacki, K. (2006). Optimising Web design across Europe: Gender implications from an interactionist point of view. *International Journal of Applied Marketing, 2*(1). Retrieved from http://www.managementjournals.com/journals/marketing/article217.htm

Nachmias, R., Mioduser, D., & Shemla, A. (2001). Information and communication technologies usage by school students in an Israeli school: Equity, gender, and inside/outside school learning issues. *Education and Information Technologies, 6*(1). Retrieved from http://muse.tau.ac.il/publications/ICT.pdf

Nie, J. H., & Erbring, L. (2002). *Internet and society: A preliminary report.* Stanford Institute for the Quantitative Study of Society, Stanford University February. Retrieved from http://www.stanford.edu/group/siqss/Press_Release/Preliminary_Report.pdf

Nielsen, J. (2002a). *Kids' corner: Website usability for children.* Alertbox, 14 April. Retrieved from http://www.useit.com/alertbox/20020414.html

Nielsen, J. (2002b). *Usability for senior citizens.* Alertbox, 28 April. Retrieved from http://www.useit.com/alertbox/20020428.html

Nielsen, J. (2005) *Usability of websites for teenagers.* Alertbox, 31 January. Retrieved from http://www.useit.com/alertbox/20050131.html

Norman, D. (1998). *Invisible computer.* Cambridge, MA: The MIT Press.

Norman, M., & Thomas, P. (1990). The very idea: Informing HCI design through conversation analysis. In P. Luff, N. Gilbert, & D. Frohlich (Eds.), *Computers and conversation* (pp. 51-65). London: Academic Press.

Payne, S. J., & Green, T. R. G. (1986). Task action grammars. *Human Computer Interaction, 2,* 93-133.

Pinckard, J. (2003). *Brenda Laurel at Stanford: Design research.* GameGirlAdvance, May. Retrieved from http://www.gamegirladvance.com/archives/2003/05/08/brenda_laurel_at_stanford.html

Powazek, D. M. (2001). *Design for community: The art of connecting real people in virtual places.* New Riders.

Ramirez, C. E. (2003). Online games attract more women: Females becoming dominant group with Web gaming sites. *The Detroit News.*

Ray, S. G. (2003). *Gender inclusive game design: Expanding the market.* Hingham, MA: Charles River Media.

RedPolka.org. (n.d.). *Design, gender and equity.* Retrieved from http://www.red-polka.org/blog/archives/001544.html

Reisner, P. (1982). Further developments toward using formal grammar as a design tool. *Proceedings of the Conference on Human Factors in Computing Systems,* Gaithersburg, MD. New York: ACM Press.

Rheingold, H. (2000). *The virtual community: Homesteading on the electronic frontier.* Cambridge, MA: MIT Press.

Sacks, H. (2001). Lecture 1: Rules of conversational sequence. In M. Wetherell, S. Taylor, & S. J. Yates (Eds.), *Discourse theory and practice: A reader.* London: Sage.

Shany, N., & Nachmias, R. (2001). The relationship between performance in a virtual course and thinking styles, gender, and ICT experience. *World Conference on Educational Multimedia, Hypermedia and Telecommunications* (Vol. 1, pp. 1698-1702). Retrieved from http://dl.aace.org/8851 (See also Research Report No. 64, Tel Aviv University, Israel. Retrieved from http://muse.tau.ac.il/publications/64.pdf)

Sørensen, K. H. (2004). *Gender and inclusion policies for the information society*. IST-2000-26329 SIGIS, Strategies of Inclusion: Gender in the Information Society, D07. Retrieved from http://www.csmb.unimo.it/adapt/bdoc/27_04/SIGIS_D07_EC.pdf

Tan, D. S., Czerwinski, M., & Robertson, G. (2003). Women go with the (optical) flow. *Proceedings of the SIGCHI Conference on Human Factors in Computing Systems* (pp. 209-215). Fort Lauderdale, Florida, USA. New York: ACM Press.

Tauber, M. J. (1990). ETAG: Extended task action grammar, a language for the description of the user's task language. *Interact '90*, Cambridge University, UK. Amsterdam: North Holland.

Taylor, T. L. (2003). Multiple pleasures: Women and online gaming. *Convergence: The Journal of Research into New Media Technologies, 9*(1) 21-46.

Taylor, T. L. (2004). The social design of virtual worlds: Constructing the user and community through code, In M. Consalvo et al. (Eds.), *Internet Research Annual Volume 1: Selected Papers from the Association of Internet Researchers Conferences 2000-2002*. New York: Peter Lang.

Tysome, T. (2005). Institutions show manly face on net. *The Times Higher Education Supplement, 1704*, 7, August 12.

Venkatesh, V., & Morris, M. G. (2000). Why don't men ever stop to ask for directions? Gender, social influence and their role in technology acceptance and usage behavior. *MIS Quarterly, 24*(1), 115-139.

Vila, J., Beccue, B., & Anandikar, S. (2003, January 6-9). The gender factor in virtual reality navigation and wayfinding. *Proceedings of the 36th Annual Hawaii International Conference on System Sciences (HICSS'03)*, Track 4, 101b. IEEE Computer Society. Retrieved from http://doi.ieeecomputersociety.org/10.1109/HICSS.2003.1174239

Vogiazou, Y., & Eisenstadt, N. (2005). *Designing multiplayer games to facilitate emergent social behaviours online*. Technical Report KMI-04-23. Knowledge Media Institute, The Open University, UK.

Chapter VII

Interpreting the Female User:
How Web Designers Conceptualise Development of Commercial WWW Sites to Satisfy Specific Niche Markets

Noemi Maria Sadowska, Regents Business School London, UK

Abstract

This chapter presents an investigation into the commercial WWW portal, "BEME. com," as an example of gendered Web design targeting female users. It argues that Web designers need to be aware of processes implicated in such gendered outcomes. Thus, an analysis of the BEME.com design process is used to identify threats and opportunities in designing for female online users in order to formulate appropriate design guidelines. The chapter outlines several underlying factors that illuminate these processes, and their social, cultural, and political origins. It is argued that the prevalence and accessibility of WWW makes it a powerful vehicle of change both within design practice and in terms of gender structures more widely. It is in this context that the author seeks to contribute to the existing research by offering a feminist critique of Web design, arguing that Web designers have an opportunity and a responsibility to affect and effect changes to a gendered status quo.

Introduction

Following the threat of economic collapse in 2001, technological development and new forms of access have revitalised interest in the Internet. Recent developments, such as the availability of "always on" connections via broadband, reduced cost, and an ever-growing population of users have had implications for the nature and reception of the Internet. In these circumstances, the role of Web designers has also shifted from that of "creative explorers" to a far more responsible, meaningful, and embedded position within the development of the World Wide Web (WWW). Furthermore, constant refinement of online niche markets has prompted further questioning and fine-tuning of Web designs to suit the needs of particular users. To facilitate a discussion of these issues, an investigation into a commercial WWW portal entitled BEME.com has been conducted as an example of Web design practice targeting female users. A product of IPC Media (IPC), BEME.com developed directly out of traditional women's magazine publishing in response to a boom in dot.com industries at the end of the 1990s. This investigation questions how Web designers conceptualise development of such Web sites intended to meet the needs of their female audience. It draws on an analysis of public relations publications and interviews with the BEME.com design team.

Early studies of women's WWW use focused primarily on raising awareness of a significant disparity between the number of male and female online users (Harcourt, 1999). However, as Martinson, Schwartz, and Walker Vaughan (2002) point out, "[w]hile current numerical parity on the Internet is one measure of progress, issues of gender equality are more complex than simple counts of who is logging on to the Internet" (p. 31). Recently, a number of scholars, including Rommes (2002) and Spilker and Sørensen (2000), have investigated various ways in which the WWW could become more inclusive of female users, and initiatives such as *Strategies of inclusion: Gender and the information society* (2000-3) have sought to address the complexity of women's participation in the WWW (Faulkner, Sørensen, Gansmø, Rommes, Pitt, Lagesen Berg, et al., 2004). The issues discussed in this chapter sit between recognition of a need for strategies of online inclusion, and belief in and knowledge of the capacity of Web design practice to continually develop and innovate. An argument is constructed for the potential of portal design to offer alternative ways of communicating to female users in such a way as to resist and combat the gendered status quo. Contemporary design, Internet, and feminist theory provide illuminative lenses through which to explore these issues.

Background

The investigation requires addressing the specificity of female audiences of the WWW, and feminist theorising on gender provides the tools with which to do so. Hence, the underlying focus is on the relationship between gender and design within the context of the WWW. Warwick (1999) believes that it is important to recognise "… [how] the entrenched masculine practices of the [design] profession have constricted the development of work by women, both as practitioners and theorists, though there have been some important recent contributions" (p. 14). For example, Matlow (1999) suggested that the introduction of new technologies was symptomatic of a paradigm shift from "modernist graphic design towards fragmented postmodern approach" (in Warwick, 1999, p. 15). This shift was exemplified by "… the consequent movement away from rigid structures and principles to the transparent and ephemeral which exists for the most part within virtual dimensions" (Warwick, 1999, p. 15). Matlow's (1999) observations are valuable as they illuminate the relationship between gender, and the professional and individual practice of design. Therefore, the relationship between gender and design within the context of the WWW could be characterised as being at a crossroad. On the one hand, literature available points to a conservative gendered approach to design for the Internet (Martinson et al., 2002; Rommes, 2002). On the other hand, it has been identified that there is a need to investigate alternative ways of tackling gender ideology and its influence on the design of the WWW technologies (Spilker & Sørensen, 2000). The following paragraphs provide examples of various ways design is implemented within the WWW, and the gendered consequences of these designs.

The first example is a case where design processes are used to insert gendered assumptions about products, and consequently about users, in order to achieve broader market coverage. In their discussion of design and computer entertainment technologies, Martinson et al. (2002) observed this practice. Their focus on women and leisure investigated the reasons why women would or would not engage with Internet technologies. Their findings pointed towards design as the key reason why women would not consider online participation and activities as part of their leisure. Martinson et al. (2002) advocated that computer entertainment technologies, in general, (including the Internet) were designed for "all" participants. However, "all participants" equated to "mainly men" (Martinson et al., 2002). Such a design approach allowed for a variety of gendered assumptions to be built in to the product, rendering it "uninteresting" for other users. Therefore, Martinson et al. (2002) suggested that due to a generalising design approach, these technologies "… are not compelling for women" (p. 46). Furthermore, "[d]esigning with women in mind might lead to adaptable entertainment technologies that will appeal to broader market segments. Conceivably, computer-based leisure needs to become more versatile in order to meet the needs of a more diverse population and wider audience" (Martinson et al., 2002, p. 46). The argument put forth envisages the Internet becoming gendered by design because of longstanding assumptions about what constitutes a user (Martinson et al., 2002). These assumptions are rarely questioned by designers, who are preoccupied with meeting deadlines and accommodating clients.

Another example of gendered design for the Internet is offered by Rommes (2002), who questioned the number of women designers involved in new technologies. Rommes (2002) observed that initial reasons for low female Internet participation stemmed from lack of online spaces designed for women. She argued "[i]n the course of time, some places for the empowerment of women were created. But why did it take so long before places for women were created on the Internet?" (p. 401). In her view, the problem rested with design. Initially, Rommes pointed to the male-dominated design of Internet technologies themselves. However, she did acknowledge Henwood's (1993) argument that cautioned against such gener-alisations: "… we should be wary of arguments that suggest that more women in systems design will, in and of itself, effect change in the design process itself and lead to new and more progressive priorities being adopted …" (Henwood, 1993, p. 43). Therefore, women who design within masculine environments, as in the early stages of Internet development, might not be in position to address issues of gender discrimination (Rommes, 2002). However, the situation would be changed if "…women's organizations [were given] influence in the design process of new technology with the specific task of paying attention to women's issues" (Rom-mes, 2002, p. 421). However, it is important to realise that "[d]esigners, women's organizations and subsidizing organizations should … take care that this influence is given space from a very early stage in the development of the technology" (Rom-mes, 2002, p. 21).

The generally termed "third wave" of research points toward another way of looking at the issue of women and computers that recognises that computers are increas-ingly part of everyday communication and cultural exchange (Spilker & Sørensen, 2000). Such recent studies of gender, design, and ICT highlight "… acknowledge-ment of flexibility in the frames of reference" (Spilker & Sørensen, 2000), as well as realisation, gender-wise, that these technologies form part of quite a varied set of practices (Aune & Sørensen, 1998; Berg, 1996; Lie, 1998). Thus, these studies identify and legitimate a relationship between gender and technology, where one is constructed by the other, and vice versa (Spilker & Sørensen, 2000).

A case study presented by Spilker and Sørensen (2000) is an example of the devel-opment and implementation of design strategy that would be in position to manage gender in this technological context. As Spilker and Sørensen observed, JenteROM (a CD-ROM targeting female users) demonstrated "… a clear cut example of a mutual reconfiguration of technology and gender" (p. 280). The CD-ROM marked an attempt to transform this type of technology into a "feminine artefact," along with what Spilker and Sørensen referred to as an "… effort to change some aspects of the definition of femininity" (p. 280). On the other hand, the HjemmeNett Web service, they observed, used design strategies to create spaces for both male and female participation, relying on gender as an important consideration in developing such outcomes. Each artefact used different design strategies informed by what both researchers termed, "action concepts." As Spilker and Sørensen (2000) indicated, JenteROM inscribed its technology with the dichotomous opposition of female vs. male as a way of acknowledging gender, whereas HjemmeNett saw male and female genders as end points of a continuous scale. Thus, contrary to Rommes (2002), who argued for the inclusion of women per se in the practice of design, Spilker and Sørensen (2000) believed that the design process itself had to address gender exclusion. "… JenteROM and HjemmeNett indicate a profound change in gender dynamics of computers and multimedia" (p. 281) and this phenomenon is starting to appear in a variety of geographical and cultural locations (Sadowska, 2003). Moreover, Sørenssen (1997) insists that mass media consumption of the Internet and related technologies, with its need to constantly attract new users, redefines these technologies as less "leading-edge," and more a mainstream medium of communication and information retrieval. Such a shift offers an opportunity for the technology to become a nurturing ground or a starting point for alternative means of inclusion. However, cases such as JenteROM or HjemmeNett are rare, and, more often than not, researchers come across discourses suggesting a dichotomous gender divide when investigating the WWW as a medium of information and communication.

Historical Account of the BEME.com Portal

BEME.com began to take shape in the summer of 1999. At that time, there was growing interest in the creation and production of online sites for female users, evidenced by the launch in the UK of three portals for female users in the autumn of 1999. However, "IPC [were] characteristically happy to sit back and watch others make the mistakes." "Contrary to Internet wisdom, it will benefit and inform us to launch later," says IPC with quiet confidence. "There will be room for smaller communities, however, with stronger identities" (D-PREA2a, 1999). Initially planned for January 2000, the BEME.com launch was delayed due to the enormity of the design task. However, prior to its launch, there was a billboard and poster campaign running in London to inform and promote the new site. The campaign was not restricted to the printed medium only. The popular TV show "Ally McBeal" (created by David E. Kelley as a mixed comedy-drama show about the trials and tribulations of a 28-year-old female lawyer fresh out of Harvard Law School) running on Channel 4 at that time was co-opted into the promotional sponsorship deal. The campaign was characterised by the projection of BEME.com logo and a voice-over mentioning the sponsorship at the beginning, end, and during commercial breaks of each episode. The executive and marketing members of the team believed the association with Ally McBeal was a perfect fit that would "… distinguish BEME.COM from [its]

... competitors, making a clear and distinct statement regarding its position within the marketplace" (D-CP1c, 2000, ll. 15-18).

The site was launched by IPC Electric, the newly established Internet business within IPC. At the time of the launch, the site was seen as an important step made by IPC towards "... creating significant new media brands and building the definitive digital business" (D-CP1a, 2000, ll. 17-19). Within IPC's portfolio of 97 consumer magazines, the company publishes 25 women's titles with a combined readership of over 12.5 million readers categorised as predominantly women. The women-focused magazines cover a range of lifestyle interests that "... appeal to modern women, from health to fashion, parenting to home" (D-CP1c, 2000). IPC defined the BEME.com target audience within the same parameters as their magazine readership, as mostly female. In 2000, the figures showed that BEME.com was attracting 1.5 million page impressions and approximately 120,000 unique users each month (D-CP1f, 2000). Although this research has not been privy to a detailed breakdown of users due to nondisclosure of commercial information, as with women's traditional magazines, any male user numbers would have been considered negligible compared to the overall female target audience.

By June 2000, BEME.com started to flourish. Simultaneously, IPC changed its focus from being a magazine publisher to becoming "a management of brands across many platforms" (D-CP1b, 2000). This change in strategy on the part of the parent company only strengthened the position of BEME.com. Developed from the outset as an online branded environment, BEME.com could only benefit from such an investment in brand-led business. A month later, BEME.com won one of its first awards: in the category for Best General News Presentation, BEME.com received the *NetMedia European Online Journalism Award*. This recognition meant prestige for BEME.com. Success continued with another award nomination for *Best Design Magazine on the Web*. The nomination was part of the Magazine Design Awards presented by Total Publishing. It gave BEME.com credibility as design outcome, providing recognition from its own peer group.

The beginning of 2001 was, as Vickers (2001) wrote, "... a tumultuous time for the online women's market." BEME.com re-evaluation occurred amidst drastic changes to other sites for women, such as the abandonment of plans for uk.women.com, and the closure of CharlotteStreet.com in favour of femail.co.uk (D-PREA2k, 2001). With Internet business plummeting, IPC chose to review its online portfolio. In an interview with MediaGuardian.co.uk, the IPC communications director admitted that IPC "... no longer believes in the broad portal model for the women's market" (D-PREA2k, 2001); a shift that prompted not only changes in design of the BEME. com portal, but also an integration of its content with the paper-based women's magazine portfolio. In addition, reassessment of the target audience meant catering to a much smaller bracket of users, namely "... aged 20-35 ABC1 women, with a high disposable income..." (D-CP1i, 2001, ll. 7-9). The site was refocused to include "... channels which mirror [users'] lifestyles and interests" (D-CP1i, 2001 ll. 7-9).

In the middle of August 2001, IPC announced a review of its online business and resulting cut-backs. Following IPC's consolidation with AOL Time Warner and the plummeting business in women's online sites, BEME.com was one of the casualties of the brutal reality of e-commerce. As the chief executive of IPC commented, "[t]his review has clearly identified where the commercial and strategic opportunities lie for our business, and IPC is now moving forward with a smaller, yet stronger and robust portfolio of digital brands on which we can drive future profit growth" (D-CP1j, 2001, ll. 17-20). In an interview with GuardianUnlimited, the IPC Group strategy director admitted that their launch of BEME.com as a new brand was a mistake (D-PREA2m, 2001). Furthermore, the GuardianUnlimited article states: "BEME and Uploaded.com, which both launched three year ago, enjoyed relatively healthy traffic figures but were understood to be struggling to compete for advertising revenue. Despite some fantastic editorial and commercial innovations, both sites suffered from not having a clear focus'" (D-PREA2m, 2001). However, IPC denied that any of the closures were connected to their AOL Time Warner consolidation. The IPC Group strategy director argued that "… the cuts were made to ensure commercial viability, protect key brands and maintain a presence in the market" (D-PREA2m, 2001). Nonetheless, experts in the field observed that the demise of BEME.com was due to its rather unfortunate timing and failure to generate advertising revenue: "They [IPC] put far too much money in and, arguably, pulled the plug too early" (D-PREA2l, 2001). After BEME.com's closure, *The Guardian* wrote, "[i]ndeed, while relatively successful commercially and popular with its user base, BEME.com was never going to draw the kind of traffic it needed to pay for itself" (D-PREA2l, 2001).

Designing BEME.com to Satisfy a Specific Niche Market

The design process of BEME.com portal was lengthy, and comprised of number of design stages. The key design phases were: research into the women's portals and market positioning; concept development and brand design; interface design including back-end database programming, testing and launch; and redesign based on performance review. To support this design process, IPC drew on external expertise by commissioning three agencies (Wolff Olins, Pres.co, and Aspect), limiting their own role to that of overseeing the process and approving design choices. It was only once the portal became live online that IPC used their in-house team to provide content and general maintenance. The contracted agencies supported the design phases based on their respective expertise.

The following paragraphs present the different phases in detail, highlighting the underlying factors that have influenced design of the BEME.com portal. The purpose of such an approach is to draw attention not only to the actual act of designing of an online portal, but also to indicate the existence of other factors that had a fundamental impact on the design decision making.

Research

Generating knowledge of the market and appropriate audiences is a widely accepted practice prior to launching a new product. This allows designers to investigate what is already out there in order that a new project builds on, deviates from, and improves on, already existing artefacts. It is supposed to minimize the number of mistakes when generating new ideas and physical outcomes. At the same time, it serves to validate generated concepts for prospective investors. In terms of research, IPC was therefore no exception. The research located the portal within a larger context, and identified examples of already existing women's portals. At a later date, these examples were used to identify opportunities and weaknesses that, in turn, informed BEME.com as a product.

The potential audience was identified from an investigation of what the proposed female users might find interesting and attractive in online activities. However, during the interviews conducted with BEME.com design team, it became apparent that research was not seen as a crucial undertaking in formulating an understanding of women's portals. The female marketing consultant, who joined the team at a later date, described it in passing: "As I understand, extensive consumer research was undertaken prior to development of the site" (I-PT1,2002, ll. 40-41). She made no further reference to any of the results, which is surprising for a marketing consultant whose expertise often relies on extensive knowledge of the initial research. Similarly, the male brand designer did not seem to give the research stage much credence:

Yeah, we did research but we kind of like had the whole thing in mind that it was specifically gonna be designed for the Web. ... from the research that we got [it was] just sort of general feed back. (I-PT4, 2001, ll. 98-102)

He seemed to acknowledge the presence of research as part of the overall design process, but did not assign this stage any great value. His reference to the production of "general feedback" went hand in hand with his subsequent statement reiterating women's stereotypical relationship with technology. "I think men were a bit more ... keen just to get stuck in and pretend that they new everything even if they didn't. But women were just a bit more wary of the medium" (I-PT4, 2001, ll. 104-107). In the end, this research was only partially used, since many decisions were based on the professional expertise of the BEME.com creators and their tacit knowledge of what a women's portal *should be*. As the senior producer observed:

And the funny thing was ... a lot of research was done and reams and reams of reports ... statistics about how women were using the Net and all that kind of stuff. Very little of it was ever referred to ... [Editorial/creative director], I don't think [she] had ever referred to it. She just knew what her project was, and that was going to be that. (I-PT5,2001, ll. 507-512)

That the production team and IPC did not use the research as a backbone for generating ideas left BEME.com open to the introduction of many gendered assumptions. These assumptions were evident in the description of the concepts behind the BEME. com brand. They surfaced in the site's visual language, and informed the midpoint redesign. Neglect of the research in the later activities informing the design process resulted in the portal losing credibility on two levels. The site was developed based largely on the personal experiences and understandings of the design team. This resulted in an outcome defined by a narrowed-down and highly partial view that was supposed to satisfy a multitude of individuals in a variety of circumstances. On the other hand, marketing credibility was also taken away. In an environment where a project like BEME.com was testing out "new waters," the lack of research back up created doubts. And at a time when the market seemed to look unfavourably on women's portals, research could have offered a credible justification for the initial choices. But as there was no great reliance on the research in the first place, this possible safety net did not exist.

Lack of integration of the research into the design process also indicated another underlying factor: an overreliance on tacit knowledge. The interview data and press releases indicate that on all levels of the design decision-making process, everyone offered expertise unsupported by any significant BEME.com design related research. Aspects such as participants' professional expertise, their reflective commentaries/observations, and personal histories were brought together to supplement the understanding of what BEME.com design required. For example, IPC, as a client, relied on its timely expertise in the field of women's publishing, design, and branding, supported by belief in their "...unique position within the Women's market ..." (D-CP4, 2001). The design team drew upon their design expertise and reflective observation in conjunction with their own previous personal or design experiences. Such an approach to the research stage of the design highlighted an intrinsic problem in the way the commercial Web design process was informed in the early days of the WWW. Consequently, it indicated the level of concern for the users' role within the development of the portal design. Design decision making was based on the tacit knowledge of the publishing house and the design team whilst the voice of the user was not considered. The design decisions were symptomatic of, what Oudshoorn, Rommes, and Stienstra (2004) refer to as "I-methodology." This meant that "[i]nstead of assessing the interests and competencies of users by formal procedures, designers ... generally took their own preferences and skills as major guidelines in the design" (Oudshoorn et al., 2004, p. 53).

Concept Development and Brand Design

Once the editorial/creative director joined the team, the branding agency (Wolff Olins) was given the go-ahead to create and develop the BEME.com brand. Wolff Olins was responsible for creating the BEME.com name, its visual representation, and the array of meanings that would be associated with the brand. The process of developing these took place through a series of branding workshops where designers from Wolff Olins worked together with IPC representatives. It was during these workshops that the brand proposals were created, discussed, and evaluated, defining the direction of the overall "look and feel" of the portal. An example of decisions made at the time concerning design was the rejection of a proposal for the portal title, Poppy.com, in favour of BEME.com. Once the conceptual stage was approved by IPC, the visual elements were generated to represent the look and feel of BEME.com based on its brand. The male brand designer described his experience of developing certain aspects of the visual language in the following manner:

... [we] took two sets [of colours] to research, one quite bright, quite young feeling ones. Another set, which was the set we worked with ... quite nice subtle sort of pastel hues. They weren't necessarily girly colours or anything ... but they were quite calming and they were quite ... nice shades, sort of pastel shades ... they reached ... sort of all women focus groups and ... I think they felt right as well. [It was] quite calming experience going there. It didn't feel like you were looking at too much data because the colours were quite sort of like soothing in a way and they worked quite well on the Web , which was good. (I-PT4, 2001, ll. 142-154)

His description revealed clear links between the actual development of BEME.com brand and gendered assumptions about the likes and dislikes of female users. As the initial research did not form a strong part of the conceptual design development either, there was no real evidence with which to counter such assumptions. Thus, in the final outcome, these conjectures went unchallenged and became an integral part of the understanding of the brand targeting online female users. Furthermore, BEME.com brand and the sales pitch were mutually reinforcing; where the brand generated and communicated ideas that would be appealing to BEME.com users, the sales pitch allowed IPC to turn the brand into a revenue generating concept. The sales pitch turned ideas that might be considered alternative into consumer norms. For example, the editorial/creative director, in her interview stated that:

... [the] personality of the brand [is] based on a non-stereotypical representation of women. Having had a background in women's magazines, I felt liberated by the opportunity the Web has given women to escape the shackles of advertising and

fashion driven imagery of women in magazines and the media in general. (I-PT2, 2002, ll. 12-16)

The editorial/creative director supported the alternative approach of the original BEME.com mission. Nevertheless, commenting for a press release, she stated, "BEME is born of the women's market. We are an editorially led site from a 100-year-old women's magazine publisher at the forefront of new media. We know women. We can be trusted. And trusting the online editorial voice is crucial to trusting the online shopping experience" (D-CP1a, 2000, ll. 11-15). A comparison of these comments reveals that a set of corporate intentions was asserted every time BEME.com was scrutinised or presented to the public. Depending on who was asking the questions, the sales pitch varied, either to promote the portal in an acceptable manner or to justify design decisions. As official owner of the site, IPC was in a position of power not only in terms of the design, but also in seeking to control how the design was publicly interpreted.

Interface Design and Back-End Programming

With final approval of the brand strategy and its marketing, Pres.co (an interface design agency) and Aspect (a back-end programming agency) were contracted to implement the visual language into a design of the portal. Web page designs were presented for daily approval to the editorial/creative director, who acted as the representative of IPC, the official client. The process was supported by daily discussions as to how the brand strategy should be implemented in the visual layouts of the portal:

... we just basically broke it down into batches of pages. ... They all had slightly different look about them to reflect channels but they had the same structure. So we'd start by doing all of the top level pages that look the same ... Go through that process of designing them sign off by [editorial/creative director] so we'd ... talk about what was right what was wrong. Go back make amendments. And then basically from there once they'd been totally signed off by [editorial/creative director] it's a case of ... coding them into html ... And then that was all supplied to Aspect ... to bring the whole thing together with the back end of the database driving it ... It's a long, sort of drawn out process. (I-PT5, 2001, ll. 218-234)

The three phases of designing the necessary portal pages, signing them off with IPC followed by back-end programming, progressed in a circular pattern until the entire portal was constructed into Web-ready documents. Unfortunately, visual material presenting BEME.com Web pages has become unavailable due to portal closure and copyright agreements. The final outcome launched by IPC, in February 2000, resulted in the following design. The original BEME.com layout invited the viewer to enter the site through a slick, simple homepage. The page contained the site title located at the top of the page supported by six images of women. The images functioned as content indicators and entry links into the further site structure, representing the six different channels contained by the portal. The choice of the six channels was drawn directly from the structures available in women's traditional paper magazines. These were: news; work and spend; home life; culture and trends; entertainment; and "my BEME." On the right-hand side of the images, a selection of buttons acted as further information links. The homepage did not contain any other elements or advertising.

The images on the homepage representing women reflected a certain level of diversity. They portrayed young women from white, African, and Asian ethnic backgrounds to invite cultural reading of variety. The idea of diversity was also stressed by the types of clothes these women were wearing—from business suits to casual bedroom attire—indicating a variety of life situations. This was further underlined by the layout of the images themselves. Each of the images had a different colour value and a different cropping, where some presented close-ups of the faces, some just the torso, and some most of the body. The choice of images and the treatment of the design aspects stressed the idea of diverse choice of audience. However, there were other elements within the layout of the images that undermined that variety. All women were more or less the same age, predominantly young with no reference to middle-aged or elderly women. All images portrayed women with a particular body size, highlighting an aspiration to a particular fashion ideal.

The inside pages were similarly designed. The overall template divided the Web page into four sections based on a distinctive vertical layout. The first section contained the navigational menu, giving access to the other channels and links pertaining to the specifics of the viewed page. Moving from left to right, the menu column was followed by an image representing a female form offset by a medallion image containing only decorative text. The female image was the same one as on the homepage to indicate the chosen content channel. To the right of the image was a listing of articles pertinent to the selected channel. These were represented by headlines that functioned as links supported by a brief introduction. One had only to click on the link to read the full story. To the right of the article section was a space dedicated to promotional advertising. The adverts were designed in vertical rather than horizontal format, as it is commonly done, to accentuate the overall vertical design. While the homepage was centre justified, the inside pages flowed from the top left hand corner. The overall layout was uncluttered, which meant empty space supporting quick page loading and page scanning. Each channel was assigned a colour scheme for easy navigation. Visually, the site set itself apart from other women's portals through this carefully constructed and arranged Web page layout.

All these design choices were driven by two factors: the previous knowledge of how to create and design women's magazines instilled by the creative/editorial director who, as the female senior producer explained, had "... a lot of experience in women's magazines" (I-PT5, 2001, l. 22). Secondly, the evaluation of what the female target audience would respond to. The female senior producer explained that they looked at, "... who the target audience would be ... how women use the Internet, how long they spend, where they access it from, how long they would be on the Internet in any one time ... so we do some kind of profile of what we thought the average user was ..." (I-PT5, 2001, ll. 24-31). In both cases, the crucial underlying factor was a gendered understanding of who the audience was. Therefore, the look and feel of the portal was driven by the design team's understandings of gender, combined with their beliefs about the category "women." Considering that the BEME.com experience was aimed at female users, it became crucial in socially defining what constituted BEME.com as a "female" experience. Unfortunately, BEME.com was created by a traditional women's publishing house, characterised by quite stereotypical notions of men and women. These, in turn, defined the understanding of how to deal with a women's Web site design, and the ways in which to communicate ideas to female users; a particular understanding of the "character" of its female audience informed conceptual, corporate, and usability aspects of the portal. The marketing consultant observed:

The idea was to offer a site, which caters for all facets of women's lives. It recognised that women were not just mothers, lovers or had careers but were all of these things at one time. Therefore the structure of the site with [wide-ranging] channels ... was designed to cater for all their needs. (I-PT1,2002, ll. 19-23)

The ideas driving the original brand were based on this notion of diversity. The recognition of female users as being multifaceted individuals through the notion of "AND" and "OR" accommodated this within the design. On the other hand, following the traditional women's paper magazines, the site set out to offer advice to its female users. The given information was specifically women focused to attract the target audience "... to get advice and help to be able to ... ask questions and get answers." However, as the female senior producer said "... that was an area that was chucked, talked about and it wasn't ... developed ... there's ... a lot of ambitions, like major ambition. But [they] just ran out of money and time ..." (I-PT5, 2001, ll. 174-182). The desire to offer such service was not implemented in BEME.com due to technological requirements and cost. The small part that was generated had to be relevant to female users, and was often conceived through a gendered lens. The design manager/designer remarked, "... it has to ... do with content as well. At the end of the day the user is going to the Web site for content, content is King ... but I think idea of having a women's site is a great one, every traditional media suggests there is a market because Cosmopolitan has been going for years, look at Vogue ..." (I-PT3, 2001, ll. 350-356).

The female senior producer advocated yet another reading of BEME.com design associated with the notion of an online female community, as she described:

... if you want to focus on a particular group ... [you offer] something that's going to interest a certain amount of people and they'll go there because they want to talk to each other and they almost create their own community in their own site and ... then you add content and build around information about your users as they sort of come on board. (I-PT5, 2001, ll. 348-349)

For the female senior producer, BEME.com should have promoted an understanding of the target audience as intelligent, comprehensive individuals engaging with worth-while content. These opposing views demonstrate that the design team represented a variety of positions. Whilst mainly trading in stereotypical notions of femininity, there were alternative interpretations. The female senior producer framed notions of gender as a limitation based on her belief that gender driven sites do not attract users. While there was a lot of attention paid to women's portals, the press treated their appearance as a passing phenomenon. And as BEME.com history has shown, female users were not attracted to online portals that did not offer anything beyond the content and outlook of a glossy magazine purchased on their way home.

Another very important factor affecting the design decision-making process stemmed from the power structures defining BEME.com portal as a project. These were strongly dependant on each participant's position and relationship to the whole project. The interviews revealed that a number of power struggles occurred at a point at which participants felt they needed to maintain their own individual standpoint. Through observations like "... she would have a tantrum actually ... she was in control and had to be ... in control" (I-PT5, 2001, ll. 311-313), the female senior producer made reference to the difficulties for the team arising from the actions of one particular member. However, problems were not only to do with individual characters. There is evidence of a quite strong institutional power structure that generated hierarchies of decision making and understanding of the positioning of the portal. There was then a dynamic between personal agendas and these hierarchies. The tensions between editors, artistic directors, or advertising directors regarding power and control over decision-making processes, undeniably generated the platform of the BEME.com design. Individual members began to believe that they were the vital link in the production, which undermined the team, created disharmony, and dispersed the guid-ing vision. Comments such as, "[w]hen the Managing Director of IPC Electric (the digital division of IPC) resigned just before the launch of BEME due to a change in the board of IPC, and his role was taken over by a magazine publisher who didn't understand the Web and hadn't been involved in BEME's launch. In short, politics at the top of a big company started the writing on the wall" (I-PT2, 2002, ll. 63-67), are evidence of the power structures in operation.

Testing

The testing phase began once all the pages were designed and programming had been executed. In theory at least, this phase is central to any Internet site, and should be given a lot of time and attention to yield useful results. The success of this stage affects the whole project: "... it's like from an agency point of view once we build the site also there is a massive amount of testing that you had to go through. Testing phases, which we did with Aspect" (I-PT5, 2001, ll. 139-142). However, in the case of the BEME.com design process, time was running out due to approaching launch deadlines, resulting in the site going live before the end of the testing. Reflecting on this stage, the female senior producer highlighted that the portal was launched before all technical problems were sorted out. But as the project was taking too long, the testing phase was regarded by IPC as a safe stage to cut short and launch the site.

Although this research has not been privy to the results of the testing, due to the nondisclosure on the part of the agencies, an important underlying factor emerged from review of the interview data. Participants' brief reference to the testing phase demonstrated a level of awareness from a "historical perspective" of success or failure of BEME.com as a piece of technology in relation to WWW developments. As with any product that has undergone a process of design, the WWW was evaluated on its ability to satisfy, fit, or adapt to already existing human needs. Of course, as pure novelty, it generated interest and curiosity; however, that did not mean it was going to be accepted as free of its own limitations. The Web designers needed to have a historical perspective in order to best apply the developing technology to their work, paying close attention not only to the equipment, but also the usability of the interface and content:

... a lot of the UK Web sites are done by ex-magazines people, who have no idea about Web usability ... So they are not customer focused and they don't really understand usability because they employ these Flash companies who will do them really nice Web sites which are not usable by your average man on the street kind of surfer ... although it is very nice it is totally useless. (I-IP1, 2002, ll. 240-256)

The historical perspective, therefore, provided a common point of reference for the BEME.com design team. It allowed all participants to define what might potentially constitute a unique WWW experience. It also provided a common thread in understanding of the BEME.com technological environment and the type of experience BEME.com offered to its online female users.

Launch

The final stage of design and production was the launch. With the site live and running, IPC took over the content production and site maintenance, as originally agreed with the contracted agencies. However, information about the success of the site was not always passed on to the people who designed it, as the female senior producer commented:

[Once the site was launched] ... IPC became very protective about it. They didn't want to give us, like the people who've been involved ... you give up sort of 6 months of your life to working on something ... no kind of feedback on statistics ... How many people go in there. They kept it all very closed to their chest, which is their total right 'cause they were the buyer and they were paying us. (I-PT5, 2001, ll. 144-149)

As is often the case in design practice, once the requested outcome is considered finalised, the client takes over, with no intrinsic need to give feedback to the agency. However, in the case of Internet technologies, designers place enormous value on learning from previous experiences. By withholding such information, IPC was not seen favourably by the design agencies, as was manifest in the interviews. The design team was considered in an inferior position because they were merely creators rather than owners.

Performance Review and Redesign

It is unfortunate that when BEME.com arrived on the scene, the dot.com boom was starting to deflate, as one of the pioneering Internet investors in the UK observed, "… it was late to the market first of all … it was not a first mover and I think that that was a disadvantage" (I-IP2, 2002, ll. 122-124). By February 2001, there were already warning signs of a possible closure. It was becoming obvious to IPC that a broad, editorially driven portal was not necessarily the best way to attract female customers (D-PREA2k, 2001). At this point, BEME.com implemented a change in strategy and a redesign, strengthening the connection between the portal and traditional women's paper magazines. From an online portal that prompted high quality of design, visually, BEME.com became just another site amongst many. The clean and spacey design was replaced by a generally available and often used online template. The new layout was based on the regular structure of a masthead supported by a three-column grid. The masthead contained the site logo buried amongst advertising banners and links to the six interest channels. The supporting three columns contained navigation buttons and adverts on the left-hand side, content in the middle, and a promotional column on the right-hand side. On the homepage, the content column was divided into subsections representing introductions to feature articles from each channel. In the redesigned portal, the images used emphasised only further the portrayal of women with beautiful toned bodies or photographs of the latest celebrities. The images communicated types of body and appearance that were unquestionably approved and acceptable within the assumed social context. Sometimes polysemic in nature, the aim of the photographs was to provide a model of comparison for female users. Before its closure, and following in the "best" traditions of women's periodicals, BEME.com positioned itself as a perfect example of a guidebook on how to become the "ultimate feminine norm." These changes were undertaken in-house by IPC, where none of the original designers were available to offer consultation.

However, the change of focus and redesign did not make for drastic improvement. BEME.com, along with other IPC online ventures, was closed down in order to recover profits. According to a senior production staff member employed by IPC, the financial gains achieved by portals like BEME.com are very limited, providing no incentive for further investment: "Anything that didn't make any money got the chop" (I-IP4, 2001, l. 104). The reason for such a discrepancy between the need to generate money and the BEME.com mission can be found in the vision supporting the portal. BEME.com was not product centred, but a branded digital environment. The underlying ideas centred on creating an online community and establishing online customer loyalty. BEME.com offered news, advice, and entertainment, and not an opportunity to buy the latest gadget or consumable product. It was a content/editorially driven portal putting e-commerce strategy-common to online businesses-on the back burner. Thus, the advertising revenue the site was capable of generating in the conventional publishing industry fashion was not there to provide necessary financing. BEME.com, as a financially viable online venture, required a new approach to commercial strategy to sustain its unique profile.

Lessons to be Learned

In review, the BEME.com design was influenced by a number of factors that, at times supported, and at other times contradicted one another. To the publisher, BEME.com was firstly a place for women online; to the producer a digital meeting space; to the designer it was an excellent new technology experiment; whilst to the diversity of female users, it was received and engaged with based on a multitude of personal interpretations. Therefore, BEME.com became embroiled in a process of continuous negotiation of different understandings of what a commercial WWW space for female users ought to be. Moreover, socially, culturally, and politically placed underlying factors informed the design team's conceptualisation of the BEME.com experience. These were central to the visual, designed outcomes, supported by a collective knowledge used to rationalise the existence of BEME.com as a design product. These factors illustrate how deeply design processes are rooted in the social, cultural, and political conditions of everyday reality. At the same time, the designed products/experiences are implicated in the perpetuation of these factors, leaving minimal room for searching out alternatives. Moreover, the design process and the underlying factors offer important insight as to how Web designers interpreted the tasks at hand in relation to the audience and the client. Considering that BEME.com was created at the beginning of the WWW boom, these underlying factors functioned as primary sources of understanding of the unknown and newly developed WWW technologies. In this case, the motivation of the client to bring in Web design expertise derived from a need to maintain their position of power within a specific marketplace; a need which became the driving force. However, it was also something that limited the knowledge of those involved in the production process. Moreover, this need defined the way in which users were interpreted by both the client and the Web designer. In the case of BEME.com, this interpretation was based on gendered understandings grounded in historical continuities derived from both the design industry and women's magazine publishing.

Although the nature of Web designers' knowledge changes throughout the design process, it does not mean that by expanding their knowledge, they gain more power to affect the design processes and their outcomes. On the contrary, the traditional context of women's magazines from which BEME.com originated only further perpetuated the historically established hierarchy between users, designers, and clients. Therefore, a study of the design process and the underlying factors offers ways of understanding how knowledge could be seen as both promoting and limiting innovation. In the case of BEME.com, knowledge served to maintain the gendered status quo. However, it had another potential not greatly explored by the early Web designers: interactivity. Burnett and Marshall (2003) argue that online interactivity encourages users to engage in a different kind of literacy encompassing simultaneous reception and production. Such an understanding will have a profound impact on the role Web designers will play in constructing online experiences in the future. As Cameron (1998) aptly pointed out, interactivity within the context of the WWW offers experiences "in potential" (in Julier, 2000, p. 179) that are replacing a sequential narrative offered by other types of communication media. Hence, Web designers have to focus on consciously generating "what-if" experiences, allowing online users to formulate their own outcomes. Under such circumstances, historical and traditional assumptions will not necessarily be in a position of power to dominate or determine the interactive process. The combination of simultaneous reception and production with "what-if" types of experiences will carry the authority to encourage more pronounced dialogue. In practical terms, such a shift in the conceptualisation of Web design has the potential to generate a scenario in which future outcomes will be based on a much more informed processes on the part of users, designers, and clients; processes that might include, among other things, dialogue between often very complex and conflicting agendas.

Conclusion

The media landscape is changing, where "... the popular ... media now promote ... a new rhetoric of freedom and independence for young women ..." (McRobbie, 1999, p. 11). This suggests that Web designers may no longer be able to use the commercial context and its imperatives as an alibi or justification for lack of innovation. BEME.com provides an example of the need for far more radical design in this commercial sector.

'Women aren't a niche market and it's time online publishers stopped treating them as if they were,' ... Part of the problem ... is that many new sites are being offered by existing offline publishers, rather than truly innovative businesses. 'They're using traditional business models, trying to move a business model online which is aimed at protecting their existing territory.' (D-PREA1a, 2000)

Three key suggestions for better design for a female niche market emerge from the BEME.com case study. They are (a) centre all aspects of the design process on the actual end-user; (b) consciously recognise the folly of using gender alone as an appropriate description of female audiences; (c) be aware of social, cultural, and political factors that exert influence over the design process.

Lack of understanding of the user can be detrimental to the design outcome. Although the audience is defined through the process of designing for a female niche market, these definitions cannot be based solely on designers' implicit knowledge. They need to reflect real people who will interact with these design outcomes. There is also additional value in recognising the significance of the users' participation within the design process. The ever-growing focus on online interactivity brings into spotlight the role users play in co-designing of the WWW sites. This is a crucial factor and can no longer be omitted from design process. With specific reference to female users, reliance on gender as the defining factor on the part of Web designers only perpetuates stereotypes and does not respond to real needs. Reliance on gender as a guiding tool in designing for female online users in the UK market has proven to be misguided. Female audiences have already demonstrated active participation in forms of online cultural production. Therefore, targeting female users does not need to rely on gender for its appeal and success. Design outcomes that focus on the particular needs of female users rather than their gender, in combination with innovative e-commerce strategies, promise greater potential for success than current solutions. Finally, in creating design outcomes for the WWW, today's Web designers cannot ignore the growing influence of information and communication technology as a tool of cultural production. Understanding of the design process as an exclusive interaction between user, designer, and client around a potential design solution is far too simplistic and does not acknowledge other factors that can make or break a design outcome. In particular, when designing for female audiences, awareness of social, cultural, and political factors can reveal implicit reliance on gender. If acknowledged early on within the design process, such awareness can lead to far more informed design outcomes based on strategies of inclusion.

The issues raised in this chapter are situated within broader public debates around the question of women's everyday uses of the WWW (see Vereniging voor Gender en Technologie or Strategies of inclusion: Gender and the information society {SI-GIS} – A project funded by the EU Information Society Technologies Programme {IST}). Prompted by research that has revealed that the division between the information rich and information poor does, in some circumstances, equate to a division between men and women, discussion of women's use of, and access to, the WWW leans on or overlaps with other debates in which inequitable access to information has grave consequences (Hawthorne & Klein, 1999). Participation in such debates opens up an opportunity for Web designers to engage with the social and cultural implications of inclusion. Seen in this light, designing for the WWW can also be seen as an open invitation for individual and collective reflection and ensuing action that has the potential to result in Web design knowledge that is not based exclusively on gendered understandings of everyday life.

References

Aitchison, C., & Jordan, F. (2001). *Beauty and the beach: Discourses of tourism and the body.* Paper presented at the Conference Programme; Women's Studies Network 14th Annual Conference, Cheltenham and Gloucester College of Higher Education, UK.

Aune, M., & Sørensen, K. H. (1998). *Teaching transformed: The appropriation of multimedia in education: The case of Norway.* Unpublished manuscript, Trondheim: Centre for Technology and Society.

Berg, A. J. (1996). *Digital feminism* (STS Report No. 28). Trondheim: Centre for Technology and Society.

Burnett, R., & Marshall, P. D. (2003). *Web theory: An introduction*. London: Routledge.

Cameron, A. (1998). Dissimulations: The illusion of interactivity. Retrieved April 23, 2003, from http://www.hrc.wmin.ac.uk/hrc/theory/dissimulations/t.3.html

Faulkner, W., Sørensen, K., Gansmø, H., Rommes, E., Pitt, L., Lagesen Berg, V., et al. (2004). *Strategies of inclusion: Gender and the information society* (No. IST-2000-26329 SIGIS). Edinburgh: The University of Edinburgh UK, Norwegian University of Science and Technology, Dublin City University Ireland Studio Metis Italy, University of Twente, NL.

Harcourt, W. (Ed.). (1999). *Women@internet; creating new cultures in cyberspace*. London: Zed Books.

Hawthorne, S., & Klein, R. (Eds.). (1999). *Cyberfeminism; connectivity, critique and creativity*. North Melbourne: Spinifex Press Pty Ltd.

Henwood, F. (1993). Establishing gender perspectives on information technology: Problems, issues and opportunities. In E. Green, J. Owen, & D. Pain (Eds.), *Gendered by design? Information technology and office systems* (pp. 31-52). London; Washington, DC: Taylor and Francis.

Julier, G. (2000). *The culture of design*. London: SAGE Publications.

Lie, M. (1998). *Computer dialogues: Technology, gender and change*. Trondheim: Centre for Women's Studies.

Martinson, A. M., Schwartz, N., & Walker Vaughan, M. (2002). Women's experiences of leisure: Implications for design. *New Media and Society, 4*(1), 29-49.

McRobbie, A. (1999). *In the culture society*. London; New York: Routledge.

Oudshoorn, N., Rommes, E., & Stienstra, M. (2004). Configuring the user as everybody: Gender and design cultures in information and communication technologies. *Science, Technology, and Human Values, 29*(1), 30-63.

Rommes, E. (2002). Creating places for women on the Internet: The design of a "women's square" in a digital city. *The European Journal of Women's Studies, 9*(4), 400-429.

Sadowska, N. (2003). *Mystery and magic behind BEME.com: An internet environment where female users negotiate gender through design*. Paper presented at the Symposium Gender and ICT: Where are we at? Amsterdam, NL.

Sørenssen, B. (1997). Let your finger do the walking: The space/place metaphor in online computer communication. *Mediekultur, (27)*, 46-52.

Spilker, H., & Sørensen, K. H. (2000). A ROM of one's own or a home for sharing? Designing the inclusion of women in multimedia. *New Media and Society, 2*(3), 268-285.

Vickers, A. (2001). IPC media loses faith in women's portals. Retrieved October 26, 2001, from http://www.guardian.co.uk/Archive/Article/0,4273,4142374,00. html

Warwick, A. (1999). Introduction. In Cutting Edge: The Women's Research Group (Ed.), *Desire by design: Body, territories and new technologies*. London: I. B. Tauris Publishers.

Additional Reading

D-CP1a. (2000). IPC launches BEME.com. Retrieved September 17, 2001, from http://www.ipcmedia.com/frameset.html

e D-CP1b. (2000). IPC unveils new name to spearhead brand-centric strategy. Retrieved September 17, 2001, from http://www.ipcmedia.com/frameset.html

D-CP1c. (2000). BEME.com to sponsor Ally McBeal on Channel 4. Retrieved September 17, 2001, from http://www.ipcmedia.com/frameset.html

D-CP1d. (2001). BLM AND IPC agree Thomas Cook sponsorship agreement. Retrieved 17.09.2001, from http://www.ipcmedia.com/frameset.html

D-CP1f. (2000). Fitzgerald joins IPC Electric. Retrieved September 17, 2001, from http://www.ipcmedia.com/frameset.html

D-CP1i. (2001). New strategy, new look and new structure for BEME.com. Retrieved September 17, 2001, from http://www.ipcmedia.com/frameset.html

D-CP1j. (2001). IPC reviews online business. Retrieved September 17, 2001, from http://www.ipcmedia.com/frameset.html

D-CP4. (2001). BEME.com. Retrieved November 15, 2000, from http://www. ipcmedia.com/frameset.html

D-PREA1a (2000). Women on the Web. J. Matthews, BBC. Retrieved April 2, 2000 from http://news.bbc.co.uk/1/hi/uk/626947.stm

D-PREA2a. (1999). C-cups through E-tailing. I. O'Rorke (Ed.): The Guardian. Retrieved July 31, 2003, from http://shopping.guardian.co.uk/newsandviews/ story/0,5804,101074,00.html

D-PREA2k. (2001). IPC media loses faith in women's portals. In A. Vickers (Ed.): The Guardian. Retrieved November 26, 2001, from http://www.guardian. co.uk/Archive/Article/0,4273,4142374,00.html

D-PREA2l. (2001). Growing pains. In O. Gibson (Ed.): The Guardian. Retrieved November 26, 2001, from http://www.guardian.co.uk/Archive/Article/0,4273,4249304,00.html

D-PREA2m. (2001). IPC axes loaded Web site. In O. Gibson (Ed.): The Guardian. Retrieved November 26, 2001, from http://www.guardian.co.uk/Archive/Article/0,4273,4244453,00.html

I-PT1. (2002). Marketing consultant: Female. Interview: April 29, 2002

I-PT2. (2002). Editorial/creative director: Female. Interview: March 20, 2002

I-PT3. (2001). Design manager/designer: Male. Interview: December 11, 2001

I-PT4. (2001). Brand designer: Male. November 30, 2001

I-PT5. (2001). Senior producer: Female. November 28, 2001

Section IV

Cultural Issues

Chapter VIII

From Computer-Mediated Colonization to Culturally Aware ICT Usage and Design

Charles Ess, Drury University, USA

Abstract

A number of examples demonstrate that technologies of computer-mediated communication (CMC) embed and foster specific cultural values and communicative preferences. Differences between the values and preferences embedded in CMC and those of a given cultural group thereby lead to communication failures. Hofstede's and Hall's theories partially explain these failures and, by contrast, examples of successful online cross-cultural communication via CMC designed to incorporate important cultural and communicative differences.

Introduction: Cultural Clashes on the Electronic Frontier

As early as 1998, when approximately 84% of the population of the Internet world still hailed from North America (GVU, 1998), Lucienne Rey (2001) (among others) demonstrated that as the Internet diffused in Switzerland, it did so along culturally and linguistically defined lines. In her study of the development of home pages by Swiss towns and cantons, Rey discovered that while the German-speaking towns and cantons of Switzerland enjoyed greater economic and political power in Switzerland (e.g., the German-speaking population outvoted, barely, the Latin-speaking population regarding membership in the vote on whether to join the European Economic Area), along with a better-developed infrastructure, consistent with their comparatively more positive attitudes towards technology in general, the French- and Rhaeto-romansch-speaking areas of Switzerland enjoyed higher Internet presence (in the form of a communal home page) than their German-speaking counterparts (Rey, 2001, p. 158).

What Does Culture Have to Do with It?

Prelude: What Do we Mean by "Culture"?

First of all, we must acknowledge that the very term "culture" is enormously problematic. As Terry Eagleton notes, the term is second only to the term "nature" in English with regard to the range and diversity of definitions offered for it.[1] The term is further loaded, as recent postcolonial scholars have demonstrated with especial force, by its use to sustain notions of cultural superiority and inferiority, and thereby the politics of colonialism and imperialism (see especially Bhabha, 1994; Gajjala, 2006; Spivak, 1999). Obviously, a complete discussion of either of these points is well beyond the limits of this paper. For our purposes, however, it is appropriate to follow Rey's lead here and, at least initially, operationalize our understanding of culture in terms of a language shared by a group (2001, p. 51). Even this operational definition, however, must be further qualified by at least two observations. First of all, language often defines a national culture, but language and culture are not synonymous with nation states. Secondly, while older notions of culture might have assumed (hoped?) that "culture" might emerge as a Platonic essence complete with a single, unchanging, and unequivocal definition, both language and culture are dynamic entities engaged in processes of change including (for better and for worse) processes of hybridization that result from cross-cultural encounters and engagements (cf. Kampurri & Tukainen, 2004).

That said, Rey suggests several possible cultural factors, including low ethnocentrism and what she calls a French "lightness of being," as fostering greater technology diffusion (Rey, 2001, p. 159). While Rey's study thus demonstrates cultural differences in responses to CMC technologies, further case studies will more directly provide us with important examples as to two key frameworks: Edward Hall's *communicative* distinction between high context/low content and low context/high content cultures, and Hofstede's distinction between individualist and collectivist cultures for understanding cross-cultural communication online.[2]

Cultural Clashes and Communication Misfires

Group Support Systems in Indonesia

Our first example of cultural conflict in the deployment of CMC technologies is provided by Abdat and Pervan (2000), who observed the cultural impacts of anonymity features in a group support system (GSS) deployed in Indonesia. We need to remember here that Western proponents of CMC argued, especially in the 1990s, that anonymity is a key advantage of these technologies: on this view, such anonymity will thereby ostensibly encourage more open and free communication and, it was hoped, a flattening of hierarchies. Such a view clearly reflects Western commitments to individualism, freedom of expression, and egalitarianism over hierarchy.

Abdat and Pervan found, however, that in the Indonesian context, the anonymity feature of a GSS led to communicative disaster. Given the ability to submit anonymous communications, subordinates indeed felt free to offer critical comments. Their superiors, however, operating from a Confucian framework that emphasizes the importance of "face," experienced these comments, nonetheless, as an attack upon their face. As a result, Abdat and Pervan recommended that subsequent designs for GSS include the ability to switch off anonymizing features in order to make such systems more culturally appropriate to the Indonesian context. Similarly, South Korea has recently started requiring users of public chat systems to log on using their national social security number, which is then used as their identifier in the chat system. The point is to make participants accountable for their statements online, and thereby protect the face of others, including important public officials, company executives, and so forth (Jang, 2005).

These conflicts point to a first *cultural framework* that may prove useful in attempting to understand such failures of communication. Beginning in the 1960s, Gert Hofstede (1980) developed a number of axes or dimensions for understanding cultural differences that he believed contributed to communication failures among the managers and personnel in the offices of multinational corporations, starting with his own employer, IBM. One of these axes contrasts the emphasis in many Western cultures on the individual vis-à-vis the emphasis in many Eastern cultures on the collective (1980).[3] In this light, we can see the Western enthusiasm for anonymity as facilitating free expression indeed reflects Western values, beginning with the emphasis on the freedom of the individual over such issues as "face" or public reputation, group solidarity, and so forth. Embedding anonymity as a design feature in CMC technologies such as GSS thereby embeds a specific cultural value; one clearly not shared by many Eastern, especially Confucian, cultures, as the conflicts observed by Abdat and Pervan make clear.[4]

South Africa Learning Centres

As a second example of such cultural conflicts, we can turn to South Africa and its efforts to establish Learning Centres that feature CMC technologies. Such Learning Centres are designed to empower indigenous peoples by providing them access to ICTs and, thereby, to help them take advantage of the multiple potentials and capacities of these technologies. Over several years, however, a series of observers have noted that these Centres repeatedly failed, primarily because of basic cultural conflicts. As Louise Postma initially pointed out, the Centres reflect their designer's Western emphasis on *individual* and silent learning, the learning style associated with the technology of *literacy* and the work of the individual learner in a traditional Western library. By contrast, as with many indigenous peoples around the world, the indigenous peoples of South Africa demonstrate strong preferences for learning as a group in *collaborative* and often noisy, *performative* ways (Postma, 2001). Similar contrasts have been documented with regard to efforts to work with the Maori people of New Zealand (Duncker, 2002; Keegan, Lewis, Roa, & Tarnowska, 2004).

These conflicts can be helpfully analyzed in terms of Edward T. Hall's distinction between high and low context cultures (1976). In this schema, contemporary societies such as the U.S., the United Kingdom, and the Germanic countries show a preference for *literate* (i.e., textual), high content (but low context) information transfer. By contrast, societies such as Arabic cultures, indigenous peoples, and many Asian cultures prefer instead more *oral,* low content (but high context) modes of communication. As the CMC technologies and social context of the Learning Centres favor the cultural values (individualism) and communicative preferences (high content/low context) of their Western designers, these values and preferences clash with those of the indigenous peoples the Centres are intended to serve (i.e., the preference for low content/high context communication and greater emphasis on the group), with almost total failure as a result (see Addison & Sikissoon 2004; Snyman & Hulbert 2004).

Best Practices of Culturally Aware CMC

... design indeed is highly culturally specific and ... universal principle—for example of Web site usability—are implausible. (Hans-Jürgen Bucher, 2004, p. 425)

... internationalization practices should not be reduced to the interface as the visible part and operable layer of the system, but to a consideration of the whole computing system as the 'interface' linking people to their socially constructed and determined activities. (Grudin, 1993, cited in Nocera & Hall, 2004, p. 40f)

Japanese CSCW

In fact, Hall's distinction between high content/low context and low content/high context communication preferences can be seen at work in the Japanese redesign of computer-supported cooperative work (CSCW) systems, as documented by Lorna Heaton (Heaton, 1998, 2001, 2002): briefly, Japanese engineers found CSCW systems designed in the West (as high content/low context) almost totally unsuited to the Japanese context, whose high context/low content characteristic included a strong reliance on nonverbal communication (body distance, gaze, gesture) to convey important elements of communication, including recognition of status (1998, 2001, 2002).

Marketing Discovers Hall

Moreover, advertisers have begun to pay serious attention to Hall's distinction, as it seems to be helpful in the development of marketing campaigns by multinational corporations seeking to improve market share in "local" markets. Mark Hermeking, for example, offers a schematic (Figure 1) as an initial orientation:

In particular, Hermeking argues:

In general, indirect and transformational advertising messages creating emotions through pictures and entertainment are more favoured in High-context cultures like France or Japan, for example, whereas direct and rational advertising messages providing first of all product information play a more important role in Low-context cultures like Germany or many parts of the USA, for example. (2004, p. 445)

Figure 1. (From Hermeking, 2004, p. 446; Used with permission)

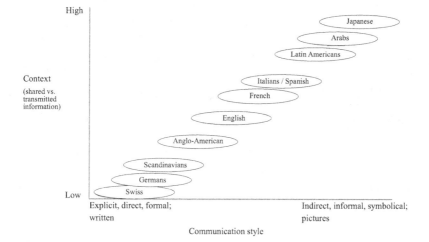

In the following, we will see further examples of how the frameworks developed by Hall and Hofstede are consistent with a number of analyses of the interplay between culture, technology, and communication.

Telephone Marketing to Hispanics and Non-Hispanics

Paul Leonardi has examined U.S. and Hispanic Web sites for U.S. and Latin American-based phone companies, along with responses to these sites by both Hispanic and non-Hispanic viewers. Leonardi draws on Hofstede's individualism/collectivism axis as a primary framework for analysis (Hoftsede, 1980). Briefly, the cultures of Latin America and U.S. Hispanics tend to be more collective in their orientation, in contrast with the more individualist culture of (white) North America. Especially with regard to the use of images and language, Leonardi's U.S. Hispanic users indeed noted these differences in the design of U.S. and Hispanic Web sites. Most strikingly, Hispanic Web sites used words (primarily, the pronoun *nosotros*, "we") and images (photographs of groups rather than solitary individuals) to reflect and foster the Hispanic cultural value of collectivism and group membership. Interestingly enough, while these differences were obvious to Hispanic users, U.S. non-Hispanic users largely failed to notice them (Leonardi, 2002).

McDonalds' Glocalizes the Web

Elizabeth Würtz (2004, 2005) has undertaken a more global study of the Web sites of one of the worlds' most successful multinational corporations: namely, McDonalds. She finds that McDonald's Web sites are indeed highly "glocalized" —that is, tuned to the local cultural values and communicative preferences of their intended customers, and in ways consistent with the frameworks developed by Hall and Hofstede. So, for example, Würtz argues that McDonald's Japanese site, as it uses animation to show four McDonalds' employees bowing to their viewer, thereby appeals to the emphasis in Japanese culture on interpersonal, *high context* communication (i.e., consistent with Lorna Heaton's findings). Similarly, both Japanese and Indian sites reflect a *collectivist* preference as these sites, like the Hispanic sites analyzed by Leonardi, emphasize photographs of people together, in activities such as sports and shopping. By contrast, the Web sites for more *individualist* cultures (Germany, Switzerland, Denmark) highlight photographs of individuals alone.

Finally, Würtz detects, in the relative *transparency* of the Web site design, important cultural differences. As we have seen, Western cultures such as the U.S., UK, and Germanic cultures favor high content/low context communication in contrast with the high context/low content preferences of many Asian and Arabic cultures, as well as Western European Latin cultures such as France, Spain, and Italy. As Hermeking (2004) argues, this contrast can be seen in preferences for more text and less image (high content), or more image and less text (low content). Würtz further amplifies this contrast by adding the distinction between monochronic and polychronic perceptions of time. Monochronic cultures–coinciding with high content preferences—see time as a valuable commodity that flows in a linear fashion, one that must be used efficiently ("time is money"). Polychronic/low content cultures, by contrast, experience time in a more accepting way (things will happen when they should), allowing persons to interrupt plans and schedules, especially for the sake of human relationships (Würtz, 2004, p. 111). Taken together, these lead to a notion of "transparency" in HCI in Western high content/monochronic cultures that stresses a comparatively brief overview of available information, making it easy for the user to navigate quickly through the links to the desired information. Such "transparency," however, is at odds with the communicative and design preferences Würtz notes in the McDonald's site for Japan. She finds that the site requires the user to "chase" information "through exploration of the site and performing 'mouse-overs' (placing the cursor over a link to reveal more content information before finally clicking it" (2004, p.118f.) She adds: "This tendency coincides neatly with the idea that in LC [Low Context] cultures, it is the *sender* that does all the work in clarifying information and getting the point across, while in HC [High Context] cultures, it is the *receiver* who has to work to retrieve the information" (p. 119: emphasis added, CE). Similar contrasts are reported between German (as a low context culture) and Chinese (as a high context culture) Web sites by Hans-Jürgen Bucher (2002).

Tone Online?

We can note that even if countries and cultures use the same language, important cultural differences, nonetheless, manifest themselves online as well. Mary Evans and her colleagues sought to examine whether *tone* on Web sites might correlate with specific cultural variables including the Hofstede dimension of power distance (Evans, McBride, Queen, Thayer, & Spyridakis, 2004). Their analysis included 320 university Web sites from 20 countries divided into "inner" and "outer" circles in terms of English use, that is, countries in which English is the first language or a second language, respectively. They focused on tone, defining formal tone as including an emphasis on passive voice rather than active voice, and informal tone as marked by greater use of informal punctuation and personal pronouns. Interestingly enough, their analysis indeed shows a strong correlation between power distance and formality, that is, high power distance countries (such as India and the Philippines) manifest higher formality online than low power distance countries such as the UK, Australia, and the U.S.

Designing for China

My colleagues at Trier University, Karl-Heinz Pohl (Chinese Studies) and Hans-Jürgen Bucher (Media Studies), have undertaken extensive cross-cultural comparisons between German and Chinese Web sites over a number of years now, including research involving eye-tracking devices and software that show how Chinese and German students "read" Web sites in different ways. Many of their findings help reinforce, but also point out the limits of, Hall's distinction between high context/low content and low context/high content cultures.

To begin with, the Chinese Web sites Pohl and Bucher have studied are generally more complex and more oriented towards entertainment, in keeping with what we would expect from a high context/low content society. Bucher explains that this complexity derives in part from the guiding principle of Chinese Web site design: to "give the people what they want at once":

... clearness and transparency in Chinese (yi mu liaoran) not only means, to 'get an overview' but also means 'to find quickly what one is looking for'. ... In contrast to western Web sites that are characterized by a deep hierarchy and fewer elements on each level, Chinese Web sites have a flat hierarchy with as many elements on each level as possible. (Pohl, 2004, p. 424)

As well, as Karl-Heinz Pohl has also demonstrated, Chinese Web sites appear more complex because of a preference for the "aesthetics of abundance" characteristic of Chinese popular culture, for example, in New Year's pictures, calendars, and paintings. This aesthetics of abundance is marked by "… strong and rich colour, density, and opulent presentation symbolize happiness and wealth" (Bucher, 2004, p. 424).

We can see this apparently greater complexity by comparing how Yahoo constructed a Chinese version of its U.S. Web site, that is, in a one-to-one correspondence that basically translates the 14 page elements making up the U.S. page into Chinese. By contrast, the Sina.com page, with 23 page elements, exemplifies the design principle of "finding quickly what one is looking for," that is, much more information is available immediately on the surface of the page, making it look more complex and confusing, especially to a Westerner expecting a few organizational elements that serve as portals to a deeper, hierarchical structure "behind" the opening page (Bucher, 2002).

Because of the graphical nature of Chinese characters, Chinese Web site design can blur the Western boundaries between text and image, that is, so as to use texts *as* images. Blurring this distinction complicates, for example, the simple distinction we have seen in Hermeking between text as associated with high-content/low context cultures and image as associated with high-context/low content cultures. Nonetheless, the important distinctions noted by Bucher and Pohl are consistent with recent research that demonstrates that U.S. and Chinese Web users are faster in finding information when searching among Web resources created by designers from their own cultures (Faiola & Matei, 2005). By now, I hope, we should not find such a discovery surprising.

Designing for Arabic Societies?

In response to an earlier presentation of these materials, Erika C. Linke, associate dean of the Carnegie Mellon University Libraries, asked for my suggestions regarding design for Arabic-language Web sites. This became the opportunity to test the guidelines presented here. While I had not undertaken any direct study of Arabic-language Web sites, nor had the CATaC conferences (so far) included such a study, I was, nonetheless, willing to risk a hypothesis regarding what culturally aware Web site design might look like for Arabic-language cultures, based in the first instance on Hall's original analysis of Arabic cultures as "high context/low content" (1976).

I wrote to Dean Linke:

I would be willing to make some predictions, based on analogues with other high-context cultures (such as China and Japan), for example, less text/linearity/information—more pictures, more "entertainment" elements.

What I'm not sure about here would be use of colors. As well, if designing for a high uncertainty avoidance culture, then it would probably be best to use relatively controlled navigation structures. (e-mail, August 5, 2004)

I then asked for assistance in this matter from several colleagues working in Arabic-language cultures: first of all, from Dr. Deborah Wheeler, who has done "on the ground" research on ICTs and culture in the Middle East for many years now. She responded to my hypothesis:

... Web site design must be culturally compatible, which means that Web sites, for a company say, are highly graphics based, use lots of flash and java, and have very little text or data. Another constraint is the tendency to want to keep information private, only shared with those who are trustworthy or need to know something. Your observations of Asia apply to the Arab region. (e-mail, August 5, 2004)

Of course, this reply does not *prove* my hypothesis—and thereby, it does not *prove* the validity of Hall's framework as applied to Arabic cultures at large. But it at least demonstrates that the hypothesis was not false. This suggest that the general frameworks developed here, based on Hall's schema (which, nicely enough, began with his work on Arabic-language cultures) may be at least generally helpful, in an initial way, when developing frameworks for culturally-aware design and communication online.

Moreover, Dr. Wheeler's reply helpfully goes beyond my general hypothesis to provide important additional information that should be useful to Web site designers, and to those of us "surfing" such sites: we should know better what the presence and absence of graphics and text, respectively, signifies. To say it differently: the absence of text is not simply an artifact of a high-context/low content communication preference, it is also a marker of a society in which information is shared only carefully.[5]

Conclusion

I hope these examples make clear that if we make the usual assumptions that technologies, including the technologies of computer-mediated communication, are somehow neutral in terms of communicative preferences and cultural values, we thereby overlook multiple ways in which CMC technologies, in fact, embed and foster the communicative preferences and cultural values of their (overwhelmingly) Western designers. To ignore these cultural and communicative dimensions of the technologies we use on a daily basis in such fields as education is not only to run the risk of using these technologies in ways that will not be effective as we seek to communicate with "Others," with human beings whose cultural values and communicative preferences may differ significantly from our own. Worse still, to ignore these dimensions of these technologies, especially as they become more ubiquitous in our lives, is to run the risk of thereby imposing a specific set of cultural values and communicative preferences upon such "Others," a form of what I have called computer-mediated colonization.

Happily, such communication misfires and colonization are avoidable simply through the effort to become aware of such dimensions of culture and communication as those developed by Hall and Hofstede, and to take these into account as we extend our efforts to communicate cross-culturally online. Of course, these frameworks must be used with caution: I would be the first to point out that, as tools for helping us better understand the ten thousand details of culture and communication, they are very crude and limited. At the same time, however, it is a somewhat astonishing fact that, at least within the English-speaking world, research and literature on effective cross-cultural communication online is only in its infancy.[6]

Nonetheless, based on these examples and additional recent research, it is possible to suggest here, by way of conclusion, some at least initial guidelines for such culturally aware HCI design.

To begin with, the frameworks developed by Hall and Hofstede are shown to work best specifically with regard to *advertising* Web sites: indeed, these frameworks appear to work best with advertising for fast-food, such as those developed by McDonald's (Würtz, 2005), and for universities (Callahan, 2005)—in contrast, say, with those developed for durable goods (Hermeking, 2004). Within this genre, designers should determine whether their intended audience comes from more *individualist* or from more *collectivist* cultures. Generally, sites designed for *individualist* cultures stress images of the individual alone, while sites more successful for *collectivist* cultures (including U.S. Hispanics and Latin American cultures) use more images of groups and families. *Color* preferences also vary from country to country: see Calahan (2005) for a representative overview. In terms of *text,* as we saw in Leonardi (2002), individualist country sites emphasize "I" and "you," in contrast with the greater use of "we" (*nosotros* in Spanish) in more collective societies.

By the same token, Hall's distinction between high context and low context cultures suggests that marketing Web sites oriented towards *low context* (LC) cultures (which tend to correlate with *individualist* cultures) should emphasize content and what Hermeking (2004) characterizes as *rational* information (conveyed primarily through *text*) about the product to be sold. By contrast, sites oriented towards *high context* cultures should emphasize *images* that appeal to strong emotions, including images stressing time spent with family and friends (cf. Würtz, 2005).

These guidelines, however, are likely to be useful only in appealing to an audience whose membership within a given national culture is largely straightforward and unproblematic. Somewhat paradoxically, perhaps, thanks precisely to the manifold cross-cultural encounters and resulting hybridization facilitated by the Internet and the Web, more and more people are more completely and accurately characterized in terms of being members of multiple and hybrid cultures, as creating their own "third" identities whose particular cultural dimensions must be carefully considered. Such persons are, in an important sense, beyond the frameworks developed by Hall and Hofstede, as these frameworks assume largely fixed and homogenous national communities as the primary unit of "culture."

To begin with, even within relatively homogenous populations, more recent research suggests that the frameworks developed by Hall and Hofstede should be extended in more complex ways in order to accurately capture important cultural elements. So, for example, Triandis (2001) has developed a refinement of Hofstede's *individualism* axis, one that distinguishes between *horizontal* and *vertical* individualism. One recent study has shown that "horizontal individualistic" individuals, that is, individuals who seek to be unique, in contrast with vertical individualistic persons who seek to be unique while simultaneously striving to be the very best in competition with others, have more *negative* views towards Web advertising than other groups (Lee & Choi, 2005). More broadly, Faiola and Matei (2005), using a framework of cultural cognition theory, show that users from within a given culture (e.g., U.S. or Chinese) are able to navigate more easily through a Web site designed by someone from the same culture, especially, in their view, as cultural background shapes choices regarding the *graphical* elements of Web sites including "… page format, imagery, color, information architecture, and system interaction" (2005). This suggests that, beyond whatever explicit guidelines we may be able to develop for HCI, there remains an important range of *tacit* cultural knowledge that cannot easily be made explicit and articulate, and that may resist reduction to general rules in the first place.

In any event, much work remains to be done. For example, Brock (2005) has developed a cultural framework that seeks to articulate cognitive approaches and preferences of U.S. African-Americans. But as important as this work is, it is simply a starting point. Moreover, especially as "culture" changes rapidly under the pressures of globalization, and so forth, any proposed guidelines will remain, at best, provisional and temporary. Finally, as globalization and hybridization generate an explosion of "third cultures" and hybrid identities, especially among young people who may share a global culture shaped by mass entertainment, but one that is directly refracted and reshaped through the lenses and experiences of their own local culture(s), guidelines resting on assumptions of relatively fixed and homogenous cultures will have, at best, a limited scope.

With these caveats and limits firmly in mind, I hope, however, that these examples and suggestions will serve as helpful and fruitful starting points for the development of "culturally-aware" design in HCI.

References

Abdat, S., & Pervan, G. P. (2000). Reducing the negative effects of power distance during asynchronous pre-meeting with using anonymity in Indonesian culture. In F. Sudweeks & C. Ess (Eds.), *Proceedings of the Second International Conference on Cultural Attitudes towards Technology and Communication* (pp. 209-15). Murdoch, Western Australia: Murdoch University Press.

Addison, T., & Sirkissoon, E. (2004). User interfaces: Black South Africans' preferences re some language, icon and usability features. In F. Sudweeks & C. Ess (Eds.), *Proceedings Cultural Attitudes Towards Technology and Communication* (pp. 469-481). Murdoch, Western Australia: Murdoch University Press.

Ang, I. (1990). Culture and communication: Towards an ethnographic critique of media consumption in the transnational media system. *European Journal of Communication, 5*(2-3), 239-260.

Barnett, G., & Sung, E. (2005). Culture and the structure of international communication. In C. Ess & F. Sudweeks (Eds.), Culture and computer-mediated communication: Towards new understandings. Special issue of *Journal of Computer-Mediated Communication, 11*(2: October). Retrieved from http://jcmc.indiana.edu

Bhabha, H. K. (1994). *The location of culture.* London; New York: Routledge.

Brock, A. (2005). A belief in humanity is a belief in colored men: Using culture to span the digital divide. In C. Ess & F. Sudweeks (Eds.), Culture and computer-mediated communication: Towards new understandings. Special issue of *Journal of Computer-Mediated Communication, 11*(2: October). Retrieved from http://jcmc.indiana.edu

Bucher, H-J. (2002). The power of the audience: Interculturality, interactivity and trust in Internet Communication. In F. Sudweeks, & C. Ess (Eds.), *Proceedings of the Second International Conference on Cultural Attitudes Towards Technology and Communication* (pp. 3-14). Murdoch, Western Australia: Murdoch University Press.

Bucher, H-J. (2004). Is there a Chinese Internet? In F. Sudweeks & C. Ess (Eds.), *Proceedings Cultural Attitudes Towards Technology and Communication* (pp. 416-428). Murdoch, Western Australia: Murdoch University Press.

Callahan, E. (2005). Cultural similarities and differences in the design of university Web sites. In C. Ess & F. Sudweeks (Eds.), Culture and computer-mediated communication: Towards new understandings. Special issue of *Journal of Computer-Mediated Communication, 11*(2: October). Retrieved from http://jcmc.indiana.edu

Duncker, E. (2002). Cross-cultural usability of computing metaphors: Do we colonize the minds of indigenous Web users? In F. Sudweeks & C. Ess (Eds.), *Proceedings of the Second International Conference on Cultural Attitudes Towards Technology and Communication* (pp. 217ff). Murdoch, Western Australia: Murdoch University Press.

Eagleton, T. (2000). *The idea of culture*. Oxford: Blackwell.

Ess, C. (Ed.). (2001a). *Culture, technology, communication: Towards an intercultural global village*, with F. Sudweeks. Foreword by S. Herring. Albany: State University of New York Press.

Ess, C. (2001b). Introduction: What's culture got to do with it? Cultural collisions in the electronic global village, creative interferences, and the rise of culturally-mediated computing. In C. Ess (Ed.), *Culture, technology, communication: Towards an intercultural global village* (pp.1-50). Albany: State University of New York Press.

Ess, C. (2005). Lost in translation?: Intercultural dialogues on privacy and information ethics. Introduction to special issue on privacy and data privacy protection in Asia. *Ethics and Information Technology, 7*(1), 1-6.

Ess, C. (Forthcoming). Can the local reshape the global? Ethical imperatives for humane intercultural communication online. In J. Frühbauer, R. Capurro, & T. Hausmanninger (Eds.), *Localizing the Internet. Ethical aspects in an intercultural perspective* (Volume 4, ICIE Series).

Ess, C., & Sudweeks, F. (2005). Culture and computer-mediated communication: Towards new understandings. Special issue of *Journal of Computer-Mediated Communication, 11*(2: October). Retrieved from http://jcmc.indiana.edu

Evans, M., McBride, A., Queen, M., Thayer, A., & Spyridakis, J. (2004). Has the tone of online English become globalized? In F. Sudweeks & C. Ess (Eds.), *Proceedings Cultural Attitudes Towards Technology and Communication* (pp. 135-139). Murdoch, Western Australia: Murdoch University Press.

Faiola, A., & Matei, S. (2005). Cultural cognitive style and Web design: Beyond a behavioral inquiry of computer-mediated communication. In C. Ess & F. Sudweeks (Eds.), Culture and computer-mediated communication: Towards new understandings. Special issue of *Journal of Computer-Mediated Communication, 11*(2: October). Retrieved from http://jcmc.indiana.edu

Gajjala, R. (2006). Cyberethnography: Reading South Asian diasporas. In K. M. Landzelius (Ed.), *Going native on the Net: Indigenous cyberactivism and virtual diasporas over the World Wide Web* (pp. 449-484). London: Routledge.

Goonasekera, A. (1990). Communication, culture and the growth of the individual self in Third World societies. *Asian Journal of Communication 1*(1), 34-52.

Graphic Visualization and Usability Center (GVU). (1998). *GVU's 10th WWW user survey graphs.* Retrieved from http://www.gvu.gatech.edu/user_surveys/survey-1998-10/graphs/general/q50.htm

Grudin, J. (1993). Interface: An evolving concept. *Communications of the ACM, 26*(4), 112-119.

Hall, E. (1976). *Beyond culture.* New York: Anchor Books.

Hannerz, U. (1992). *Cultural complexity: Studies in the social organization of meaning.* New York: Columbia University Press.

Harris, R., Bala, P., Songan, P., Khoo Guat Lien, E., & Trang, T. (2001). Challenges and opportunities in introducing information and communication technologies to the Kelabit community of North Central Borneo. *New media and society, 3*(3), 271-296.

Heaton, L. (1998). Preserving communication context: CSCW design in Japan. *Electronic Journal of Communication/Revue électronique de la communication, 5*(3&4: Fall).

Heaton, L. (2001). Preserving communication context: Virtual workspace and interpersonal space in Japanese CSCW. In C. Ess (Ed.). *Culture, technology, communication: Towards an intercultural global village* (pp. 213-240). Albany: State University of New York Press.

Heaton, L. (2002). Designing work: Situating design objects in cultural context. *Journal of Design Research, 2*(2). Retrieved from http://jdr.tudelft.nl

Hermeking, M. (2004). Cultural influences on Internet diffusion and Web site acceptance: Some findings from cross-cultural marketing research. In F. Sudweeks & C. Ess (Eds.), *Proceedings Cultural Attitudes Towards Technology and Communication* (pp. 442-453). Murdoch, Western Australia: Murdoch University Press.

Hofstede, G. (1980). *Culture's consequences: International differences in work-related values.* Beverly Hills, CA: Sage.

Hofstede, G. (1983). National cultures in four dimensions. *International Studies of Management and Organization, 13*, 52-60.

Hofstede, G. (1984). The cultural relativity of the quality of life concept. *Academy of Management Review, 9*, 389-98.

Hofstede, G. (1991). *Cultures and organizations: Software of the mind.* London: McGraw-Hill.

Hofstede, G., & Bond, M. H. (1988). The Confucius connection: From cultural roots to economic growth. *Organizational Dynamics, 16*(4), 5-21.

Jang, S. (2005). Personal communication to the author.

Kampurri, M., & Tukainen, M. (2004). Culture in human-computer interaction studies: A survey of ideas and definitions. In F. Sudweeks & C. Ess (Eds.), *Proceedings Cultural Attitudes Towards Technology and Communication* (pp. 43-57). Murdoch, Western Australia: Murdoch University Press.

Keegan, T. T., Lewis, R., Roa, T., & Tarnowska, J. (2004). Indigenous language in an e-learning interface: Translation of PLACE™ into the Māori language. In F. Sudweeks & C. Ess (Eds.), *Proceedings Cultural Attitudes Towards Technology and Communication* (pp. 250-254). Murdoch, Western Australia: Murdoch University Press.

Lee, W., & Choi, S. M. (2005). The role of horizontal and vertical individualism and collectivism in online consumers' response toward persuasive communication on the Web. In C. Ess & F. Sudweeks (Eds.), Culture and computer-mediated communication: Towards new understandings. Special issue of *Journal of Computer-Mediated Communication, 11*(2: October). Retrieved from http://jcmc.indiana.edu

Leonardi, P. (2002). Culture inside the technology: Evidence for paying attention to user-end cultural practices in Web design. In F. Sudweeks & C. Ess (Eds.), *Proceedings of the Second International Conference on Cultural Attitudes Towards Technology and Communication* (pp. 297-315). Murdoch, Western Australia: Murdoch University Press.

Lübke, E. (2005). Cultural dominance through communicative "censorship": About necessary research in the CMC of virtual teams. In C. Ess & F. Sudweeks (Eds.), Culture and computer-mediated communication: Towards new understandings. Special issue of *Journal of Computer-Mediated Communication, 11*(2: October). Retrieved from http://jcmc.indiana.edu

Macfadyen, L. P., Roche, J., & Doff, S. (2004). *Communicating across cultures in cyberspace: A bibliographical review of online intercultural communication.* Hamburg: Lit-Verlag.

Maitland, C. (1998). Global diffusion of interactive networks. In C. Ess & F. Sudweeks (Eds.), *Proceedings: Cultural attitudes toward technology and communication* (pp. 51-69). Sydney, Australia: Key Centre of Design Computing, University of Sydney.

Maitland, C., & Bauer, J. (2001). National level culture and global diffusion: The case of the Internet. In C. Ess (Ed.), *Culture, technology, communication: Towards an intercultural global village* (pp. 87-128). Albany: State University of New York Press.

Nocera, J. L. A., & Hall, P. (2004). Global software, local voices: The social construction of usefulness of ERP systems. In F. Sudweeks & C. Ess (Eds.), *Proceedings Cultural Attitudes Towards Technology and Communication* (pp. 29-42). Murdoch, Western Australia: Murdoch University Press.

Pohl, K.-H. (2004). *Aesthetics of the Chinese Internet.* Paper presented at "Internetkulturen: – regionale – nationale – globale Ausprägungen" [Internet Cultures: regional – national – global expressions], November 5, Universität Trier, Trier, Germany.

Postma, L. (2001). A theoretical argumentation and evaluation of South African learners' orientation towards and perceptions of the empowering use of information. *New Media and Society, 3*(3: September), 315-28.

Rahmati, N. (2000). The impact of cultural values on computer-mediated group work. In F. Sudweeks & C. Ess (Eds.), *Proceedings of the Second International Conference on Cultural Attitudes towards Technology and Communication* (pp. 257-74). Murdoch, Western Australia: Murdoch University.

Rey, L. (2001). Cultural attitudes toward technology and communication: A study in the "multicultural" environment of Switzerland. In C. Ess (Ed.), *Culture, technology, communication: Towards an intercultural global village* (pp. 151-160). Albany: State University of New York Press.

Snyman, M., & Hulbert, D. (2004). Implementing ICT Centres for Development in South Africa: Can cultural differences be overcome?" In F. Sudweeks & C. Ess (Eds.), *Proceedings Cultural Attitudes Towards Technology and Communication* (pp. 626-630). Murdoch, Western Australia: Murdoch University Press.

Spivak, G. C. (1999). *A critique of postcolonial reason: Toward a history of the vanishing present.* Cambridge, MA: Harvard University Press.

Sudweeks, F., & Ess, C. (Eds.). (2002). *Proceedings of the Second International Conference on Cultural Attitudes towards Technology and Communication.* Murdoch, Western Australia: Murdoch University.

Sudweeks, F., & Ess, C. (Eds.) (2004). *Proceedings Cultural Attitudes Towards Communication and Technology 2004.* Murdoch, Western Australia: Murdoch University.

Sy, P. (2001). Barangays of IT: Filipinizing mediated communication and digital power. *New Media and society, 3*(3), 297-313.

Triandis, H. C. (2001). Individualism-collectivism and personality. *Journal of Personality, 69,* 907-924.

Wheeler, D. (2001). New technologies, old culture: A look at women, gender, and the Internet in Kuwait. In C. Ess (Ed.), *Culture, technology, communication: Towards an intercultural global village* (pp. 187-212). Albany: State University of New York Press.

Würtz, E. (2004). Intercultural communication on Web sites: An analysis of visual communication in high- and low-context cultures. In F. Sudweeks & C. Ess (Eds.), *Proceedings Cultural Attitudes Towards Technology and Communication* (pp. 109-122). Murdoch, Western Australia: Murdoch University Press.

Würtz, E. (2005). Intercultural communication on Web sites - A cross-cultural analysis of Web sites from high-context cultures and low-context cultures. In C. Ess & F. Sudweeks (Eds.), Culture and computer-mediated communication: Towards new understandings. Special issue of *Journal of Computer-Mediated Communication, 11*(2: October). Retrieved from http://jcmc.indiana.edu

Zakaria, N., Stanton, J. M., & Sarkar-Barney, S. T. M. (2003). Designing and implementing culturally sensitive IT applications: The interaction of cultural values and privacy issues in the Middle East. *Information Technology and People, 16*(1), 49-75.

Endnotes

[1]   2000. See especially chapter 1, "Versions of Culture."

[2]   It should be noted at the outset that while, as we are about to see, the frameworks for cultural analysis developed by Hall and Hofstede indeed work in a range of examples and are thus suggestive for culturally aware HCI design, these frameworks have been extensively criticized and shown in important ways not to always succeed. See Ess and Sudweeks (2005) for discussion and additional studies that both confirm the utility and demonstrate the limitations of Hall and Hofstede. In particular, Callahan (2005), in addition to her own research, is especially useful for additional positive examples of Hofstede vis-à-vis HCI, while Lübke (2005) is especially useful for literature and examples critical of Hofstede.

We will see how Hofstede and Hall can be used to develop guidelines for specific applications in HCI in the conclusion.

[3]   Lorna Heaton (1998) describes Hofstede's additional axes most succinctly:

The first dimension, that of power distance, refers not to the actual distribution of power, but to the extent to which the less powerful members of institutions and organizations within a country expect and accept that power is distributed unequally. This dimension has implications for hierarchy, centralization, privilege, and status symbols. The individualism/collectivism dimension identifies the strength of ties to, and belonging in, a group. One might expect this dimension to be correlated with loyalty, trust, shared resources, even the relative importance of verbal or nonverbal communication. The masculinity/femininity dimension measures the clarity of gender role distinction, with masculine cultures having clearly defined gender, and feminine cultures considerable overlap. Finally, the uncertainty avoidance dimension measures the tolerance (or intolerance) of ambiguity, the way in which people cope with uncertain or unknown situations. In the workplace, one might expect correlations with the way the environment is structured; rules, precision, and punctuality; toleration of new ideas, as well as with motivation (achievement, security, esteem, belonging). (1998, ftn. 5, 169.)

Carleen Maitland points out that a fifth "Confucian" dimension, the contrast between short-term and long-term orientation, discovered originally by Michael Bond, is frequently included with Hofstede's original four dimensions (1998, ftn. 2, 55), and describes it helpfully:

Characteristics of long-term oriented societies include respect for social and status obligations within limits, thrift, high savings rates, and perseverance. Countries scoring high on this index include China, Hong Kong, Taiwan and Japan. Short-term orientation cultures are characterized as having respect for social and status obligations regardless of cost, social pressure to 'keep up with the Joneses' even if it means overspending, and low levels of savings. Countries with a short-term orientation include Canada, Philippines, Nigeria, and Pakistan. (1998, 56)

4   These findings are consistent with those of Nasrin Rahmati's analysis of basic contrasts in responses to such GSS systems in Malaysia and Australia (2000). Taken together, these studies point to a cluster of South Asian cultural values that conflict with Western CMC:

- *face-saving (Confucian)*
- *high uncertainty avoidance (low risk tolerance)*
- *high collectivism/low individualism*
- *high power distance*

These findings, moreover, correlate with Maitland and Bauer's demonstration that:

- *low uncertainty avoidance* and
- *gender* emp owerment

are significant *cultural* factors promoting diffusion of IT (2001).

These findings, in turn, are at least consistent with those of Barnett and Sung (2005) who, in their analysis of the hyperlink structure of the Web, determine that both individualism and low uncertainty avoidance correlate with what they identify as centrality (defined as "the mean number of links or the social distance [the inverse of the frequency of communication] required to reach all other countries in a network, such that the lower the value the more central the nation").

In turn, Lee and Choi (2005) helpfully complicate Hofstede's individualism/collectivism axis by drawing on Triandis' distinctions between horizontal and vertical individualists, and horizontal and vertical collectivists, and again find correlations between these four types of cultural orientation and Web skills and attitudes towards Web advertising.

Callahan (2005), by contrast, finds a much weaker correlation between Hofstede's axes and design elements from her extensive study of university Web sites from around the world.

Finally, we can note that similar contrasts between Western (U.S./E.U./Scandinavian) and Asian (Japan/Thailand/China) cultures manifest themselves with regard to privacy expectations and data privacy protection laws: see Ess (2005).

[5] Dr. Wheeler also recommends Zakaria, Stanton, & Sarkar-Barney (2003), as a useful resource.

[6] The most important of these is the bibliography developed by Macfadyen, Roche, & Doff (2004). But to my knowledge, no one has developed a comprehensive, systematic, and theoretically well-grounded set of guidelines and best practices for cross-cultural communication online along the lines, for example, of the best practices in Web site design I attempt to summarize here.

Chapter IX

A Case Study:
Creating and Designing a Bilingual Resource Web Site for Somali Immigrants

Sauman Chu, University of Minnesota, USA

Mauricio Arango, University of Minnesota, USA

Charles Earl Love Yust, University of Minnesota, USA

Abstract

This chapter addresses the design and procedural variables of creating a bilingual Web site information portal for an audience of culturally diverse immigrants. A Web site developed as a resource for a diverse Somali community (http://www.somaliresource.net) is used as a case study for this chapter. The Somali community, which includes immigrants, refugees, and asylees, faces difficulties associated with language barriers. They struggle with the adjustment of life in a completely new system in Minnesota. The aim of this resource is to address some of the Somali's informational needs in the form of a one-stop bilingual Web site. It is our goal to describe our design process, and offer recommendations on design and procedural variables for working with the Somali cultural group. We envision that graphic designers and other researchers will find it useful to reference this material when they address design issues related to different cultural groups.

Introduction

For the past 15 years, the state of Minnesota, in the United States, has received one of the largest waves of Somali immigrants in North America. Most of these immigrants are located in and around the Minneapolis/St. Paul metro area. The majority of these individuals have come to the United States as refugees fleeing political unrest in their homeland.

The 2000 U.S. Census (U.S. Census Bureau, 2000) estimated the number of Somalis in Minnesota to be approximately 15,000. However, less conservative figures reach as high as 50,000 (Burke, 2001).

According to the Minneapolis Foundation (2004), many immigrants arrived in other U.S. states before relocating permanently to Minnesota. The primary reason for this relocation is that an established Somali community, as exists in Minnesota, is better prepared to address the particular needs of Somalis, including the need for unskilled jobs that do not require English fluency or literacy.

These new immigrants experience many difficulties adjusting to their lives in a new country. They face language barriers, culture shock, religious differences, and a sense of loss and isolation. Additionally, many of them must cope with traumatic experiences that they survived in war-torn Somalia or refugee camps. There are few resources readily accessible to facilitate a smooth transition to their new environment.

The objectives of this bilingual Web site project were to create an online community resource for the Somali immigrants, especially in Minnesota, and to examine the design and procedural variables of creating a bilingual Web site for this population.

The Collapse of Somalia

Somalia, a former British and Italian colony, became an independent nation in 1960. By 1969, General Siad Barre overthrew Somalia's nascent democratic institutions; he maintained political and military power for the next 20 years. His repressive regime centralized all of the economic activities in Mogadishu, Somalia's capital, while ignoring the rest of the country. This imbalance gave rise to tensions in Somalia's regions for the control and distribution of increasingly scarce resources, and to the creation of militias accountable to faction leaders.

In 1991, Barre was overthrown, but the opposing factions failed to agree on a replacement. This plunged the country into lawlessness and clan warfare, which was exacerbated by the large arms remnants from the Cold War. In the early 1990s,

Somalia's plight was worsened by a famine that cost the lives of nearly 300,000 people (Lewis, 2002).

In 2004, after protracted talks in Kenya, the main warlords and politicians signed a deal to set up a new parliament that would appoint a new president. In October 2004, the interim parliament chose Abdullahi Yusuf as the country's new president. Mr. Yusuf pledged to do his best to promote reconciliation and rebuild the country. He called upon the international community to provide aid and peacekeepers.

Difficulties Encountered by Somali Immigrants

The Somali immigrant community in Minnesota faces many challenges as they acclimate to life in the United States. These challenges include learning about American culture and the complex legal system; transcending language barriers; finding employment at a livable wage (while attempting to transfer job skills and qualifications from their homeland to the United States); supporting family members overseas; and accessing affordable housing, education, healthcare, and technology.

Although some of these cultural, economic, and social barriers have been overcome by Somalis in Minnesota, there is still much to be accomplished in making the transition to the United States less difficult for new immigrants.

English as a Second Language

Becoming fluent in English is, arguably, the single most important step that an immigrant can take if he or she wants to be successful in the United States. The Somali Resource Web site directs visitors who are seeking information about learning English to many educational offices and organizations including the International Institute of Minnesota, the English Learning Center, public school organizations, and the Minnesota Literacy Council. The Minnesota Literacy Council is a nonprofit, statewide organization that provides direct and indirect literacy services to adults, children, volunteers, and community programs around Minnesota (The Minnesota Literacy Council, 2004).

Employment and Transferring Job Skills

The vast majority of Somali immigrants are refugees who have roots in diverse echelons of Somali society. Some possess postgraduate degrees and a history of high professional positions in Somalia. Because certification and qualifying exams were in Italian, Somali immigrants experienced difficulty transferring their job skills to similar employment positions in the United States.

Gwendolyn Freed (2003), of the Minneapolis *Star Tribune,* wrote about the difficulties that some of these highly skilled immigrants have experienced. One story was about Marian Hussein. Once a physician in Somalia, she now works as an interpreter in Minneapolis. When she is not taking care of her six children, she is keeping up on her effort of many years to get back into doctoring.

Many Somali immigrants struggle to learn a new language, find jobs to support themselves and their families back home, and acquire technological skills required in today's workplace. Obtaining the necessary credentials to continue their career in this country can be a Sisyphean task (Freed, 2003). The struggle experienced, even by highly skilled Somali immigrants looking for work, exemplifies the hardship that all Somali immigrants, skilled or unskilled, face while seeking employment in the United States.

Access to Technology

It became apparent in this study (see method section) that many Somali immigrants have only limited opportunities for accessing the Internet and publicly available technology. Such access is usually limited to libraries, Internet cafes (which primarily provide wireless access to the Web for people who own laptops), community centers, universities, and schools. Many of these resources are not located near Somali population centers, making it difficult, if not impossible, for those lacking transportation to use the available resources, especially during long winters of inclement weather.

A few Somalis obtain high-speed Internet access at home if they can afford it. Otherwise, they use dial-up modems to access the Internet over phone lines. Somalis who do not have a personal computer at home may, alternatively, obtain Internet access through their place of employment or a university, if they attend school.

Obtaining Assistance

Somali immigrants seek solutions to these challenges from a variety of sources. Many rely on a network of family and communal contacts or local Somali community centers. Some of the services available at Somali community centers include youth services, advocacy and intervention services, education and outreach services, and capacity building. Persons at these community centers will assist in document translation, application and letter writing, employment verification, housing referrals,

ESL classes, medical/legal/housing services, and other social services. These centers also sponsor numerous community forums and cultural events, and are developing an East African Business Development Collaborative that assists East Africans who are interested in starting their own businesses (Confederation for Somali Community of Minnesota, 2001). There are only a handful of Somali community centers in the Twin Cities that offer assistance to the Somali immigrant community.

In addition to information found on a Somali community center Web site, a number of online resources have been made available to the Somali immigrant community over the last decade. The most in-depth online resource for the Somali immigrant community in existence, prior to the production of the Somali Resource, was the online immigrant guide published by the Minnesota Council of Churches (MCC). Refugee Services at the MCC published this guide in English, Somali, and Spanish (Minnesota Council of Churches, 2002).

Additionally, both the state of Minnesota, and governmental and educational institutions in the Twin Cities have published online resources. The state developed a comprehensive Web site devoted specifically to refugee health in Minnesota. The state works with local health departments and private health care providers to offer each new refugee a comprehensive screening examination, including appropriate follow-up or referral (Burke, 2001).

The city of Minneapolis provides a general guide for newcomers to the city. Other Minnesota organizations-most notably the League of Women Voters, various colleges and universities, and the Minneapolis Foundation-provide reports on Somali immigration to Minnesota. Additionally, Law Help Minnesota published a notable online resource in 24 different languages, including Somali.

In researching the Somali Resource project, we soon saw that access to helpful information existed for Somali immigrants in numerous locations and mediums. However, there was no central directory from which to link and explore all of the available online information.

Case Study:
The Bilingual Somali Web Site

Minnesota is home to one of the largest Somali communities in North America. Surprisingly, there are few accessible resources that facilitate an easy transition to this new environment.

The objective of the bilingual Web site project is to address Somalis' needs by creating an online community resource. This project is a collaborative work between the University and the Somali community. The Web site provides a centralized directory to the large amount of information (about employment, health services, housing, transportation, etc.) that recent immigrants need to know in order to adapt to their new life. Currently, such information is dispersed among various organizations, and is often only available in English. The new Web site also provides a Somali business directory, cultural facts, and information about the history of Somalis in Minnesota.

The authors recently completed this Web site. The Web site's content is written in two languages, English and Somali, that are arranged in a side-by-side format. All of the Somali text was translated and edited twice by professional translators.

Objectives and Goals of the Study

The objectives of this project are (a) to address some of the Somalis' needs by creating a centralized online directory that would help new immigrants learn information in a one-stop manner, and (b) to examine the design and procedural variables of creating a bilingual Web site for the Somali population. Creating a bilingual format offered two benefits. First, by viewing the English text and Somali text side-by-side, immigrants might be able to understand the English text, as well as develop this overall comprehension of English. Second, the Somali text is necessary for more recent immigrants or people who have limited or no English skills. Therefore, a bilingual format promotes the learning of English, and ensures that the information reaches the target audience.

Research Questions

This study addressed the following questions:

1. Is a bilingual format preferable for presenting online information?
2. What are design guidelines and procedures for designing online material for a specific immigrant group?
3. Does an online bilingual resource portal help to address the informational needs of Somali immigrants?

Method

This study consisted of collecting information for the Web site, conducting a focus group discussion to ascertain preferences about content and design elements, developing the Web site, and conducting a focus group discussion/workshop to gather feedback on the Web site.

Stage I: Information Gathering

The authors obtained the majority of the information, with consent, from numerous organizations such as Lutheran Social Services, Minnesota Council of Churches, and Minnesota Extension Services. We then grouped the information into different categories. Some of the information needed to be rewritten into English. All of the information was later translated into Somali. The authors presented the English content during the first focus group discussion.

Stage II: First Focus Group Discussion

We held the first focus group discussion for 2 hours at a Somali community organization in Minneapolis. A Somali translator, with experience running focus group discussions, recruited subjects. She also served as a translator during this focus group discussion. The discussion began by talking about Internet access issues and the use of computers. We then presented the purpose of the project and the concept of a bilingual Web site.

- **Subjects:** Eight people (three males and five females) participated in the focus group discussion. Their ages ranged from 18-50 years old. Six of the participants had been living in the United States for 4 to 8 years. One participant had lived in the United States only 1 month, and another participant had been living in the United States for about 1 year. Six of the participants could speak English, except for the two newest immigrants. Two of the five female participants were high-school students, and the other three were stay-at-home housewives. The three male participants held different types of jobs, but all provided services to the African community.

- **Technology discussion:** In regard to technology usage, six participants indicated that they used computers or accessed the Internet through work, home, or school. The three participants who had full-time jobs tended to use computers at work because they used e-mail quite often. The two participants who were students used computers at school since they did not have computers at home. Out of all eight subjects, four of them had computers at home. Additionally, three participants used their friends' computers. Participants suggested that approximately 50% of Somali households have computer access.

  Most participants indicated that public access to computers is very limited. For instance, public libraries can limit computer usage to 1 hour. Additionally, the nearest library branch may be inconveniently located for immigrants without a car. Public transportation is particularly difficult for families with young children who must wait and ride on a bus for 15-30 minutes. Some community centers have computers that can be used by people enrolled in ESL courses. However, these computers are not available to the general public.

Participants with access to computers said they tended to use the Internet quite frequently. In particular, they used the Internet to search for jobs and to find information related to their community.

During the focus group discussion, the last question asked was what method do Somalis prefer to use when they search for information. New immigrants stated that their preference would be to talk with friends or look in a newspaper. However, if they had convenient computer access, their first choice would be the Internet.

- **Organization of the Web site:** All of the participants were in consensus about the bilingual presentation of the Web site. They felt that having English and Somali presented side by side (rather than in two different Web sites) was an effective solution. For someone who does not know English, he/she can read the Somali text while learning English at the same time.

  Participants agreed that topics of health, education, employment, public service, and cultural and historical information are essential. Participants also agreed that it is critical to centralize these topics in one site. Participants indicated that including ESL information is very important since language barriers are a major problem for new immigrants. They felt that language is the primary obstacle for obtaining a job. In fact, some of the participants indicated that they do not know how to look for a job.

  Two younger participants also suggested that there should be separate Web sites for different age groups. For instance, there could be an educational Web site aimed at helping teenagers to succeed in school. Such a Web site could also provide information about social services available to teens.

- **Color and type:** In regard to font preference, participants emphasized that the font must be bold, very clear and easy to read, and must have good contrast with the background. For the preference of color, there seems to be less color symbolism in the Somali culture than in other cultures. Participants emphasized that high contrast is essential. One participant indicated that several Somali Web sites use yellow for the graphic elements, and they are very ineffective due to the lack of contrast.

- **Translation:** All participants agreed that accurate translation is very important. They agreed that some Web sites contain inaccurate translations. They recommended that two to three translators proofread the material before it is published. It is also important to note that there are different dialects in Somali culture, and the difficulty of reaching a consensus on any one translation necessitates the services of multiple Somali editors.

Figure 1. Web site's information structure

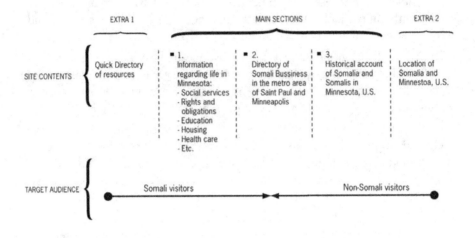

Stage III: Web Site Development

- **Information structure:** The project goal was to create a one-stop Web site containing information related to the Somali experience in Minnesota. Visitors to the Web site could be either Somali immigrants in need of basic information or non-Somalis who are interested in learning more about their community.

  With that premise in mind, the authors divided the Web site's information into three main categories (see Figure 1).

  1. Information for Somali immigrants about life in Minnesota. Based on the focus group discussions, this information was grouped into eleven categories: (1.1) Immigration, (1.2) Legal Rights and Responsibilities, (1.3) Identification Documents, (1.4) Public Benefits, (1.5) Employment Resources, (1.6) Learning English, (1.7) Housing Information, (1.8) Transportation, (1.9) Personal Finance, (1.10) Healthcare, and (1.11) Education.

  2. Information for the general public about the history of Somalia and Somalis living in Minnesota.

3. Information about Somali businesses in the St. Paul/Minneapolis metro-
    politan area.

In addition, an extra section, a directory of resources, was devised with the
aim to conveniently find names and contact information of many agencies and
offices that are of interest to Somali immigrants (see Figure 1, Extra 1). This
way, when a Somali visitor is looking for contact information for a specific
agency or institution, he or she could quickly find it without having to delve
onto the more extensive resources sections.

Finally, to highlight the origins of Somali immigrants in Minnesota, the authors
added a hyperlink to maps that display the location of Somalia and Minnesota
in the world (see Figure 1, Extra 2). Figure 1 illustrates the type of information
available in the Web site and the Web site's target audience.

•   **Design considerations:** The most important constraints for the design of the
    Web site were access to technology and information.

1. **Technology limitations:** According to information gathered in the first
    focus group and conversations with social workers and advocates of
    the Somali community, many members of this community have lim-
    ited access to computers and the Internet. Many Somalis do not own a
    computer; they must go to community centers or libraries to access the
    Internet.

    Computers in community centers are functional, but often do not have
    up-to-date software or hardware. The situation in libraries is similar;
    their Internet browsers do not allow the running of certain cgi-scripts or
    Internet applications that require third-party plug-ins. Also, the connection
    speed is an important concern for users who have Internet access only at
    community centers.

    These technology limitations defined the profile for the Web site. Due
    to uncertainties about Internet access and technologies that might not be
    up-to-date, we decided that the Web site should be based on the most
    elemental components of Internet technology: HTML and cascading style
    sheets (CSS).

    The authors opted against using more advanced technologies (video, ani-
    mations, audio clips, etc.) that may have been useful for communicating
    with the audience, due to the low probability of the audience being able
    to view them.

    Many community centers do not yet have access to broadband Internet.
    Hence, the graphics content of the Web site was reduced to streamline
    download times. A 56-kb dial-up modem could download the initial page
    in about 7 seconds. Once the initial graphics, menu items (rollover im-

ages), and navigational elements are downloaded to a user's computer, the time it takes to load additional pages becomes negligible, as the site is mainly text based.

2. **Access to information:** Since many individuals in the target audience are still in the process of learning English, it was necessary to present the Web site contents in both English and Somali. This ensured full accessibility to the information.

The initial design response (before first focus group discussion) was to create two separate versions of the same Web site: one for English speaking viewers, and one for Somali speaking viewers. However, since the spirit of the project was to create a feeling of inclusion, this design direction was aborted. Instead, the design team decided to create a Web site in which the English and Somali languages coexisted.

This decision (for a bilingual format) meant that every button and link, and all of the text, had to be presented simultaneously in two languages. Given the large amount of information presented in the Web site and the use of two languages, the design team opted to greatly reduce the number of graphics, and take advantage of the vertical axis of the page. As a result, the languages were presented in a two-column design: one column for English and one column for Somali.

- **Site layout:** The layout for the content of the Web site reflects the hierarchies of information. The Web site content is separated into three tiers.

The first tier is dedicated to information that requires immediate access. A resource directory and a "site credits and contact" link were allocated to this tier.

The second tier contains navigation buttons for the Web site's three main sections: information for immigrants, directory of Somali businesses, and history of Somalia and Somalis in Minnesota. The content for these links opens in the third tier.

The third tier is divided into two main areas: a navigation section to access subsections and a bilingual section (see Figure 2).

- **Colors:** The colors of the Web site were selected to ensure readability, maintain sufficient contrast between the two languages in the navigation bars, establish and separate different hierarchies, and create a sense of cultural connection to the Somali community.

Somalia's flag comprises two colors: white and light blue. Because of their cultural significance, these colors were chosen for the Web site. However, the light blue color did not provide enough contrast with white, so a much darker shade of it was used predominantly throughout the Web site; the light blue

Figure 2. Information visual hierarchies

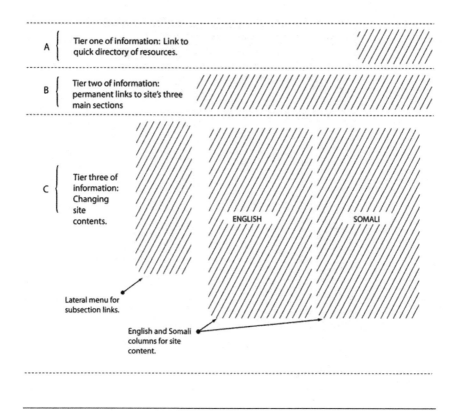

was used to accentuate the navigation buttons (e.g., to show event changes such as roll over).

The background of areas that contained large amounts of text was left white; the text was made dark gray.

- **Final design:** Figure 3 shows the first page of the Web site. Its layout conforms to the hierarchical organization depicted in Figure 2. The final design includes graphic elements, such as headings and a map showing the location of Somalia and Minnesota. The map serves as a hyperlink to a larger, more detailed

Figure 3. Site's front-page template

version of the map. Despite the addition of these graphics, the hierarchical organization of links and sections is still easy to identify.

One of the limiting factors in the final design was the large amount of information that needed to be accommodated in some of its subsections. The Web design team opted to follow the common practice in other Web sites that deal with large quantities of text-based contents (i.e., newspapers and blogs), of presenting that information along the vertical axis of the page. This vertical orientation also helped the purpose of presenting English and Somali translations side by side.

Figure 4. Site's navigation scheme for subsections

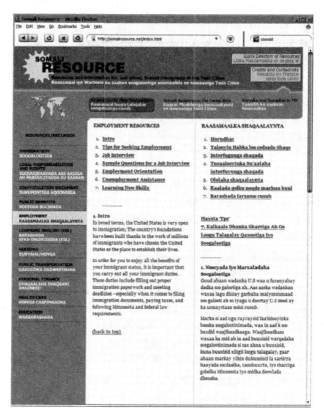

Visual distinctions between the different hierarchies of information were achieved by spatially separating sections and using other visual hints like different color backgrounds for each tier of information (see Figure 4).

Finally, another deciding factor for the Web site's layout was the decision to minimize, as much as possible, the area taken by fixed elements in the design (Web site heading, links to the directory of resources and credits, and navigation bar linking to the sites three main sections) while maintaining a clean and uncluttered layout.

Stage IV: Second Focus Group Discussion/Workshop

The second focus group met for 2 hours at the University's computer lab. The location was selected so that participants would not have to use transportation; the lab was within walking distance to most participants' homes.

Ten participants participated in this focus group. There were six men and four women ranging in age from 20-50 years old. For all of the participants, English was their second language. Most of the participants had limited English proficiency, and only two could speak English fluently. A translator facilitated communication between the researchers and the participants.

- **Process:** Participants were asked to review the prototype Somali Web site (http://www.somaliresource.net) for 30 minutes. They were allowed to ask questions for clarification while reviewing the site. All participants were given a piece of paper to write down their thoughts and comments about the Web site. At the end of 30 minutes, the researchers asked participants for a list of questions regarding the Somali Web site, in particular, as well as Internet use in general. The translator verbally translated each question to ensure that all participants had fully understood the communication. Two researchers served as notetakers.

  In response to the question about the frequency of Internet use, six participants indicated that they used the Internet every day at work or at home. Three participants accessed the Internet about once a week, and one participant never used the Internet. In response to the question about obtaining information on health or educational materials, two men and two women indicated that they found such information on the Internet or in printed brochures. Others had never tried to find this information or did not know where to look for it.

- **Responses to the bilingual format:** All participants liked the bilingual format. They thought it was very easy to read and easy to access both languages. They liked the layout of parallel columns that contained English and Somali text.

- **Other feedback:** Participants indicated that the navigation was easy to follow and there was no confusion about which button to click. They did not have any problems looking for specific content. However, a particular "quick link button" was identified that none of the participants knew existed. A redesign of this button (by increasing its contrast with the background) was necessary in order to make it more visible. All participants were very positive about the structure of the site. They thought the content was very clear and logical. There was no area of the Web site that participants felt had to be reorganized.

  In response to the questions about colors and fonts, participants indicated that the colors were very appropriate and the typeface was clear. Participants felt that they would like to see more images/pictures on the Web site.

- **Translation:** The accuracy of the translation was a major issue. Participants pointed out that the translation still needs work. Many felt that the inaccuracy of the Somali text made the content difficult to understand. It is absolutely essential to get a good and concise translation. We assured participants that a second editor was still working on proofreading the translation.

- **Summary of the second focus group discussion:** The overall perception of the Web site was extremely positive: one participant said, "I'm speechless, the site is just great! I have never seen anything like this before." Participants felt that the site was very informative and extensive.

Several participants asked about the marketing strategy for the Web site. We then distributed a few copies of the full-color postcard we designed to announce the Web site. We explained that our goal was to distribute 4,000 copies of the postcard to Somali community organizations, restaurants, and shops.

Participants offered several suggestions for improving the content of the Web site. First, several of them indicated that they would like to see more images in several of the content areas. For instance, on the page about education, an image of a student in a graduation gown would be helpful. This addition would enhance a viewer's understanding of the content, as would a photo gallery featuring various Somali festivals or events. Second, one subject suggested that the color of the Somali and English text differ from each other to further distinguish the two languages. Third, two participants suggested placing more links to other international Web sites targeted at the Somali population.

Accuracy of translation seems to be a major problem. Most participants indicated that more editing needed to be done. It is important to note that translation from English to Somali is very time-consuming: it takes 3 to 4 hours to translate a single page of words of English into Somali.

Web Site Marketing

The Somali Resource was officially launched with the initial distribution of 4,000 printed postcards to the Somali community in the Twin Cities (see Figure 5). The

Figure 5. The two-sided postcard to announce the Web site

two-sided 5X7-inch postcards reflect the identity and content of the Web site, as well as provide the address of the Somali Resource Web site. Awareness of the Somali Resource will spread, as the postcards were distributed to various locations, including Somali businesses, residence buildings, and community centers.

The Somali community centers currently hand out many printed materials, and several Somali businesses have Somali newspapers and informational pamphlets in their entryways. Putting Somali Resource postcards at these locations will further facilitate the distribution of information within the Somali community. The Somali Resource was also featured in the University of Minnesota's Office of the Vice President of Research's annual publication titled "Research and Inventions 2004."

Discussion

Effectiveness of Bilingual Web Sites

If one examines current Web sites in the United States that are targeted at Somali immigrants, one commonly finds that most are written in only one language; bilingual formats rarely exist.

Chu, Martinson, McNaughton, and Lawton (2000) suggested that a bilingual/multilingual publication for visual projects targeted at immigrants is a preferable format. Their study, focusing on two-dimensional printed publications, provided the foundation and guidance for the design process of the Somali Resource Web site project. We extended that study to the bilingual presentation of online information.

Based on the Somali Resource Web site project, we have concluded that new immigrants prefer a bilingual format when they search for information online. Focus group subjects suggested that a bilingual presentation assists in the learning of English equivalencies, and helps the site reach a wider audience (i.e., those with better, limited, or no English proficiency).

Translation

Translation is the dominant factor that determines the successfulness of bilingual publications. If the text is poorly translated, it can cause misunderstandings and miscommunications. According to some subjects, a poor translation, in addition to being unclear, shows disrespect toward the particular culture, and implies that the information is not important.

It is highly recommended that at least two translators proofread the translated text. Additionally, based upon our discussion with the subjects, it is important that translators have a good understanding of the particular culture and its people. Furthermore, translators need to be aware that different written forms of a dialect may exist. In such cases, translators must determine the most appropriate or popular form.

Suggestions for Designing Online Material for Immigrant Groups

Layout

In their study, Chu et al. (2000) found that participants prefer to read English on one side, and Hmong or Somali on the other side of a bilingual printed brochure. This format is feasible for printed materials. To transfer the similar criteria for presenting online information, we proposed the side-by-side format for two different languages. The Somali participants indicated that positioning the two languages side-by-side seemed logical and reasonable; we decided that such a layout might be easier to reference, particularly for lengthy content. In fact, if someone can read English, that person could read the entire text in English, and someone who prefers reading Somali could read only the Somali text without interruption.

Type

Based on our first focus group discussion, participants preferred a simple and clean typeface. The most important criterion for choosing a font was that it is easy to read.

Color

Color carries significant meaning in different cultures. Various cultures may have different interpretations for the same color. For instance, in Western culture, white is used for wedding ceremonies. However, in Chinese culture, white is used for funerals and mourning.

When discussing color preferences, participants indicated that most colors are appropriate for Somali culture. In fact, color does not carry much of either a positive or negative connotation in Somali culture. We decided to use blue as the predominant color for graphics since the Somali National flag is also blue and harbors a connection to Somalia; we also set the majority of text against a white background to ensure high contrast.

Images

It seems that the majority of participants wanted more images on the Web site. They also preferred images that represent the Somali culture. In particular, they wanted costumes of the Somali people to be represented appropriately. There did not seem to be any gender preferences for the images that were used; images should be used in accordance with the content.

Navigation

Most participants indicated that they understood the navigation of the Web site and that the structure was clear. A couple of participants in the second focus group, who had limited knowledge and use of the Internet, indicated that it was difficult for them to navigate the Web site. This difficulty was because they did not realize what parts of the content were hyperlinks, and they did not understand how the Internet works.

Procedures for Designing Online Material for Immigrant Groups

Although multicultural and international education have been incorporated into some major disciplines at colleges and universities, most design students have not been trained or provided the opportunity to work with audiences from different cultural groups. We hope that this study will provide guidance for research and the creative process.

Based upon the findings of this study, we suggest the following procedural steps for producing bilingual online material: (1) collect and develop the necessary content and images relevant to the targeted cultural group; (2) conduct focus group discussions with members of the targeted cultural group to review the content and images; (3) select a qualified translator to translate all of the text, and have at least one additional translator to review and proofread the text; (4) develop and design the Web site based on the focus group discussions; (5) conduct a final focus group discussion to review the Web site design, content, translation, and usability; (6) revise and prepare the final Web site based on feedback from the final focus group discussion; and (7) launch the Web site.

Based on the focus group discussions, it is important to note that computers are not widely used among Somali immigrants. This use contrasts sharply with the majority of the U.S. population. Only about 50% of Somali households have a computer. Many Somalis rely on using computers in public places such as libraries and community organizations. Many gain access to computers due to the nature of their jobs. This type of access implies that men have more access to computers then women do because Somali men are more likely to work outside of the home and provide the major source of financial support for their families. Additionally, Somali women indicated that it is difficult to use public transportation with their children. In turn, this makes it difficult for Somali women to get to the library where they could access a computer. This difficulty is especially true during the cold and snowy winter: most families have just one car or none at all.

Conclusion

The goal of this project was to create a centralized online directory for Somali immigrants. The Web site connects Somali immigrants to essential information that may help them adapt to their new life in the United States.

We examined the design and procedural variables of creating a bilingual Web site for the Somali immigrant population. Focus groups were conducted to gain an understanding of Somali culture and design preferences. Both of the discussion sessions were mixed gender (men and women). It was noted that men tended to express their opinions more frequently than women did. The team of researchers and the translator were consistent throughout both sessions to ensure validity and reliability. Additionally, at the end of the concluding discussion, validity was achieved by asking participants to verify researchers' perceptions of the information. A debriefing session was conducted after each discussion with the translator, and the two notetakers compared notes. These debriefings helped to ensure that the researchers clearly understood the discussions.

This study encountered some limitations. First, the participants' differing backgrounds and experience with using the Internet were variables that were difficult to control. Such differences among the participants can influence their expectations about what they want to see on the Web site. For example, experienced users might have higher expectations than inexperienced users regarding design and the amount of information included in the Web site. Second, the accuracy of the text translation is always a major issue for any research team that works with different cultural groups. Third, we learned that expectations about deadlines may vary greatly among different cultural groups. This particular project was delayed 4 to 6 months due to delays with the translation process.

An additional component to the initial proposal of this project was the issue pertaining to the site's longevity and updating. The Confederation for Somali Community of Minnesota is a Somali community organization located near a large Somali immigrant neighborhood in Minneapolis. They were consulted during the course of the project development about what services they provide to the Somali community and what other services and information venues existed at the outset of the project for Somali immigrants; they assisted the project by facilitating a location to house the first focus group discussion. They also agreed to assume responsibility for updating the site with new information, and for the continued editing of the Somali language translations, provided the project developers fund the project for the first 2 years. Securing a stable environment in which the project could be updated was important due to the increase in Somali-owned businesses, and adjustments to services provided to the Somali Community and immigrant population in general.

We envision that graphic designers and other researchers will find it useful to reference this material when they address design issues related to different cultural groups.

References

Burke, H. (2001). *Immunization and the Twin Cities Somali Community: Findings from a focus group assessment.* Minneapolis: Refugee Health Program, Minnesota Department of Health.

Chu, S., Martinson, B., McNaughton M., & Lawton, D. (2000). Designing multilingual communications. *Journal of Applied Communications, 84*(2), 7-28.

Confederation for Somali Community of Minnesota. (2001). *Our services.* Retrieved June 27, 2005, from http://www.cscmn.org/xoops/modules/wfchannel/index.php?pagenum=4

Freed, G. (2003). Minnesota's East Africans have difficulty transferring job skills from there to here. *Minneapolis Star Tribune.* Retrieved July 1, 2003, from http://www.startribune.com/stories/462/3962933.html

Lewis, I. M. (2002). *A modern history of the Somali.* Oxford: James Currey Ltd.

Minnesota Council of Churches (2002). *Immigrant guide.* Refugee Services. Retrieved June 27, 2005, from http://www.mnchurches.org/refugees/

The Minnesota Literacy Council. (2004). Retrieved December 12, 2004, from http://www.themlc.org/

U.S. Census Bureau. (2000). Ancestry: 2000. *Data set: Census 2000 summary file 3 (SF 3) - Sample data.* Retrieved June 18, 2000, from U.S. Census Bureau database.

U.S. Committee for Refugees. (2004). *World refugee survey 2004 country report.* Retrieved June 20, 2005, from http://www.refugees.org/countryreports.aspx?id=165

Section V

Accommodating Disabilities

Chapter X

Web Site Design for People with Dementia

Nada Savitch, Innovations in Dementia, City University, London, UK

Panayiotis Zaphiris, Centre for HCI Design, City University, UK

Abstract

This chapter describes the current thinking around designing Web sites for people with dementia. It is important that people with dementia are involved in the development of Web sites that are designed for them to use. The chapter offers advice for both researchers and practitioners who may not have thought about this user group. Symptoms of dementia are described, and the design needs of people with the condition are discussed. A list of design considerations for Web site designers covering simplified displays, avoiding distractions, consistent and familiar page design, contextual support, the use of colour, graphics, icons and sound, language and content, and navigation and menus is presented. Appropriate methodologies for working with people with dementia are also described.

Introduction

People with dementia have not traditionally been seen as a user group for Web site development. However, due to the availability of drug treatments that slow the progression of the disease, and patterns of increasing early diagnosis, the numbers of people in the early stages of dementia are increasing. Involvement of people with dementia in their own treatment and care, and in voluntary organisations such as the UK Alzheimer's Society is also increasing (Litherland, 2004), as is the amount of information about the condition and the social, legal, and health issues associated with it available specifically for people with dementia. Web sites of organisations for people with dementia now have sections specifically targeted at this user group. However, there is little evidence that the design of these Web sites takes into account any special needs people with dementia may have when using the Web (Savitch & Zaphiris, 2005).

One of the most significant developments in the field of dementia care has been the focus on personhood (Kitwood, 1997). The Alzheimer's Society also promotes the idea of hearing the voice of people with dementia, and developing communities of people with dementia, including online communities (Litherland, 2004; Savitch, Zaphiris, Smith, Litherland, Aggarwal, & Potier, 2006).

Computer interfaces can and should be designed in a way that maximises their accessibility, and enables people with early-stage dementia to benefit from this enabling technology, should they wish to do so.

Dementia is a complex progressive condition that affects not only memory, but also language and perception. This chapter describes the symptoms and experience of dementia, and how designers might help people with dementia to overcome some of these difficulties.

In the past, people with dementia have been excluded from research. Appropriate methods for involving this user group in designing accessible Web sites are also discussed.

Dementia

Dementia has been defined as a syndrome characterised by the development of multiple cognitive deficits including progressive deterioration of specific functions such as language (aphasia) or perception (agnosia), and/or a disturbance of executive functioning (Cummings & Khachaturian, 1999). The cognitive domain that is impaired first and foremost in Alzheimer's disease is memory (Kertesz & Mohs, 1999).

There are an estimated 18 million people worldwide with dementia. Dementia primarily affects older people. The chance of having the condition rises with age to 1 person in 20 over the age of 65, and 1 person in 5 over the age of 80 (ADI, 2004). Although age is the most important risk factor for Alzheimer's disease, no age-related change has been established as being mechanistically important in the causation of Alzheimer's disease (Poirier, Danik, & Blass, 1999).

There are many causes of dementia including Alzheimer's disease, vascular dementia, and dementia with Lewy bodies. Alzheimer's disease is the most common cause of dementia (Alzheimer's Society, 2006). Probable Alzheimer's disease is characterised by deficits in two or more areas of cognition, and progressive worsening of memory and other cognitive functions (Cummings & Khachaturian, 1999). Vascular causes of dementia have slightly different diagnostic criteria including uneven impairment of cognitive function, focal neurological signs, preservation of insight and judgement, abrupt onset, and stepwise deterioration (Cummings & Khachaturian, 1999). Dementia with Lewy bodies is a form of dementia that shares characteristics with both Alzheimer's and Parkinson's diseases. It may account for 10% to 15% of all cases of dementia in older people (Alzheimer's Society, 2006).

Early Stages of Dementia

At present, Alzheimer's disease is widely accepted to be a disease, and not a normal part of ageing (Clare, 2002). However, there is a continuing debate about whether the pathological changes in Alzheimer's disease are qualitatively different from those seen in normal ageing (Huppert, 1994). The distinction between severe dementia and normal ageing is obvious, but establishing the difference between early, mild Alzheimer's disease and age-related cognitive loss can be more difficult (Jones & Ferris, 1999). In the early stages, there may be very minor changes in a person's abilities or behaviour that are often mistakenly attributed to stress, bereavement, depression, or the normal ageing process (Alzheimer's Society, 2006).

Memory (particularly episodic memory) is usually the first cognitive function to be affected by Alzheimer's disease, but attention, executive function, and wording finding may also be compromised (Clare, 2002).

Memory Problems in Dementia

Memory is usually the first cognitive function to be affected by the onset of Alzheimer's disease, although impairments are initially evident only in certain memory systems, especially episodic memory (Clare, 2002). This characteristic loss of memory distinguishes Alzheimer's disease from other cortical degenerative diseases such as Pick's disease where memory is not affected in the early stages (Kertesz & Mohs, 1999).

Working memory may be lost in dementia. However, the patchy progression of dementia means that even people in the later stages may retain early learning and access to long laid down memories (McIntosh, 1999). Delayed recall is often severely impaired even in early Alzheimer's disease (Clare, 2002; Kertesz & Mohs, 1999). Perhaps the most substantial deficits in people with Alzheimer's disease are found on short-term memory tasks that require divided attention (Morris, 1994). Alzheimer's disease is also associated with deficits in various aspects of semantic memory functioning, for example, categorical organisation (Backman, 1998). However, procedural memories are relatively spared in Alzheimer's disease (Zanetti, 2001).

Episodic memory, or memory for events recent or remote, is impaired in Alzheimer's disease the earliest. The progressive failure of memory forms a gradient from the most severely affected recent to the relatively preserved distant memories, the opposite of the gradient seen in normal controls (Kertesz & Mohs, 1999). In the early stages of dementia, unlike episodic memory, semantic memory is quite preserved. Implicit or procedural memory is generally spared until late in the disease when people with Alzheimer's lose their ability to use utensils and other overlearned mainly motor functions (Kertesz & Mohs, 1999).

Dementia and Language

Subtle language impairment is usually detectable early in the course of Alzheimer's disease (Kertesz & Mohs, 1999). Language impairments include word finding difficulties and circumlocutions with normally fluent, articulated and syntactically preserved speech (Kertesz & Mohs, 1999).

Virtually all people with Alzheimer's disease show language changes, with problems with naming being especially prominent (Henderson, 1996). People with Alzheimer's disease have been shown to be impaired in their appreciation of the relationship between a word and its attributes (Grossman, Mickanin, Robinson, & d'Esposito, 1996).

Perception and Dementia

Visuospatial perception is usually only affected in the later stages, although in atypical cases, it may be observed as one of the earliest symptoms (Clare, 2002). Perceptual impairments often present as spatial disorientation (Tetewskey & Duffy, 1999). Visual symptoms have been found to precede other features of dementia (Fletcher, 1994).

The problems seen in Alzheimer's disease are higher order visual disturbances involving attention, memory, spatial localisation, and complex pattern recognition (Jackson & Owsley, 2003). While Alzheimer's disease affects higher visual functions, basic visual sensory functions are spared. People with mild Alzheimer's disease show significant impairments of visuospatial construction, higher visual perception, and processing of complex motion (Rizzo, Anderson, Dawson, & Nawrot, 2001).

Topographical disorientation, that is, difficulty in orienting to, navigating through, and feeling familiar with one's surroundings, has also been identified as a problem for people with Alzheimer's disease (Pai & Jacobs, 2004). Three-dimensional deficits are present in Alzheimer's disease that may contribute to a person's difficulty in navigating and becoming disorientated. People with Alzheimer's disease tend to omit, or inaccurately portray, local details in drawings, as opposed to distorting the picture's global configuration. These deficits may contribute to a person's difficulty in navigating in the spatial environment and becoming lost (McGee, van der Zaag, Buckwalter, Theibaus, Van Rooyen, Neumann et al., 2000).

The Experience of Dementia

The symptoms of dementia are not uniform. The types and severity of cognition impairment varies from person to person, especially in the early stages (Kertesz & Mohs, 1999). The course and progression of Alzheimer's disease is also heterogeneous (Clare, 2002).

People with Alzheimer's disease may experience different symptoms at different times. Some people may have a relatively greater impairment in one area of cognitive function than in other areas, especially in the early stages (Kertesz & Mohs, 1999).

One of the most significant developments in the field of dementia care has been the focus on personhood (Kitwood, 1997). It has been suggested that the manifestation and progression of Alzheimer's disease in any one individual is influenced by the interplay of neurological impairment, physical health, sensory acuity, personality, biographical experience, and social psychology, in terms of environment, communication, and interaction (Clare, 2002).

Dementia often leads to deterioration in functional abilities of daily life that has a major impact on quality of life. The condition also has an emotional impact. For example, feelings of incompetence and loss of control are often expressed by people with dementia (Gelinas & Auer, 1999).

Design Needs of People with Dementia

Most of the research that considers design issues for people with dementia has concentrated on designing institutional care facilities such as nursing or residential care. There has been some work on outside environments and more informal settings.

Although there are many different causes of dementia, most research into design has presumed that the differences in symptoms are not as important as the similarities (Burton & Mitchell, 2003).

Design of physical environments has been thought to have therapeutic properties in that good design can promote well-being and functionality among people with dementia (Day, Carreon, & Stump, 2000). It has been suggested that good internal design principles have a positive effect on functional and cognitive abilities of residents in care homes (Mitchell, Burton, Raman, Blackman, Jenks, & Williams, 2003).

Orientation is one of the main design considerations for people with dementia (Day et al., 2000). Orientation is particularly important, as people who have become lost often feel anxious and distressed (McGilton, Rivera, & Dawson, 2003). For people with dementia, spatial disorientation and loss of way-finding ability are major reasons why the environment constrains their autonomy. Perceptual skills are often impaired so that there may be difficulty telling right from left or differentiating between shapes and sizes, while loss of higher cognitive skills impairs decision making, spatial memory, spatial planning, and mental mapping. They may find difficulty using unfamiliar environmental cues. Overall, dementia is associated with progressively decreasing abilities to plan a route, to remember or try different options, to recall previous mistakes, and to remember to use mental maps, spatial information, and signs (Blackman, Mitchell, Burton, Jenks, Parsons, Raman, & Williams, 2003).

Burton and Mitchell (2003) have identified six requirements of dementia-friendly design. Designers should create places that are familiar, legible, distinctive, physically accessible, comfortable, and safe. The first three of these concepts have direct relevance to designing computer interfaces.

Familiarity

People with dementia have a reduced ability to understand their surroundings or to follow or plan a route. They are more likely to get lost. Dementia friendly environments should therefore contain environmental cues that are familiar and easily understood (Burton & Mitchell, 2003). Simple, small, familiar surroundings play an important role in preventing and alleviating spatial disorientation, confusion, and impaired memory problems (Mitchell et al., 2003). People with dementia tend to feel more comfortable in informal places. They recognise and remember streets, places, buildings, and features that they have seen regularly for a long time (Mitchell, Burton, & Raman, 2004).

Interventions, which have provided people with moderate to severe dementia with the opportunity to learn a route focussing on landmarks as environmental cues, have been demonstrated to help people to find an intended destination in the short-term. It was found to be important to let people with dementia find their own landmarks (McGilton et al., 2003).

Legibility

People with dementia may have problems following directions. Way-finding and orientation can be encouraged by design features that are easily understood and memorable (Burton & Mitchell, 2003).

A person with dementia who has forgotten the route to a specific place may be able to relearn this information, but will probably need to use reminders such as written notes. However, remembering to use such prompts is a further challenge (Mitchell et al., 2003).

People with dementia are most likely to become disorientated at decision points, such as junctions and corners; it is therefore recommended that designers enable people with dementia to go from one decision point to the next without having to plan for future decisions (Mitchell et al., 2003).

Landmarks and features are easier to remember if their function is obvious and they are seen regularly (Mitchell et al., 2004). Grid patterns, which have been thought to be the simplest urban layout to understand, have been found to be confusing for people with dementia because the streets, turnings, and junctions are identical or similar to one another (Mitchell et al., 2003). Being able to see the end of a short street, or having the view ahead constantly open up helps people with dementia to find their way (Mitchell et al., 2004).

Busy patterns, such as chessboard squares or repetitive lines, can cause confusion, and sharp colour or pattern contrasts can be misinterpreted (Blackman et al., 2003). And it is recommended that the number of signs is kept to a minimum, as an abundance of signs may increase rather than alleviate confusion and disorientation (Mitchell et al., 2003).

Distinctiveness

The presence of distinctive features has also been found to be important in navigation (Burton & Mitchell, 2003). There should be appropriate levels of sensory stimulation, striking a balance between overstimulation and deprivation (Day et al., 2000).

Cues that require the ability to read and comprehend are effective only in the early stages of the disease. Single-word signs rather than compound words have been found to be effective (Brawley, 1997).

In the physical environment, short corridors with uninterrupted visual access and frequent environmental cues have been found to be more navigable than long, uniform corridors with repetitive elements, fixtures, and fittings (Blackman et al., 2003). Distinctive cues at decision points act as a form of reference, leading the person on to the next destination (Mitchell et al., 2003). Visual cues or landmarks need to be recognisable, identifiable, and meaningful, and architectural features need to give information about their role or features (Mitchell et al., 2003). Streets and buildings with few distinguishing features have been found to be more difficult to recognise (Mitchell et al., 2004). These finding may have relevance for the design of hierarchical navigation systems and orientation cues in Web sites. Web designers need to create "features" that people with dementia will understand and recognise.

It has been suggested that colour can provide a latent cue for orientation and wayfinding. However, although colour may attract the attention of people with dementia, they may not be able to determine the significance (Brawley, 1997). Using colour can also be problematic as older people may not be able to differentiate between colours, and people with dementia are often unable to understand colour-coding systems (Mitchell et al., 2003). Therefore, it cannot be assumed that the use of colour for orientation or navigation purposes in Web site design will be beneficial for people with dementia.

Computers and People with Dementia

People with dementia are increasingly being exposed to computer technology for diagnosis and to aid daily living. Computers have been used in diagnostic and other assessment tests of people with dementia. The computer permits consistent presentation of the task, easy and accurate recording of the results, and rapid data analysis. Personal computers are used because they are easily portable and require no special environment (Sano, 1988). Various sensor and detector systems have been developed, or are being developed, for use in the care of people with dementia. For example, sensors which can be put under a mattress to alert care staff when someone moves to get out of bed, or more sophisticated sensor systems that alert staff only if a particular person does something outside their normal routine (Marshall, 1999).

There has also been some research into memory aids (Goodman, Brewster, & Gray, 2002; Grandmaison & Simard, 2003), but the application of these technologies for people with dementia is not clear.

The nonjudgemental nature, user friendliness, repetitive capabilities, and adaptability of computers have been described as making them suitable for helping residents in nursing homes with moderate memory loss. However, most studies tend to exclude people with dementia (Sherer, 1996, 1997). Alm et al. (Alm, Astell, Ellis, Dye, Gowans, & Campbell, 2004) have described a multimedia reminiscence "scrapbook" including text, photographs, videos, and songs, arranged by subject, with a simple screen display. This multimedia presentation has produced a great deal of interest and motivation from people with dementia themselves, and has been successfully used as an effective support for satisfying conversation for people with dementia, with the emphasis on failure-free reminiscence activities. Some researchers have observed that people with dementia like using computers, and seem to profit from a sense of achievement that was "quite different from the feeling of getting worse in every other aspect of life" (Hofmann, Hock, Kuehler, & Mueller-Spahn, 1996). It has been acknowledged that older people benefit from computer use for communication and social interaction, access to information, entertainment and learning, healthcare, and to assist them to remain independent and in control (Ryan & Heaven, 1986). However, this principle does not appear to have been widely extended to people with dementia.

People with Dementia and the Web

Some people with dementia, however, are actively using computers and the Internet (Alzheimer's Forum, 2006; DASNI, 2006).

For example, the Alzheimer's Forum is a Web site that is run by people with dementia for people with dementia. It was established and is run by a small group of people with dementia at the West Kent branch of the Alzheimer's Society (Alzheimer's Forum, 2006).

The aim of Alzheimer's Forum is to "communicate with people with dementia across the world." The site features "contributions from friends" and a "predicament of the month." Both features encourage contributions from people with dementia across the country.

There are also a number of Web sites offering information about the condition and ways of coping. However, although the content of these Web sites is written specifically for people with dementia, there is no evidence that they have been designed specifically for this user group. A preliminary study has investigated the design issues for Web-based information for people with dementia looked at the Web sites of four English-language Alzheimer's associations around the world. The study found that there are design issues for people with dementia, and that the general design guidelines for older people may not be usefully applied for this user group. More work is needed to ascertain the needs of people with dementia (Savitch & Zaphiris, 2005).

Web Site Design for
People with Dementia

As dementia rarely affects anyone under the age of 40, and is associated with older age (especially over 65), guidelines for designing Web sites for older people should be followed when designing for people with dementia. However, as outlined previously, there are particular issues around memory, perception, and language that need to be further considered.

It is important to remember that people with dementia are not a homogenous group, and not everyone with dementia will have the same impairments to the same level.

Design of personalised or adaptive interfaces for disabled users assumes that we know their usability requirements. Little is known about how cognitively disabled users learn and operate computers, and there has been very little usability research with adults with cognitive impairments (Sutcliffe, Fickas, Sohlberg, & Ehlhardt, 2003).

There has been even less research into Web site design for people with dementia. The following suggestions are made on the basis of the research so far, and of research into general design for people with dementia. It is important to remember that assumptions that user interface designers make for able-bodied users rarely hold for cognitively disabled users (Sutcliffe et al., 2003).

From their work with people with cognitive disorders (but not dementia), Sutcliffe et al. (2003) have identified five cognitive variables that impact on design: limited attention span, working memory disorders, learning/problem solving disorders, impaired long-term memory, and impaired linguistic abilities/aphasias. They recommend design guidance for each impairment separately, and suggest mapping the design guidance to a user group profile. However, people with dementia will often display all the variables described by Sutcliffe et al. (2000), and elements of their design guidance for one variable is the opposite of that recommended for another disorder. For example, use of icons is recommended for people with language problems, but not for people with learning disorders.

It is the aim of good Web site design to enable people to use the site. When designing for people with dementia, it is important to concentrate on the abilities that may remain, rather than concentrating on what people cannot do. Bad design for people with dementia may have harmful consequences for the user. People with dementia may lose confidence in their remaining abilities. Bad design may reinforce negative feelings about the abilities of someone with dementia, whereas good design may enable them to continue to function for as long as possible.

The following design features and guidelines are the most likely to help people with dementia to use Web sites. Many of these design ideas discussed here have been identified as being important when designing for older people in general, or for people with other specific disabilities. They may therefore be of benefit for people with dementia as well.

It should also be remembered that impairments with age and with dementia are not uniform, and so there is no specific pattern of reduced ability to design for (Hawthorn, 2000).

The main design ideas identified as playing a part in making a Web site more accessible to people in the early stages of dementia are simplified displays, avoiding or eliminating distractions, having consistent and familiar page designs, and providing contextual support. The use of graphics, icons, and sound, and the importance of the language and content of Web sites are also stressed. Navigation and menu design is identified as perhaps the most important issue when designing Web sites for people with dementia. Finally, it is recognised that dementia is a progressive disease, and that people with dementia may need support and assistance when using Web sites.

Simplify Displays

The problems that people with dementia may have with attention, concentration, and especially divided attention (Morris, 1994) have fundamental implications for designing Web site displays. Simple Web site designs will be easier for someone in the early stages of dementia to use. Indeed, it has long been agreed that older users in general are more likely to benefit from interfaces that reduce the complexity of the task that the user is attempting (Hawthorn, 2000). Simplified displays may be especially appropriate for people with Alzheimer's disease because of the problems they may have with impaired perceptual recognition (agnosia) and visuospatial perception (Jackson & Owsley, 2003).

When communicating with people with dementia it is important to reduce cognitive load. For example, by reducing the need to multitask, eliminating distractions, and asking individuals to recognise rather than recall (Bayles, 2003). While in the HCI field, Sutcliffe et al. (2003) recommend that designers of assistive technologies should keep tasks and dialogue complexity to a minimum; simplify screens, prompts, and menus, and provide clear progress status displays. These principles can be applied to Web site design for people with dementia.

Visuospatial abilities are needed to scan through information on the page for the information that is important. For example, older adults with higher spatial scanning ability scores have been shown to perform better on word processing tests than those with lower scores (Dyck & Smither, 1995). As these abilities may be impaired in dementia, displays should be simplified to ensure that important information is not missed. From their work on assistive technologies in general, Sutcliffe et al. (2003) recommend clear and simple prompts, simple screen layouts, the elimination of icons and complex graphics, and the clarification of metaphors.

Avoid Distractions

People with dementia often have problems with visual attention and difficulties with motion perception (Rizzo, Anderson, Dawson, Myers, & Ball, 2001). It may therefore be important to avoid distractions, particularly moving text or images.

Searching for important or relevant information on a screen involves selective attention because information that is relevant must be selected from the visual field, while inhibiting the information not relevant to the search goal. Typically, the eyes skim over the screen, guided by the attributes of the information. If information is not relevant to the search goal, it may be a source of distraction. This is particularly true of blinking or moving text (Echt, 2002). It has been stated that older users in general will be more easily distracted by extraneous design detail or background noise than younger users (Hawthorn, 2000). As people with dementia have trouble with attention, avoiding distractions on the screen will be even more important.

It has been an assumption that in order to participate in computer activities people must be able to maintain visual attention (O'Leary, Mann, & Perkash, 1991). However, designers have been urged to help older users to find items easily and to keep their attention focused on them (Hawthorn, 2000). For people with dementia to be included in the digital age, designers must find ways of overcoming problems with visual attention. From their work on an e-mail system for cognitively impaired users, Sutcliffe et al. (2003) recommend limiting distractions, keeping continuous engagement, and giving status reminders.

It is possible that even the use of colour may have a distracting effect (Mitchell et al., 2003), but this needs more investigation when designing Web sites.

Consistent and Familiar Page Designs

The concept of familiarity has been shown to be important in design of the built environment for people with dementia (Burton & Mitchell, 2003), and older users are also thought to function best with a stable well-known interface environment (Hawthorn, 2000). Problems with retaining and recalling new information have been seen in dementia; however, implicit and procedural types of memory appear to be relatively intact, and there appears to be more access to laid-down memories (McIntosh, 1999). Priming—the facilitation by prior stimuli—is an unconscious form of memory that is relatively spared in people with Alzheimer's disease (Bayles, 2003). Therefore, the learnability features of Web site design, including predictability, familiarity, and consistency (Dix, Finlay, Abowd, & Beale, 1997), are more important for people with dementia than for a general user group.

Contextual Support

In dementia, recognition may be impaired, as well as recall, so cues may not be as helpful as in general interface design. It is generally recognised that age-differences in learning and recall are more pronounced if the learning problem exists in an unfamiliar cognitive domain where there is little contextual support (Czaja, 1997).

The context in which an item is encountered while being memorised is important as a cue to later remembering. Older adults appear to have problems in making use of contextual cues if the context is only loosely related to the target item, or there is competing cognitive load during the memory task (Hawthorn, 2000).

Well-designed visual cues such as text links, buttons, and icons could significantly support older users (Ellis & Kurniawan, 2000). More salient markers of previously following hypertext links (e.g., a salient colour change), and perceptual cues on Web pages, such as colour-coding or graphics, have been suggested for older people using Web sites (Mead, Batsakes, Fisk, & Mykitshyn, 1999).

Contextual help needs to be designed, which supports someone with dementia to use a Web site without distraction or confusion.

Use of Colour, Graphics, Icons, and Sound

The use of graphics, icons, colour and sound in Web sites for people with dementia needs more research.

Colour is often used in Web design to emphasise important information and increase comprehension and memorability (Brink, Gergel, & Wood, 2002). However, use of colour in Web site design for people with dementia needs to be considered carefully. Colour has been found to be of limited use in the design of the built environment because of possible problems associated with older people differentiating different colours, and with people with dementia not understanding the significance of colour changes (Mitchell et al., 2003). However, the relevance of this work to younger people or people in the earlier stages of dementia using Web sites has not yet been investigated.

It has been assumed that when designing interfaces for older users, graphics need to be carefully selected for relevance rather than decoration (Hawthorn, 2000). Sutcliffe et al. (2003) recommend that for people with cognitive difficulties, display design should link to existing everyday knowledge, for example by using metaphors and everyday images.

Icons are traditionally viewed as giving cues for recall, but it is not clear whether this is true of older users as well as younger ones (Hawthorn, 2000). People with Alzheimer's disease often have difficulty in naming pictures (Nicholas, Obler, Au,

& Albert, 1996). Therefore, although the use of icons in Web site design may be attractive, it may not be appropriate for Web sites designed for people with dementia. The use of icons and graphics may also prove to be distracting or confusing.

Multiple sensory modes for information provision have been put forward as a way of improving learning in older adults, but other studies have found that sound may make certain applications more difficult to use for older people, and synthesised speech may be difficult to understand (Morris, 1994). Multiple sensory output (e.g., text of screen and sound) could aid attention, but might lead to a confusing interface (Morris, 1994).

Guidelines for older people with regard to font size, for example, using 14 point rather than 12 point, should be followed (Bernard, Liao, & Mills, 2001; Liao, Groff, Chaparro, Chaparro, & Stumpfhauser, 2000); however, this recommendation is based on the average age of people with dementia, rather than on the condition itself.

Language and Content

The source of language comprehension impairments in Alzheimer's disease is a matter of debate. Deficits in lexical semantics, syntactic ability, and memory may all play a role. If the problem is due to attention and memory deficits, intervention strategies might include repetition of the input. However, if syntactic deficits are involved, intervention might involve linguistic simplification and/or alternative communication modalities (Kempler, Almor, Tyler, Andersen, & MacDonald, 1998).

Memory problems characteristic of Alzheimer's disease cause, or at least aggravate, sentence comprehension deficits. Therefore, sentences that put extra demands on memory are likely to exacerbate comprehension problems for people with dementia. Strategies such as repetition and paraphrasing, which are thought to compensate for memory impairments, have been shown to improve comprehension (Kempler, 1998).

Singh, Domonkos, and Rho (1998) have stated that understanding Web information can be exhausting for elderly users, or for users with illnesses that affect language, or for those who are stressed or anxious. People with dementia will often fall into all three categories. Therefore, some of the problems identified by Singh et al. (1998) should be considered when designing Web sites for people with dementia. These include use of technical, abstract or unfamiliar words; use of words or sentences with more than one meaning; use of words with high semantic specificity; words that are difficult to spell or pronounce; adjectives that are ambiguous or imprecise; overuse of pronouns; sentences in the passive tense or long and compound sentences; strange word order; phrases that are intended to be interpreted metaphorically; words that are used in an abstract manner; or sentences that require detailed processing with respect to temporal and spatial information.

Many of these issues have been addressed by Bayles (2003), who recommends ways for facilitating communication with people with Alzheimer's disease. These include using shorter commands that are easier to remember and follow; allowing the person with dementia time to complete one portion of the task before giving the next instruction; using simple, active, declarative sentences and avoiding embedded relative clauses; using high-frequency common words that are more easily assessable to everyone; and avoiding the overuse of pronouns, because processing pronouns requires remembering their antecedents (Bayles, 2003).

For people with cognitive difficulties, Sutcliffe et al. (2003) recommend using simple commands and prompts, simple and clear text eliminating dense text, and using visual metaphors and icons. They conclude that people with cognitive difficulties need step-by-step instructions, with diagrams and images.

The organisation of the information on the screen is also important. Proper organisation and the amount of information on a screen are important for people with impaired visual search skills and selective attention (Ellis & Kurniawan, 2000). Older users are likely to find lists easier to work with than paragraphs (Hawthorn, 2000).

Navigation and Menus

Navigation has been identified as a problem for people with Alzheimer's disease (Pai & Jacobs, 2004). And as memory loss is an early and important symptom of most types of dementia, the design of clear navigation systems for people with dementia is vitally important.

Users need tools to answer questions like "Where am I?", "What have I seen?", and "What else is there to see and how can I see it?" However, it is difficult to provide conceptual navigation if users are unable to conceptualise their questions (Singh et al., 1998).

Designing menu systems may be challenging, as people with dementia may have conceptual problems that might have implications for the use of menus and hierarchical navigation that relies on grouping concepts together. Broader category names are remembered easier than specific names (Spaan, Raaijmakers, & Jonker, 2003).

Clear navigation aids and location cues would therefore appear to be important for people with dementia. The navigation needs to stand out from the rest of the information on the screen.

Some design features that might seem to help older people may create problems for people with dementia; for example, keeping pages short will lead to increased screen sequences that could lead to navigation problems (Morgan Morris, 1994).

Efficient browsing through a Web site requires good episodic memory for whether or not a particular page has been visited. Episodic memory failures should cause browsers to follow the same hypertext links and visit the same Web pages repeatedly while performing a single task (Mead et al., 1999).

Older adults have been found to have difficulty recalling previous actions and the locations of previously viewed information (Mead et al., 1999). However, the recency effect appears to be less impaired in people with dementia, which may mean that they are able to remember the last few actions (Morris, 1994). Therefore, there may be a design solution to help people with dementia to navigate successfully through a Web site.

Support and Training

Sutcliffe et al. (2003) have highlighted the importance of training and assistance for people with cognitive problems, and Hawthorn (2000) has suggested that successful learning for older users will involve a lot of practice.

Designers should be producing Web sites that will be used by people in the early stages of dementia independently; however, it is important to remember that dementia is a progressive disease. As the condition progresses, people may find that they need support from carers or others to use computers successfully.

Many of the problems encountered by people with cognitive disorders, in a study by Sutcliffe et al. (2003), were caused by learning difficulties associated with standard computer operations such as mouse movement or cursor selection. An interesting area of research would be the training and support needs of people with dementia.

Appropriate Research Methods

When working with people with dementia, appropriate research methodologies are vital. Both in the area of dementia care and in dementia research, a more person-centred approach to working with people with dementia has been adopted (Kitwood, 1997). How this person-centred approach can be incorporated into user-centred design and research methodologies will be discussed.

A Person-Centred Approach

Once people have a diagnosis of dementia, assumptions are often made that they do not have views about their care, and are unable to express their own history (Allen, Newby, & Kennally, 2003). It is now recognised that many people experiencing mild symptoms of dementia are aware of their condition, but in the past, there had been a strong held belief that people with dementia were unable to communicate what they were really experiencing (Bond & Corner, 2001). At the same time, the concept of "design exclusion" has been put forward as a way of focussing attention on how existing designs fail to address user needs and aspirations, especially that of older people (Lebborn, Coleman, & Cassim, 2002).

However, there is growing recognition that people in the early stages of dementia are able to provide accurate and valid reports of the experience of services provided for them, such as community care (Bamford & Bruce, 2000). Although few evaluations of services carried out now do not include users' views, it is only recently that the views of people with dementia themselves, rather than those of a carer or voluntary organisation, have been sought (Cox, 1999; Stalker, Gilliard, & Downs, 1999). Traditional large studies of elderly people and care services have avoided direct interviewing altogether, and concentrated on information from third-party informants, and observation (Mozley, Huxley, Sutcliffe, Bagley, Burns, Challis, & Cordingley, 1999). Researchers have also tended to view the ethical and methodological considerations surrounding the study of people living with the early stages of dementia to have been immense, and so studies have been limited to relatively small samples (Keady, 1996).

However, when asked, people with dementia have expressed a willingness to participate in research, as they perceive it to be doing something worthwhile (Robinson, 2002). There may also be a feeling of being taken seriously as a capable person again (Dewing, 2002). People with dementia are also increasingly becoming involved in voluntary organisations such as the Alzheimer's Society (Litherland, 2004).

There is growing recognition that people with dementia should be included in research as participants, and not as subjects or objects (Dewing, 2002). However, research methodologies themselves can be a barrier to the inclusion of people with dementia into research. Some researchers believe that challenging methodology is an important part of encouraging research to be more inclusive of people with dementia. Methods need to be designed that focus on the strengths of the participants' abilities (Pratt, 2002). For example, questions themselves can be threatening to someone with cognitive impairment (Stalker et al., 1999). Dementia research calls for a collaborative style in which the person with dementia, carers, and researchers explore difficulties and options for their resolution together (Blackman et al., 2003). One of the most significant developments in the field of dementia care has been the focus on personhood (Kitwood, 1997). It is now widely accepted that the goals of care should move beyond maintenance, and focus instead on the abilities and residual interests, rather than the deficits of the person with dementia (Nolan, Ryan, Enderby, & Reid, 2002); this concept is also being accepted in research. Research into the views of people with dementia has shown the importance that people with dementia place on autonomy and being in control (Bamford & Bruce, 2000). It has been observed that although participants may not always remember the things they have been doing during the research, the positive feelings engendered from participation in an enjoyable experience remained with them after the event (Hubbard, Downs, & Tester, 2003).

Users are increasingly being involved in the design, development, and evaluations of services, but there is debate around what inclusion in research means, and the level to which it can be achieved while not cognitively and emotionally out-pacing the person with dementia (Dewing, 2002). It has also been suggested that person-centred research encounters are potentially therapeutic encounters. People with dementia cannot be regarded as objects to be examined through observation or interviews and left unchanged by the research event (Dewing, 2002).

Researchers are encouraged to reflect, respectfully, the human value, dignity, and experience of participants in research (Woods, 1997). Researchers with a person-centred approach try to respect each person's individuality in order to gain some understanding of the meaning their unique situation has for them (Howorth & Saper, 2003). One way of demonstrating personhood is to actively seek the view of people with dementia, to reflect these views in the design of services, and how the success of services is gauged (Nolan et al., 2002).

Involving people with dementia in research may require the researcher to think differently about how the research is conducted. Concluding that a person lacks autonomy purely because of dementia can be inaccurate. Autonomy may be retained for some types of decisions and lost for others (Halstead & Vernon, 2000). Through training and experience, researchers can develop a repertoire of strategies that complement the uniqueness of each person with dementia, so that each research participant received bespoke methods for exploring their experience and listening to their voice (Hubbard et al., 2003). The researcher should reach towards the person with dementia, rather than the person with dementia having to reach into a cognitively demanding reality in which they become incapacitated (Dewing, 2002).

Qualitative methods are useful when carrying out research with people with dementia because of the commitment to viewing events, actions, beliefs, and so forth, from the perspective of those being studied. This commitment is essential when carrying out studies with people with dementia. The commitment to understanding participants' perspectives implies investigating the experience, meanings, intentions, and behaviours of people with dementia on their own terms. A distinctive feature of qualitative methods is the flexibility of research designs, particularly where ethnographic methods using a range of techniques are involved (Bond & Corner, 2001).

Researchers have highlighted the inappropriateness of controlled laboratory experiments when working with highly heterogeneous populations, such as people with aphasia. They also highlight the difficulty of acquiring a sufficient sample of the population, and the unavailability of appropriate controls and difficulties in interpreting data from a population with large individual differences (Moffat, McGrenere, Purves, Klawe, 2004). The same considerations may apply to research participants with dementia.

A person-centred approach can easily be applied to a more traditional user-centred approach in which users' concerns direct development of a system, rather than technical concerns (Preece, Rogers, & Sharp, 2002). Involving users from the beginning of a Web site design process allows a holistic approach. Such an approach allows the designers to examine the context of the design in the user's life, and to examine the ways in which the user will learn to use the technology, what support will be needed, and how the user experiences and perceives it (Dickinson, Eisma, Syme, & Gregor, 2002).

It must be remembered that people with dementia will often have other impairments, possibly associated with older age, including losses in sight and hearing (Hubbard et al., 2003). Indeed, the functionality of older people, in general, varies more widely than that of younger people. Designing for such a wide variety of functionality necessitates a reexamination of design strategies and methodologies and, in particular, a questioning on the concept of universal design (Dickinson et al., 2002). Older people have been found to have a much wider range of abilities, and real needs and wants than many traditional user groups of information technology. Sensory impairments, communication difficulties, and lack of familiarity with technology also provide barriers to requirements gathering (Newell, & Gregor, 2004).

It has been argued that user-centred design methodologies have been developed for relatively homogenous user groups. Older people in general (and people with dementia in particular) encompass an incredibly diverse group of users. Gregor et al. (Gregor, Newell, & Zajicek, 2002) have put forward the concept of user-sensitive inclusive design. User-sensitive inclusive design aims to address issues of coping with:

- A much great variety of user characteristics and functionality
- Finding and recruiting "representative users"
- Conflicts of interest between user groups
- The need to specify exact characteristics of the user group
- Tailored, personalisable, and adaptive interfaces
- Provision of accessibility using additional components

Gregor et al. (2002) feel that the word "sensitive," rather than "centred," reflects:

- The lack of a truly representative user group
- Difficulties of communication with users
- Ethical issues
- That different paradigms are needed to standard user-centred design paradigms
- That there must be a different attitude of mind of the designer

This sensitive approach will be useful when working with people with dementia. A different attitude is needed from both the researcher and designer when working with, and for, this user group. The lack of a truly representative user group should not stop designers and researchers from seeking the views of people with dementia.

A Participatory Approach

The action research approach implies that research is done with people rather than on them, and uses more qualitative than quantitative methods. The democratic principles of action research imply that researchers and participants are treated as equals in the enterprise. The researcher is the facilitator of changes, consulting with participants at all stages of the research process and, in particular, feeding back findings and interpretations of findings to participants on a regular basis. This collaborative style leads to the research process adopting a spiralling sequence of planning, acting, observing, reflecting, and replanning. In dementia care, the principles of action research have been used in the technique of dementia care mapping, which changes the quality of institutional environments for people with dementia (Bond & Corner, 2001).

During the 1980s, there was a shift away from user-centred design to user-involved design (Gill, 1996). Participatory design represents an approach towards computer systems design in which the people destined to use the system play a critical role in designing it. The approach was pioneered in Scandinavia, where it was used to involve workers (Schuler & Namioka, 1993).

Participatory design methodology is a process that uses early and continual participation of the intended users to produce a technology that will realise better acceptance, and better suit the needs of its users (Moffat et al., 2004). The approach focuses on collaborating with the intended users throughout the design and development process, rather than developing a system "for" them (Ellis & Kurniawan, 2000).

Participatory design philosophy has been described as having three premises:

1. The goal of participatory design is to improve quality of life, rather than demonstrate the capability of technology.

2. The orientation of participatory design is collaborative and cooperative, rather than patriarchal.

3. Participatory design values interactive evaluation to gather and integrate feedback from intended users, thereby promoting design iteration (Ellis & Kurniawan 2000).

Newbery et al. (2003) found a participatory approach to interface design ensured the long-term engagement and enthusiasm of group members with aphasia. And in their work with nine people with aphasia, Moffat et al. (2004) describe a participatory design process that included brainstorming, low-fidelity paper prototyping, medium-fidelity software prototyping, and high-fidelity software prototyping, followed by a formal evaluation over a 7-month period.

Ellis and Kurniawan (2000) describe a participatory design project with older people. They describe a six-step process: build bridges, develop user model, map possibilities, develop prototype(s), elicit and integrate feedback, and continue interaction.

Ellis and Kurniawan (2000) emphasise the importance of building trust with the participants, communicating the importance and relevance of the project to the participants, and engendering a culture of partnership and mutual respect. They build trust and capability by offering a 12-week workshop on WWW usage to prospective participants in their study. The researchers felt that it was important that the participants felt supported and respected as partners in the effort. The researchers worked hard to avoid behaviour that could be viewed as exploitative, patriarchal, or patronising. They tried to empower all the participants to have and express their opinions. Participants in the study viewed their participation as a service to other current and potential older Web users. The researchers also highlight the role of the design sessions as social occasions involving lunch with the whole team. Placing the participatory design activity in a larger social context was seen as a key way of maintaining interest in the project.

Groves and Slack (1993) identified the key to helping older people to overcome their reluctance and fear of using computers is to show them the meaningfulness and the usefulness of using computers in their lives. Some individuals may start out in a study enthusiastically, but then lose interest. For these people, maintaining motivation could be achieved by showing them different aspects of computer function (Groves & Slack, 1993).

Savitch and Zaphiris (2005) are investigating a community-centred approach for developing an online discussion board for people with dementia. Preece and Maloney-Krichmar (2003) have identified the link between social interaction on an online discussion forum (sociability) and usability. The community-centred approach involves software design, deciding on initial social policies, and development of the community over time (Preece, 2001). Involving people with dementia at an early stage in the development of an innovative discussion forum for people like themselves is vitally important. It is only if a group of people with dementia feel ownership and responsibility for the discussion forum that it will succeed.

The think-aloud technique may be a useful tool in the person-centred approach. The think-aloud technique requires people to say out loud everything that they are thinking and trying to do, so that their thought processes are externalised (Preece et al., 2002). Think aloud has been used successfully when analysing the browsing behaviour of older people on Web sites (Mead et al. 1999). A variation of the think-aloud protocol is probably even more appropriate with participants with dementia. Cooperative evaluation (Monk, Wright, Haber, & Davenport, 1993) is based on traditional talk-aloud protocols, but involves more intervention, and the participant is encouraged to see himself as a collaborator in the evaluation and not an experimental subject. This method is appropriate for use with people with dementia because it enables the participant to be part of the research process, and to concentrate on the strengths of the individual rather than highlight their impairments. More quantitative methods would inhibit the participants and contribute to feelings of failure (Savitch & Zaphris 2005).

Cooperative prototyping is another technique that allows users and designers to participate actively and creatively in developing a prototype. It can be used in Web site design because of the flexible nature of HTML documents and WWW browsers. Observation and open-ended discussions can be used to evaluate prototypes as part of a participatory design process (Ellis & Kurniawan, 2000). Sutcliffe et al. (2003) have described a user-centred approach where simple prototype mock-ups were used in the investigation of assistive technology for cognitively disabled users.

Interviews and Focus Groups

Research into the views of people with dementia has shown the importance of autonomy or being in control (Bamford & Bruce, 2000). Many researchers have found that a qualitative design approach is most useful to explore the perspective and experience of people with dementia. Such a research design might include interviews, participant observation, and case studies (Bartlett & Martin, 2002).

Interviews and focus groups are useful to find out the needs and views of people with dementia, especially those with mild to moderate symptoms (Hubbard et al., 2003). Many interview techniques will be the same, but a more sensitive approach may be necessary. People with dementia experience profound and continual feelings of loss and fear. It is important that researchers are sensitive to participant's emotional states, provide support for those who are experiencing anxiety, and do not inadvertently contribute towards heightened feelings of loss and fear (Hubbard et al., 2003). Much of the following advice will depend on the stage of the dementia and the personalities of the people involved.

The conventional approach to conducting semistructured interviews may need to be adapted. It may be more appropriate to follow the person's lead than impose a structure on the conversation from without (Stalker et al., 1999). A researcher needs to set the complexity of the questions to a level that the person finds comprehensible (Dewing, 2002).

The relationship of the researcher to the person with dementia, and the people around him or her, is very important (Pratt, 2002). Getting to know people with dementia, and inviting them to get to know the researcher, has been found to be important (Allan, 2002). Encouraging openness requires a degree of trust that must be nurtured during the interview (Mason & Wilkinson, 2002). The first few minutes of an interview may be crucial for allaying suspicion and building trust (Keady, Nolan, & Gilliard, 1995).

Researchers need to have the flexibility to take account of the unpredictability of the impact of dementia on communicative and other capacities and, therefore, to change strategies in ways that are beneficial to the participant (Hubbard et al., 2003). For example, ample time should be set aside for interviews, as some respondents require considerable mental processing time, and it has been found to be difficult to keep other participants "on task" (Mozley et al., 1999). People with dementia themselves have highlighted that they need more time to complete tasks, and may become agitated if put under undue pressure (Robinson, 2002). A silence might be related to difficulties in memory recall (Mason & Wilkinson, 2002), or a participant may repeat himself or herself, and so an interview may last longer than usual (Hubbard et al., 2003).

When interviewing people with dementia it is important to offer breaks, especially if the person with dementia is showing signs of distress (Pratt, 2002). People with dementia have good days and bad days; therefore, engaging in multiple interviews over time allows an interviewer to observe and understand the context of each individual (Pratt, 2002). A flexible observation and interview schedule allows research to take place when the participants are at their most lucid (Hubbard et al., 2003).

People with dementia may need extra support to participate in research. For example, Bamford and Bruce (2002) used three facilitators in each focus group meeting so that someone was available to help participants to leave the discussion or go to the toilet.

The usefulness of interviews can be limited by the participant's ability to verbally communicate, and also by the researchers' own listening skills (Hubbard et al., 2003).

Pictures or cards with single emotions written on them have been successfully used to stimulate conversation and discussion (Allan, 2001a; Dewing, 2002). Interactions involving handling of props tend to enable the person to feel more confident and respond more confidently (Dewing, 2002). In focus groups settings, physical cues and prompts, such as household objects or photographs, have been found to be helpful to orientate people to the subject under discussion and help them focus their thoughts (Heiser, 2002).

It has been suggested that people with dementia may request meetings on a one-to-one basis, as they find group situations difficult (Corner, 2002). However, focus groups have also been used successfully with this user group.

Because focus groups have been found to be appropriate for research with people with limited power and influence (Morgan & Kreuger, 1993), this method of research has often been used with people with dementia. Group discussions may have a number of potential advantages over individual interviews including enhanced quality of interaction, reduced pressure on individuals to respond, mutual support, and the opportunity for shared experiences to trigger memory (Bamford & Bruce, 2000).

Focus groups are used to explore people's experiences, opinions, wishes, and concerns. The method is particularly useful for allowing participants to generate their own questions, frames, and concepts, and to pursue their own priorities on their own terms, in their own vocabulary. They are particularly suited to the study of attitudes and experiences around specific topics (Kitsinger & Barbour, 1999).

Bamford and Bruce (2002) have described a study with 15 older people with dementia, where formal focus groups discussions took place with four to nine people with dementia. They concluded that focus groups are only suitable for researching certain topics, and only with certain groups of people with dementia. For example, focus groups will be more useful for people in the earlier stages of dementia, and to discuss specific issues rather than broad experiences.

Focus groups have proved a useful tool for finding out about the views of people with dementia about their own day centre. For example, Heiser (2002) describes how a group of people with dementia quickly grasped what the session was about and were forthcoming with their views.

As with all focus groups, interaction may not necessarily be positive. Bamford and Bruce (2002) found that participants with dementia sometimes showed a lack of respect to one another. They feared that negative responses of other participants could undermine a speaker's confidence and feelings of self-worth. Bamford and Bruce have also found that there may be more potential for a dominant participant to exert a significant effect on the findings in group discussions, and found problems with parallel conversations independent of group size (Bamford & Bruce, 2002).

Using skilled dementia specialists to facilitate the group has been found to be thus important, especially in giving prompts to move people on to the next question without leading anyone with answers (Heiser, 2002).

As with one-to-one interviews, time is a big issue in focus group discussions. People with dementia often need time to communicate their thoughts, but it has been found difficult to give them this time in focus group settings (Bamford & Bruce, 2002). Researchers advise against trying to tackle lots of topics in one session (Heiser, 2002). Each person's abilities, such as speech and thought response time, need to be considered so that all contributions are valued and acknowledged. Care should be taken to make sure that people feel included, even if not playing an active verbal part, or if they do not fully understand. For such a person to feel at ease, with a sense of belonging, is important (Moyes, 2002). Some researchers who have used focus groups with older people have reported difficulties in keeping members of the focus groups "on task" and retaining their attention, and have suggested using small structured focus groups (Lines & Hone, 2002).

A layered, qualitative approach has been used by researchers at Intel who have investigated assistive technology for elderly people, including people with dementia. Their approach has involved holding focus groups first, and then recruiting individuals from the focus groups for interview and ethnographic observation. Focus troupes of actors were used to depict a technology concept via dramatic scenarios (Lundell & Morris, 2004).

Defining the User Group

When designing a Web site for a user group of people with dementia, it may not necessarily be appropriate or necessary to carry out the research or user testing with people who have a definite diagnosis of dementia. There are issues around the diagnosis process and acceptance of a diagnosis, but also, the target user group will be varied. People using the Web site may not have a diagnosis of dementia, but may have other memory problems, or may just be worried about their health. Many people with dementia remain undiagnosed, and a diagnosis does not necessarily provide an indication of the effects of the disease on the person's skills (Hubbard et al., 2003). Use of the words "dementia" or "Alzheimer's disease" has been highlighted by researchers as a problem. Either because of the stigma involved with the terminology, or because of the lack of insight of people with dementia into their condition. Many researchers have used the phrase "memory problems," unless the participant used other descriptions (Bartlett & Martin, 2002; Mason & Wilkinson, 2002).

The process for selecting people for inclusion in any research study should be flexible. Cognitive impairment is a complex phenomenon, and some components of cognitive functioning are more essential to real-life activities than others. Using an arbitrary cut-off score on the MMSE test has been shown to exclude people who were capable of being interviewed (Mozley et al., 1999).

Researchers need to assume that the person with early dementia retains the ability to manage their input into a sensitively conducted research process (Kemp, 2003). It is seen to be important to meet people on their own terms and, therefore, there is no need for participants to admit that they have a diagnosis of dementia (Reid, Ryan, & Enderby, 2001).

What We Know So Far

Small-scale pilot projects have shown that it is both possible and desirable to involve people with dementia in Web site design (Savitch et al., 2004).

A small-scale, preliminary study, with a collaborative and person-centred approach, has been undertaken (Freeman, Clare, Savitch, Royan, Litherland, & Lindsay, 2005).

Five men with probable Alzheimer's disease in the early stages participated in the study. The participants were asked to compare two different Web site designs offering the same content. The study demonstrated that people with early-stage dementia are interested in using the Internet, that it is feasible to involve people with early-stage dementia as collaborators in the development of Web-based resources aimed at people with dementia. People with early-stage dementia who have little prior experience of using computers or the Internet can be successfully introduced to this activity. The study also demonstrated that design makes a difference, and that people with dementia can become centrally involved in the evaluation process.

In another study (Savitch & Zaphiris, 2005), a cooperative evaluation method was used. Cooperative evaluation is based on traditional talk-aloud protocols, but involves more intervention, and the participant is encouraged to see himself as a collaborator in the evaluation, and not an experimental subject (Monk et al., 1993). This method was found to be appropriate for use with people with dementia because it enables the participant to be part of the research process. It also enables the researcher to concentrate on the strengths of the individual, rather than highlight their impairments. More quantitative methods would inhibit the participants and contribute to feelings of failure. The tasks chosen in this study reflected realistic information needs of people with dementia.

The cooperative evaluation method enabled the researchers to ask questions and clarify points with the participants during the tasks. This was especially useful when working with people with language and memory problems.

Participants were keen to take part in the research. Even if they were not very familiar with Web sites, they understood the importance of design for making information accessible. However, although four of the five participants had no problem understanding the tasks, one participant was obviously having difficulty with the concept of how Web sites are organised and the tasks involved. Therefore, the interview was stopped after only two sites had been evaluated. Another participant became tired before the final task was completed.

This study also highlighted the need to involve people with dementia themselves in user testing. Using general design guidelines for elderly people is not helpful, nor is relying on the thoughts and assumptions of Web site designers, or people who work with people with dementia.

The authors have also found that the terminology and phrases used when designing for people with dementia are extremely important, possibly more so than for the average Web user. They suggest that a longer list of menu items may be preferable to grouping information into abstract categories. However, further study will be needed to investigate the optimum number of headings that is possible without causing confusion. Preliminary findings have also indicated that, although each individual is different, it may be possible to elicit some general information about what makes a site easy to use for people with dementia.

Another study (Savitch et al., 2006) has demonstrated that the use of focus groups for people with dementia is a useful tool for finding out views and opinions about computer interfaces. Focus group methodology can be particularly suitable for this group of people. Often, people with dementia feel isolated. To bring a group of people with dementia together was a rewarding experience both for the participants and for the facilitators. Again, it was shown that although the participants varied considerably in their experience of using online discussion forums, there was quite high agreement in their opinions about the design options presented. Grouping people by perceived skills was found to be useful when conducting focus groups with people with dementia. The participants were able to contribute to the discussion on a level at which they felt comfortable. This is particularly important for people with dementia who may be feeling devalued by the experience of dementia (Kitwood, 1997).

Conclusion

In the future, people in the early stages of dementia will increasingly require access to the same electronic resources and information as the rest of the population. It is therefore important that researchers and practitioners start to work together with people with dementia to ensure that Web sites are designed to be as accessible as possible for this user group.

Suggestions for Researchers

The Internet is one of the main ways in which people with dementia are using computers, but little research has been carried out to enable them to use the Web effectively. The only way to understand the needs of people with dementia is to involve them in the design process. Methodologies for developing a truly partici-patory design approach for a Web site for people with dementia need to be chosen well and developed. Much can be learnt from the work of researchers into other disciplines; however, researchers into Web site accessibility need to find innovative ways of involving people with dementia in their research.

Summary of Considerations when Choosing an Appropriate Methodology

- Involve people with dementia as participants, not subjects
- Concentrate on the strengths of the participants

- Allow people with dementia to be "in control" of the research process
- Respect the participant as a unique individual
- Have a flexible approach to the research
- Avoid cognitively demanding methodologies
- Be aware of other impairments
- Have a sensitive approach to the participants
- Be aware of ethical issues
- Involve people with dementia from the start of the design process
- Focus on the needs of the participants
- Adopt a collaborative and cooperative style
- Build trust with the participants
- Allow plenty of time
- Be aware that people with dementia may need extra or external support
- Encourage and support participants to give their views and experiences

Suggestions for Practitioners

The demand for Web-based information for people with dementia has already been identified. The large English-speaking Alzheimer's associations around the world are all committed to providing information for people with dementia via their Web sites, and have produced special sections of their Web sites dedicated to providing information directly to people with dementia. However, accessible design for people with dementia should not be limited to only certain sections of specific Web sites. One comment from a participant in one study (Savitch & Zaphiris, 2005) should also not be overlooked by the Alzheimer's associations and other organizations in the field. The participant stated that the entire Web site should be for people with dementia, not just a section. This target audience needs to be helped to get the most out of information provided through the Web.

The design features and ideas discussed earlier need to be investigated more fully both by researchers and practitioners. For example, the use of visual metaphors needs to be investigated. It is unclear whether people with dementia will perceive the metaphor correctly and so, whether they are useful for navigation. The use of language in interface design also seems to be very important for people with dementia. Simple language is needed. But also, the way information is grouped together needs to be investigated. The cues and links needed to navigate through a Web site is another area for research. Design considerations for practitioners are summarised as seen in Figure 1.

Figure 1.

Simplified design	Reduce complexity Simple layouts Clear prompts Important information should be highlighted Simple menus Few graphics
Avoid distractions	Avoid moving text or images Keep information to a minimum Keep design features to a minimum Avoid excessive use of colour Don't include unnecessary information Important information should be highlighted
Consistent and familiar page design	Design should be consistent Menus should be easy to use Simple navigation system that is easy to learn
Contextual support	Clear navigation Clear use of text links Icons that are easy to understand
Use of colour, graphics, and sound	Colour should be used sparingly and not relied on Graphics and icons should be easy to understand Avoid distracting sound or graphics
Language and content	Use simple, clear, plain language Avoid long sentences Avoid technical, abstract, or unfamiliar words Use short commands Use common words Avoid unnecessary information
Navigation and menus	Provide clear location cues to support orientation Use broad category names for menu selection Use clear navigation
Support and training	Provide simple navigation that is easy to learn

Summary of Design Considerations for People with Dementia

People with dementia will continue to use the World Wide Web, and specific Web sites for them are being developed. For example, the UK Alzheimer's Society is committed to involving people with dementia at an early stage in the development of an innovative discussion forum for people like themselves, and Alzheimer's Forum will grow and develop.

The Web site design world needs to be ready for future generations of people who may develop dementia, and will automatically turn to the Web for information, advice, and support.

References

Allan, K. (2001a). Drawing out views of services: Ways of getting started. *Journal of Dementia Care*, (Jan/Feb), 23-25.

Allan, K. (2001b). Drawing out views on services: Meeting the many challenges. *Journal of Dementia Care*, (Mar/Apr), 26-29.

Allan, K. (2002). Working with staff to include people with dementia in research. In H. Wilkinson (Ed.), *The perspectives of people with dementia: Research methods and motivations* (pp. 117-137). London: Jessica Kingsley.

Allen, C., Newby, G., & Kennally, M. (2003). Forthcoming research in the Oxford region: Innovations in dementia care – The benefits of multimedia profiling for older people with dementia. *PSIGE Newsletter, 83*(May), 13-14.

Alm, N., Astell, A., Ellis, M., Dye, R., Gowans, G., & Campbell, J. (2004). A cognitive prosthesis and communication support for people with dementia. *Neuropsychological rehabilitation, 14*(1/2), 117-134.

Alzheimer's Disease International. (2005). http://www.alz.co.uk

Alzheimer's Forum. (2006). http://www.alzheimersforum.org

Alzheimer's Society. (2006). http://www.alzheimers.org.uk

Backman, L. (1998). The link between knowledge and remembering in Alzheimer's disease. *Scandinavian Journal of Psychology, 39*, 131-139.

Bamford, C., & Bruce, E. (2000). Defining the outcomes of community care: The perspectives of older people with dementia and their carers. *Ageing and Society, 20*, 543-570.

Bamford, C., & Bruce, E. (2002). Successes and challenges in using focus groups with older people with dementia. In H. Wilkinson (Ed.), *The perspectives of people with dementia: Research methods and motivations* (pp.139-164). London: Jessica Kingsley.

Bartlett, H., & Martin, W. (2002). Ethical issues in dementia care research. In H. Wilkinson (Ed.), *The perspectives of people with dementia: Research methods and motivations* (pp. 47-61). London: Jessica Kingsley.

Bayles, K. A. (2003). Effects of working memory deficits on the communicative functioningg of Alzheimer's dementia patients. *Journal of Communication disorders, 36*, 209-219.

Bernard, M., Liao, C. H., & Mills, M. (2001, March 31-April 5). The effects of font type and size on the legibility and reading time of online text by older adults. *Proceedings of CHI 2001, Extended Abstracts on Human Factorings in Computing Systems (CHI '01)*, Seattle, WA (pp. 175-176). New York: ACM Press.

Blackman, T., Mitchell, L., Burton, E., Jenks, M., Parsons, M., Raman, S., & Williams, K. (2003). The accessibility of public spaces for people with dementia: A new priority for the "open city." *Disability and Society, 18*(3), 357-371.

Bond, J., & Corner, L. (2001). Researching dementia: Are there unique methodological challenges for health services research? *Ageing and Society, 21*, 95-116.

Brawley, E. C. (1997). Designing for Alzheimer's disease: Strategies for creating better care environments. New York: John Wiley.

Brink, T., Gergel, D., Wood, S. C. (2002). *Designing Web sites that work: Usability for the Web*. San Francisco: Morgan Kaufmann.

Burton, E., & Mitchell, L. (2003). Urban design for longevity. *Urban Design Quarterly, Summer, 87*, 32-35.

Chute, D. L., & Bliss, M. E. (1994). ProsthesisWare: Concepts and caveats for microcomputer-based aids to everyday living. *Experimental Aging Reseach, 20*, 229-238.

Clare, L. (2002). Invervention in dementia of Alzheimer type. In A. Baddeley, M. Kopelman, & B. Wilson (Eds.), *The handbook of memory disorders* (2nd ed., pp. 711-739). Chichester, UK: John Wiley & Sons.

Corner, L. (2002). Including people with dementia: Advisory networks and user panels. In H. Wilkinson (Ed.), *The perspectives of people with dementia: Research methods and motivations* (pp. 83-98). London: Jessica Kingsley.

Cox, S. (1999). Exploring creative responses in housing and support. *Journal of Dementia Care*, (Mar/Apr), 15-17.

Cummings, J. L., & Khachaturian, Z. S. (1999). Definitions and diagnostic criteria. In S. Gauthier (Ed.), *Clinical diagnosis and management of Alzheimer's disease* (2nd ed.). London: Martin Dunitz.

Czaja, S. J. (1997). Computer technology and the older adult. In M. Helander, T. K. Landauer, & P. Prabhu (Eds.), *Handbook of Computer Interaction* (2nd ed., pp. 797-812). Elsevier Science BV.

DASNI. (2006) http://www.dasni.org

Day, K., Carreon, D., & Stump, C. (2000). The therapeutic design of environments for people with dementia: A review of the empirical research. *The Gerontologist, 40*(4), 397-416.

Dewing, J. (2002). From ritual to relationship: A person-centred approach to consent in qualitative research with older people who have a dementia. *Dementia, 1*(2), 157-171.

Dickinson, A., Eisma, R., Syme, A., & Gregor, P. (2002, September). UTOPIA Usable technology for older people: Inclusive and appropriate. In H. Sharp, P. Chalk, J. LePeuple, & J. Rosbottom (Eds.), *Proceedings Volume 2 of 16th HCI Conference*, London (pp. 38-39). British Computer Society.

Dix, A., Finlay, J. E., Abowd, G. D., & Beale, R. (1997) *Human-computer interaction* (2nd ed.). Harlow, UK: Pearson Education Limited.

Dyck, J. L., & Smither, J. A. (1995). Older adults' acquisition of word processing: The contribution of cognitive abilities and computer anxiety. *Human Behavior, 12*(1), 107-199.

Echt, K. V. (2002). Designing Web-based health information for older adults: Visual considerations and design directives. In R. W. Morrell (Ed.), *Older adults, health information and the World Wide Web* (pp. 61-88). NJ: Lawrence Erblaum Associates.

Ellis, D. R., & Kurniawan, S. H. (2000). Increasing the usability of online information for older users: A case study in participatory design. *International Journal of Human-Computer Interaction, 12*(2), 263-276.

Fletcher, W. A. (1994). Ophthalmological aspects of Alzheimer's disease [ABSTRACT]. *Current Opinion in Opthalmology, 5*(6), 38-44.

Freeman, E., Clare, L., Savitch, N., Royan, L., Litherland, R., & Lindsay, M. (2005). Improving Web site accessibility for people with early-stage dementia: A preliminary investigation. *Aging and Mental Health, 9*(5), 442-448.

Gelinas, I., & Auer, S. (1999). Functional autonomy. In S. Gauthier (Ed.), *Clinical diagnosis and management of Alzheimer's disease* (2nd ed.). London: Martin Dunitz.

Gill, K. S. (1996). The foundations of human-centred systems. In K. S. Gill (Ed.), *Human machine symbiosis: The foundations of human-centred systems design* (pp.1-68). Springer-Verlag.

Goodman, J., Brewster, S., & Gray, P. (2002, September). Memory aids for older people. In H. Sharp, P. Chalk, J. LePeuple, & J. Rosbottom (Eds.), *Proceedings Volume 2 of the 16th British HCI Conference,* London (pp. 32-33). British Computer Society.

Grandmaison, E., & Simard, M. (2003). A critical review of memory stimulation programs in Alzheimer's disease. *Journal Neuropsychiatry and Clinical Neurosciences, 15*(2), 130-144.

Gregor, P., Newell, A. F., & Zajicek, M. (2002, July 8-10). Designing for dynamic diversity – Interfaces for older people. In J. A. Jacko (Ed.), *ASSETS 2002. The 5th International ACM conference on Assistive Technologies,* Edinburgh, Scotland (pp.151-156). New York: ACM Press.

Grossman, M., Mickanin, J., Robinson, K. M., & d'Esposito, M. (1996). Anomaly judgments of subject-predicate relations in Alzheimer's disease. *Brain and Language, 54,* 216-232.

Groves, D. L., & Slack, T. (1993). Computers and their application to senior citizen therapy within a nursing home. *Journal of Instructional Psychology, 21*(3), 331-226.

Halstead, G. A., & Vernon, M. J. (2000). Are you confused about consent? *GM*, (July), 19-23.

Hawthorn, D. (2000). Possible implications of aging for interface designers. *Interacting with computers, 12*, 507-528.

Heiser, S. (2002). People with dementia reveal their views of homecare. *Journal of Dementia Care*, (Jan/Feb), 22-24.

Henderson, V. W. (1996). The investigation of lexical semantic representation in Alzheimer's disease. *Brain and Language, 54*, 179-183.

Hofmann, M., Hock, C., Kuehler, A., & Mueller-Spahn, F. (1996). Interactive computer-based cognitive training in patients with Alzheimer's disease. *Journal Psychiatric Research, 30*(6), 493-501.

Howorth, P., & Saper, J. (2003). The dimensions of insight in people with dementia. *Aging and Mental Health, 7*(2), 113-122.

Hubbard, G., Downs, M. G., & Tester, S. (2003). Including older people with dementia in research: Challenges and strategies. *Aging and Mental Health, 7*(5), 351-362.

Huppert, F. A. (1994). Memory function in dementia and normal aging – Dimension or dichotomy? In F. A. Huppert, C. Brayne, & D. W. O'Connor (Eds.), *Dementia and normal aging* (pp. 291-330). Cambridge University Press.

Jackson, G. R., & Owsley, C. (2003) Visual dysfunction, neurodegenerative diseases, and aging. *Neurologic Clinics of North America, 21*, 709-728.

Jones, R. W., & Ferris, S. H. (1999). Age-related memory and cognitive decline. In G. K. Wilcock, R. S. Bucks, & K. Rockwood (Eds.), *Diagnosis and management of dementia: A manual for memory disorder teams* (pp. 211-230). Oxford: Oxford University Press.

Keady, J. (1996). The experience of dementia: A review of the literature and implications for nursing practice. *Journal of Clinical Nursing, 5*, 275-288.

Keady, J., Nolan, M., & Gilliard, J. (1995). Listen to the voices of experience. *Journal of Dementia Care*, (May/June), 15-17.

Kemp, E. (2003). Maintaining connection – managing disruption: The subjective experience of early dementia, a qualitative exploration of the impact of memory changes. *PSIGE Newsletter, 83*(May), 33-42.

Kempler, D., Almor, A., Tyler, L. K., Andersen, E. S., & MacDonald, M. C. (1998). Sentence comprehension deficits in Alzheimer's disease: A comparison of off-line vs. online sentence processing. *Brain and Language, 64*, 297-316.

Kertesz, A., & Mohs, R. C. (1999). Cognition. In S. Gauthier (Ed.), *Clinical diagnosis and management of Alzheimer's disease* (2nd ed.). London: Martin Dunitz.

Kitwood, T. (1997). The experience of dementia. *Aging and Mental Health, 1*(1), 13-22.

Kitzinger, J., & Barbour, R. S. (1999). Introduction. The challenge and promise of focus groups. In *Developing focus group research: Politics, theory and practice* (pp. 1-20). London: Sage Publications.

Lebborn, C., Coleman, R., & Cassim, J. (2002, September). It's CHI Jim, but not as we know it! In H. Sharp, P. Chalk, J. LePeuple, & J. Rosbottom (Eds.), *Proceedings Volume 2 of 16ᵗʰ HCI Conference,* London (pp. 34-35). British Computer Society.

Liao, C., Groff, L., Chaparro, A., Chaparro, B., & Stumpfhauser, L. (2000). A comparison of Web site usage between young adults and the elderly. In *Proceedings of the IEA 2000/HFES 2000 Congress.* San Diego, CA: Human Factors and Ergonomics Society.

Lines, L., & Hone, K. S. (2002, September). Research methods for older adults. In H. Sharp, P. Chalk, J. LePeuple, & J. Rosbottom (Eds.), *Proceedings Volume 2 of the 16ᵗʰ British HCI Conference,* London (pp. 36-37). British Computer Society.

Litherland, R. (2004). Listen to us. *Working with Older People, 7*(4), 17-20.

Lundell, J., & Morris, M. (2004). Tales, tours, tools and troupes: A tiered research method to inform ubiquitous designs for the elderly. In S. Fincher, P. Markopoulos, D. Moore, & R. Ruddle (Eds.), *People and Computers XVIII – Design for Life Proceedings of HCI 2004* (pp. 165-177). London: Springer-Verlag.

Marshall, M. (1999). Person centred technology? *Signpost, 3*(4), 4-5.

Marshall, M. (2003). The Iris Murdoch building at Stirling. *Alzheimer's Care Quarterly, 4*(3), 167-171.

Mason, A., & Wilkinson, H. (2002). Don't leave me hanging on the telephone: Interview with people with dementia using the telephone. In H. Wilkinson (Ed.), *The perspectives of people with dementia: Research methods and motivations* (pp. 183-207). London: Jessica Kingsley.

McGee, J. S., van der Zaag, C., Buckwalter, J. G., Theibaux, M., van Rooyen, A., Neumann, U., Sismore, D., & Rizzo, A. A. (2000). Issues for the assessment of visuospatial skills in older adults using virtual environment technology. *CyberPsychology and Behaviour, 3*(3), 469-482.

McGilton, K. S., Rivera, T. M., & Dawson, P. (2003). Can we help persons with dementia find their way in a new environment? *Aging and Mental Health, 7*(5), 363-371.

McIntosh, (1999, February). Memory loss: The effects of age or dementia? *Geriatric Medicine, 29*(2), 21-24.

Mead, S. E., Batsakes, P., Fisk, A. D., & Mykitshyn, A. (1999). Application of cognitive theory to training and design solutions for age-related computer use. *International Journal of Behavioural Development, 23*(3), 553-573.

Mitchell, L., Burton, E., & Raman, S. (2004). *Neighbourhoods for life: A checklist of recommendations for designing dementia-friendly outdoor environments.* Oxford: Oxford Centre for Sustainable Development and the Housing Corporation.

Mitchell, L., Burton, E., Raman, S., Blackman, T., Jenks, M., & Williams, K. (2003). Making the outside world dementia-friendly: Design issues and considerations. *Environment and Planning B: Planning and Design, 30,* 605-632.

Moffat, K., McGrenere, J., Purves, B., & Klawe, M. (2004, April). The participatory design of a sound and image enhanced daily planner for people with aphasia. *CHI 2004, ,* Vienna, Austria (Vol. 6, Number 1, pp. 407-414).

Monk, A., Wright, P., Haber, J., & Davenport, L. (1993). *Improving your human-computer interface: A practical guide.* London: Prentice Hall.

Morgan, D. L., & Krueger, R. A. (1993). When to use focus groups and why. In D. L. Morgan (Ed.), *Successful focus groups: Advancing the state of the art* (pp. 3-19). London: Sage Publications.

Morgan Morris, J. (1994). User interface design for older adults. *Interacting with Computers, 6*(4), 373-393.

Morris, R. G. (1994). Working memory in Alzeimers-type dementia. *Neuropsychology, 8*(4), 544-554.

Moyes, M. (2002). The voice of the user group. *Signpost, 6*(3), 42-44.

Mozley, C. G., Huxley, P., Sutcliffe, C., Bagley, H., Burns, A., Challis, D., & Cordingley, L. (1999). Not knowing where I am doesn't mean I don't know what I like: Cognitive impairment and quality of life responses in elderly people. *International Journal of Geriatric Psychiatry, 14,* 776-783.

Newbery, J., Parr, S., Moss, B., Petheram, B., & Byng, S. (2003). Aphasishelp: Developing an accessible Web site for people with communications disabilities.

Newell, A. F., & Gregor, P. (2004, September). HCI and older and disabled people: Applied computing at University of Dundee, Scotland. In A. Deardon & L. Watts (Eds.), *Proceedings Volume 2 of the conference HCI 2004: Design for Life,* Leeds, UK (pp. 205-206). Published on behalf of the British HCI Group by Research Press International.

Nicholas, M., Obler, L., Au, R., & Albert, M. L. (1996). On the nature of naming errors in aging and dementia: a study of semantic relatedness. *Brain and Language, 54,* 184-195.

Nolan, M., Ryan, T., Enderby, P., & Reid, D. (2002). Towards a more inclusive visions of dementia care practice and research. *Dementia, 1*(2), 193-211.

O'Leary, S., Mann, C., & Perkash, I. (1991). Access to computers for older adults: Problems and solutions. *American Journal of Occupational Therapy, 45*(7), 636-642.

Pai, M.-C., & Jacobs, W. J. (2004). Topographical disorientation in community-Residing patients with Alzheimer's disease. *International Journal of Geriatric Psychiatry, 19*, 250-255.

Poirier, J., Danik, M., & Blass, J. P. (1999). Pathophysiology of the Alzheimer syndrome. In S. Gauthier (Ed.), *Clinical diagnosis and management of Alzheimer's disease* (2nd ed.). London: Martin Dunitz.

Pratt, R. (2002). Nobody's ever asked how I felt. In H. Wilkinson (Ed.), *The perspectives of people with dementia: Research methods and motivations* (pp. 165-182). London: Jessica Kingsley.

Preece, J. (2001).Community-centred development. In *Online Communities: design usability, supporting sociability* (pp. 203-231). Chicester, UK: John Wiley.

Preece, J., & Maloney-Krichmar, D. (2003). Online communities: focusing on sociability and usability. In J. A. Jacko & A. Sears (Eds.), *The human-computer interaction handbook: Fundamentals, evolving technologies and emerging applications* (pp. 596-620). NJ: Lawrence Erlbaum Associates.

Preece, J., Rogers, Y., & Sharp, H. (2002). *Interaction design: Beyond human-computer interaction*. New York: John Wiley & Sons.

Reid, D., Ryan, T., & Enderby, P. (2001). What does it mean to listen to people with dementia? *Disability and Society, 16*(3), 377-392.

Rizzo, M., Anderson, S. W., Dawson, J., Myers, R., & Ball, K. (2001). Visual attention impairments in Alzheimer's disease. *Neurology, 54*(10), 1954-9.

Rizzo, M., Anderson, S. W., Dawson, J., & Nawrot, M. (2001). Vision and cognition in Alzheimer's disease. *Neuropsychologia, 38*, 1157-1169.

Robinson, E. (2002). Should people with Alzheimer's disease take part in research? In H. Wilkinson (Ed.), *The perspectives of people with dementia: Research methods and motivations* (pp. 101-107). London: Jessica Kingsley.

Ryan, E. B., & Heaven, R. K. B. (1986). Promoting vitality among older adults with computers. *Activities, Adaptation and Aging 8*, 15-30.

Sano, M. (1988). Using computers to understand attention in the elderly. *American Behaviour Scientist, 31*(5), 588-594.

Savitch, N., & Zaphiris, P. (2005, July). An investigation into the accessibility of Web-based information for people with dementia. *The 11th International Conference on Human-Computer Interaction*, Las Vegas. Mira Digital Publishing.

Savitch, N., Zaphiris, P., Freeman, E., Clare, L., & Litherland, R. (2004). Learning from people with dementia to improve accessibility of Web site interfaces. In A. Deardon & L. Watts (Eds.), *Proceedings Volume 2 of the conference HCI 2004: Design for Life,* Leeds, UK (pp. 185-186). Published on behalf of the British HCI Group by Research Press International.

Savitch, N., Zaphiris, P., Smith, M., Litherland, R., Aggarwal, N., & Potier, E. (2006). Involving people with dementia in the development of a discussion forum – A community-centred approach. In J. Clarkson, P., Langdon, & P. Robinson (Eds.), *Designing accessible technology* (pp. 237-248). London: Springer-Verlag.

Schuler, D., & Namioka, K. (Eds.). (1993). Preface. *Participatory design: Principles and practices* (pp. xi-xiii). Hillside: Lawrence Erlbaum Associates.

Sherer, M. (1996). The impact of using personal computers on the lives of nursing home residents. *Physical and Occupational Therapy in Geriatrics, 14*(2), 13-31.

Sherer, M. (1997). Introducing computers to frail residents of homes for the aged. *Educational Gerontology, 23*, 345-358.

Singh, S., Domonkos, G., & Rho, Y. (1998). Enhancing comprehension of Web information for users with special linguistic needs. *Journal of Communication,* Spring, 86-108.

Spaan, P. E. J., Raaijmakers, J. G. W., & Jonker, C. (2003). Alzheimer's disease vs. normal ageing: A review of the efficiency of clinical and experimental memory measures. *Journal of Clinical and Experimental Neuropsychology, 25*(2), 216-233.

Stalker, K., Gilliard, J., & Downs, M. G. (1999). Eliciting user perspectives on what works. *International Journal of Geriatric Psychiatry, 14*, 120-134.

Sutcliffe, A., Fickas, S., Sohlberg, M. M., & Ehlhardt, L. A. (2003). Investigating the usability of assistive user interfaces. *Interacting with Computers, 15*, 577-602.

Tetewsky, S. J., & Duffy, C. J. (1999). Visual loss and getting lost in Alzheimer's disease. *Neurology, 52*, 958.

Woods, B. (1997). Talking point: Kitwood's "The experience of dementia." *Aging and Mental Health, 1*(1), 11-12.

Zanetti, O., Zanieri, G., di Giovanni, G., De Vreese, L. P., Pezzini, A., Metitieri, T., et al. (2001). Effectiveness of procedural memory stimulation in mild Alzheimer's disease patients: A controlled study. *Neuropsychological rehabilitation, 11*(3/4), 263-272.

Chapter XI

Comparing Comprehension Speeds and Accuracy of Online Information in Students with and without Dyslexia

Sri Kurniawan, The University of Manchester, UK

Gerard V. Conroy, The University of Manchester, UK

Abstract

This chapter describes some statistics of people with dyslexia. It continues with describing problems people with dyslexia experience with reading online material, and some technological aids available to help them. Three groups of university students participated in the user study of comprehension tasks using five online articles of varying complexity (as measured through Flesch-Kincaid readability grade). The study found that students with dyslexia are not slower in reading than students without dyslexia when the articles are presented in a dyslexia friendly colour scheme, but these students with dyslexia fare worse in answering correctly the questions related to the passages they read when the complexity increases.

Introduction

Dyslexia has been described as a difficulty in processing information that may be linked to a below average short-term memory and poor visual coordination. This weakness in short-term memory, whether visual or auditory, can make it particularly difficult for a person with dyslexia to learn the correspondence between the written symbol and the spoken sound. It is the most common form of learning disability. Approximately 15% to 20% of the population has a learning disability, and 60% to 80% of those with learning disabilities have problems with reading and language skills. People with dyslexia usually have difficulty with receptive oral language skills, expressive oral language skills, reading, spelling, or written expression (IDA, 2004). Fortunately, people with dyslexia respond successfully to timely and appropriate intervention.

University students with dyslexia might have problems in the following areas (Dyslexia Services, 2005):

1.   Lectures
   • Taking down information accurately in lectures
   • Carrying out multiple tasks simultaneously (i.e., listening to a lecturer, taking down information from the displayed slides at the same time as synthesising and summarising the information into a written format of notes

2.   Reading
   • Conducting literature searches
   • Skimming and scanning for information when reading
   • Making notes from essential research reading

3.   Assignments
   • Putting ideas into words
   • Sequencing ideas/information into sentences and paragraphs
   • Concentrating for long periods of time—they are easily distracted
   • Spelling and/or recognising correct spellings offered by spell checkers
   • Choosing the appropriate word—they tend to substitute less effective words because of worries about spelling

4.   General
   • Remembering facts and new terminology
   • Organising work: files, notes, essays, and so forth
   • Organising time effectively

More and more people are using the Web, and more and more sophisticated sites that use graphically oriented design and multimedia have been developed. However, one of the consequences of these advances is that, in many cases, the Web has grown considerably less accessible to those with disabilities (Hudson, 2005). Dyslexia affects a user's ability to read, write, navigate, comprehend, and recall relevant information from electronic materials for example, Web sites. Current Web accessibility initiatives (WAI) and other accessibility guidelines mainly focus on the research that affects people with visual impairments and blindness. There is, however, little research that specifically deals with the issues surrounding Web accessibility for people with dyslexia (TechDis, 2003).

It is estimated that between 1.2% and 1.5% of students in higher education in the UK are dyslexic (Singleton, 1999), but the number of these students has been steadily increasing over the last few years. When accessing online information, students with dyslexia were shown to have problems in visual concentration and/or oversensitivity to light, slow reading speeds, performing backward navigation, and becoming lost in a hypertext structure (TechDis, 2003).

There are several purposes of this study. Firstly and mainly, to compare the comprehension speeds and accuracy of students with and without dyslexia when reading online information of varying complexity.

Two established readability measures, the Flesch-Kincaid and the Gunning-Fox Index, are used. The scoring of the test material is adapted from the reading comprehension assessment of a nationwide entrance test to postgraduate level studies in the U.S., called the Graduate Record Examination (GRE). The material itself is adapted from the passages provided by the ETS or from the Web pages of National Geographic magazine (http://www.nationalgeographic.com).

The second aim of this study is to investigate the types of technological aids that students with dyslexia use. Finally, the third aim is to understand problems students with dyslexia experience when interacting with computers.

Reading Comprehension

There are many types of readability formulae; some use simple calculations, some are more sophisticated, but most are based on a similar concept. The average sentence lengths and the number of complex words are correlated to the reading level. Passages with a lower reading level theoretically can be comprehended more easily and quickly than those with a higher reading level. Although based on proven research, readability formulae should be considered as a guideline and reference point rather than a rule.

A few things apply to all formulae. Because most of them are based on an average, they require 100-word samples; anything shorter may produce a false reading level. Most formulae count any proper nouns, numbers, or dates as one. For instance, "Abraham Lincoln," "865,460," "March 23, 1998," and "Connecticut" would each count as an "easy word" or a one-syllable word. This is because most reading measures test the vocabulary of the sample, and things like names, numbers, and locations are usually understandable by anyone. For example, most children know the four-syllable word "Arizona," but not the four-syllable word "vicissitude" (Long, 2002).

Flesch-Kincaid

The Flesch-Kincaid reading assessment consists of measures of reading ease and grade level. These two measures have been around for more than 50 years, and are integrated with Microsoft Word, making it easier for computer writers to measure the readability of their articles.

The Flesch-Kincaid reading ease score is calculated using the following formula.

206.835 - (1.015 * average words per sentence) - (84.6 * average syllables per word)

The formula produces a number ranging between 0-100. The higher that number is, the easier the text is to read. Specifically:

- 0-29: Very Difficult (most postgraduate students should understand)
- 30-49: Difficult (most university students should understand)
- 50-59: Fairly Difficult (most high school students should understand)
- 60-69: Standard (most students with 8-9 years of education should understand)
- 70-79: Fairly Easy (most students with 7 years of education should understand)
- 80-89: Easy (most students with 5-6 years of education should understand)
- 90-100: Very Easy (most students with less than 5 years of education should understand)

The Flesch-Kincaid grade level is a similar calculation; however, it gives a number that corresponds to the years of education a person will need to have reached to understand it. For example, a grade level score of 8 means that most readers with 8 years of education should understand the text.

(.39 * average words per sentence) + (11.8 * average syllables per word) - 15.59

Gunning Fog Index

The Gunning Fox Index (GFI) was developed by Robert Gunning, and is one of the simplest and most effective manual tools for analyzing readability. Gunning defines hard words as those with more than two syllables. This method is usually used to determine the readability for junior-high school reading material.

The number the formula produces (called the Gunning-Fox Index or GFI) represents the approximate reading age of the text, the age someone will need to be to understand what they are reading. The following is the formula to determine the GFI:

(average words per sentence + percentage of words with more than three syllables) * 0.4

GRE (Graduate Record Examination)

The GRE consists of general and subject-specific tests. The general test measures analytical writing, verbal, and quantitative skills that have been acquired over a long period of time and that are not related to any specific field of study.

The verbal section of the general test measures the ability to analyze and evaluate written material and synthesize information obtained from it, to analyze relationships among component parts of sentences, to recognize relationships between words and concepts, and to reason with words in solving problems. There is a balance of passages across different subject matter areas: humanities, social sciences, and natural sciences.

Reading comprehension questions, which form part of the verbal test, measure the ability to read with understanding, insight, and discrimination. The type of question in this section explores the ability to analyze a written passage from several perspectives, including the ability to recognize both explicitly stated elements in the passage, and assumptions underlying statements or arguments in the passage, as well as the implications of those statements or arguments. Because the written passage upon which the questions are based presents a sustained discussion of a particular topic, there is ample context for analyzing a variety of relationships.

There are six types of reading comprehension questions, ones that ask about: (1) the main idea or primary purpose of the passage; (2) information explicitly stated in the passage; (3) information or ideas implied or suggested by the author; (4) possible applications of the author's ideas to other situations, including the identification of situations or processes analogous to those described in the passage; (5) the author's logic, reasoning, or persuasive techniques; and (6) the tone of the passage or the author's attitude as it is revealed in the language used.

Technology Aids for People with Dyslexia

There are a number of devices, which are now available, that can be of practical help, but much will depend on the nature and extent of the individual's disability (Drewe, 2004). These include:

- Spell checkers and grammar checkers. Most modern computers now have a spell-check facility, which many dyslexic people find invaluable. Spell checkers specific to some enabling technology are phonetic in nature, although there is little evidence that these are more accurate than conventional spell checkers. Some also have a grammar checker.

- Online/electronic dictionaries. These offer meaning of words or alternatives, and are quicker to use than conventional dictionaries.

- Dictating machines, voice recognition and synthesis software, and voice recording devices. Because people with dyslexia do not suffer as much from the inability to process auditory information as when visual information is involved, voice-supported input and output devices are very helpful for some.

- Calculators and spreadsheet software. Even a simple calculator can be a big help for someone who has difficulty with numbers.

- Memory telephones. Telephones that can store and automatically dial pre-entered numbers may be useful. Fortunately, most landline and mobile phones are equipped with this facility.

- Electronic schedulers or diaries, for example, Microsoft Outlook or Lotus Notes. These can be used as a reminder for appointments, meeting deadlines, or remembering important tasks.

- Tinted lenses and coloured overlays. Some people with dyslexia suffer from a condition called Meares-Irlen syndrome. Text or symbols become blurred or indistinguishable soon after reading begins. This is particularly the case when reading information presented in high contrast, such as black text on a white background. The condition varies in its severity, but in most cases it can be improved with the use of simple coloured overlays (placed over pages or computer screen) or tinted lenses.

Web Design Guidelines for
People with Dyslexia

Various studies had suggested the presentation guidelines when designing Web sites for readers with dyslexia. The following guidelines are summarised from these studies. These studies stated that these guidelines are in addition to the basic accessibility guidelines (e.g., avoid horizontal scrolling, or allow users to turn off flashing images and auto-update).

1. Present the text *in narrow columns*, that is, 60-70 characters width. Ensure the column width is set as a relative value when designing in HTML, so that when a user needs to magnify the text, the layout still makes sense.

2. Reword the sentences so that the *average sentence length is 15-20 words*.

3. Format the paragraph as *left aligned* (justified text, with its uneven spaces between words, creates visual patterns of white space that are hard to ignore. They distract readers, who might then lose their orientation).

4. Use a *plain nonwhite background*. Many dyslexic readers are particularly sensitive to the brightness of text on a pure white background. This can cause the words to appear to move around and to blur together. Patterned background distracts readers from the main content.

5. Use *sans-serif fonts*. Decorative bits added to letters (serifs) make them more complex to read. Use one or two font types only if possible.

6. Use *emboldened words for important information, not italics or underlined*. Italicized text is difficult to read for people with dyslexia. Underlining makes the words seem to "run together."

7. *Text boxes or bubbles* can be used for emphasis or to highlight important points. They also serve to break up a long section of dense text.

8. *Bullet points* can also highlight key items, especially if they are separated by an extra blank space to help clarity.

9. *Short paragraphs* surrounded by white lines also help readability.

10. Use a *minimum font size of 12pt*.

11. Use *active verbs*.

12. Use *lower case letters for information*. Using capital letters for emphasis can make text harder to read. Words entirely written in capital letters also infer that the reader is being shouted at.

13. Use *dark text on a pale background*, for example dark blue on cream.

14. *Using "Web safe" colours* (256 colours that are available on the majority of browsers) should help interoperability.

15. The most effective colour combination varies from person to person; so allowing users to *customise their colour scheme* would help readers with dyslexia choose the colour scheme that would help their comprehension the most.

16. *Don't hyphenate words* that are not usually split in order to fill up line ends, for example, "opera-tion."

17. *Navigation mechanism* should be easily understood. A site map is essential.

18. *Use graphics, images, and pictures to break up text*, while bearing in mind that graphics and tables may take a long time to download. Large images also make pages harder to read.

19. Offer *alternate pages* in a *text reader friendly* style.

20. Where possible, design Web pages that can be *downloaded and read off-line*.

21. *Do not use moving text.* It diverts the users' attention, and it creates problems for text-reading software.

22. *Differentiate* between *links* that *have and have not been visited.* Some readers with dyslexia have problems with their short-term memory and might not remember which pages they had visited.

User Study

The purpose of this study is to investigate the online reading comprehension of university students with dyslexia. The Flesch-Kincaid grade level is used as the main measure. As these students have 16-20 years of education, five articles with grade levels 16-20 were selected from the GRE reading comprehension collection. Another article of grade level 14 was chosen as a practice article. Care was taken to ensure that the Flesch-Kincaid ease scores of the articles fell into the same category. Similarly, the selection ensures that the GFI reflects students' ages. The topics of the articles vary from health to history to science to ensure that no participant will be familiar with all topics. The articles were carefully controlled to contain 440-450 words and would fit in one page so that the participants did not need to scroll.

Participants

Five students with dyslexia participated in this study (in this chapter, it will be referred to as Group 1).

Table 1. Basic demographic of the three groups

Basic demographics	Group1	Group2	Group3
Median age	20	23	30
Gender	3F/2M	3F/2M	1F/4M
Years of computer experience (median)	6	10	10

Table 2. Number of participants per group that had used the various technological aids

Technological aids	Group1			Group3			Group2		
N = Never, O = Occasionally, F = Frequently	N	O	F	N	O	F	N	O	F
1. Spell checkers and grammar checkers	0	0	5	2	0	3	0	3	2
2. Online/electronic dictionaries	0	2	3	0	2	3	0	3	2
3. Dictating machines/voice-recognition software	0	3	2	3	2	0	3	2	0
4. Software that reads out for you	2	1	2	3	2	0	5	0	0
5. Calculators or Excel software	2	3	0	0	4	1	0	5	0
6. Address book or speed dial in your phone	0	0	5	1	0	4	0	4	1
7. Electronic schedulers or diaries	1	2	2	3	0	2	0	2	3
8. Tinted overlays or lenses	5	0	0	5	0	0	5	0	0

To provide baseline data, two groups of five students without dyslexia also participated. The first group was given articles with the same colour scheme as the scheme viewed by the students with dyslexia (Group 2), the other was given articles in black and white (Group 3). All participants are university students of the University of Manchester. Group 1 participants are BSc students, while the participants of the other two groups are MSc and PhD students. Table 1 summarises the basic demographic data of the three groups. Table 2 provides an overview of the types of technological aids used by the three groups.

Stimuli

There are two sets of stimuli for this experiment, each containing five online passages and one practice article. The only difference between the first and second sets is the colour scheme. The first set has dark blue text on a greenish cream background,

Figure 1. An example passage

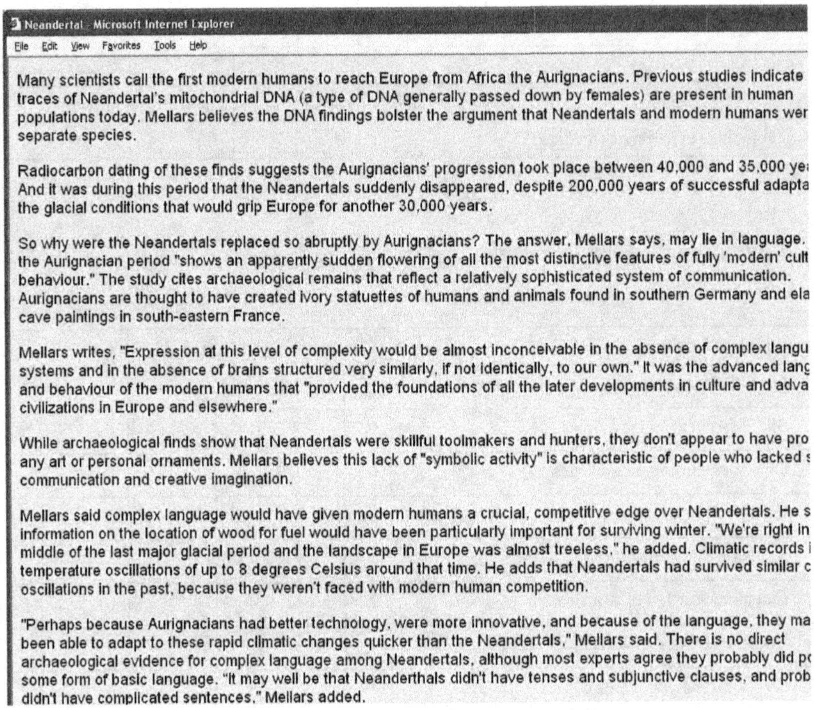
Neandertal - Microsoft Internet Explorer

File Edit View Favorites Tools Help

Many scientists call the first modern humans to reach Europe from Africa the Aurignacians. Previous studies indicate traces of Neandertal's mitochondrial DNA (a type of DNA generally passed down by females) are present in human populations today. Mellars believes the DNA findings bolster the argument that Neandertals and modern humans wer separate species.

Radiocarbon dating of these finds suggests the Aurignacians' progression took place between 40,000 and 35,000 ye And it was during this period that the Neandertals suddenly disappeared, despite 200,000 years of successful adapta the glacial conditions that would grip Europe for another 30,000 years.

So why were the Neandertals replaced so abruptly by Aurignacians? The answer, Mellars says, may lie in language. the Aurignacian period "shows an apparently sudden flowering of all the most distinctive features of fully 'modern' cult behaviour." The study cites archaeological remains that reflect a relatively sophisticated system of communication. Aurignacians are thought to have created ivory statuettes of humans and animals found in southern Germany and ela cave paintings in south-eastern France.

Mellars writes, "Expression at this level of complexity would be almost inconceivable in the absence of complex langu systems and in the absence of brains structured very similarly, if not identically, to our own." It was the advanced lang and behaviour of the modern humans that "provided the foundations of all the later developments in culture and adva civilizations in Europe and elsewhere."

While archaeological finds show that Neandertals were skillful toolmakers and hunters, they don't appear to have pro any art or personal ornaments. Mellars believes this lack of "symbolic activity" is characteristic of people who lacked s communication and creative imagination.

Mellars said complex language would have given modern humans a crucial, competitive edge over Neandertals. He s information on the location of wood for fuel would have been particularly important for surviving winter. "We're right in middle of the last major glacial period and the landscape in Europe was almost treeless," he added. Climatic records i temperature oscillations of up to 8 degrees Celsius around that time. He adds that Neandertals had survived similar c oscillations in the past, because they weren't faced with modern human competition.

"Perhaps because Aurignacians had better technology, were more innovative, and because of the language, they ma been able to adapt to these rapid climatic changes quicker than the Neandertals," Mellars said. There is no direct archaeological evidence for complex language among Neandertals, although most experts agree they probably did pc some form of basic language. "It may well be that Neanderthals didn't have tenses and subjunctive clauses, and prob didn't have complicated sentences," Mellars added.

while the second set has black text on a white background. This allowed Group 1 and Group 3 to view the passages in the colour schemes that theoretically are most effective for them. Group 2 viewed the passages in the colour scheme that is optimal for readers with dyslexia. The font type and size were carefully chosen based on the guidelines previously stated (i.e., Arial 12pt).

An example of the passages is displayed in Figure 1. The passages were displayed using a PC with Pentium IV 3 GHz running Windows XP and Microsoft Internet Explorer and a 19" screen.

Procedure

The session started with the participants filling in a demographic questionnaire on coloured paper for Groups 1 and 2 and on white paper for Group 3. An explanation was then given to them about the aim of the study and the experimental procedure. Each participant performed the reading tasks individually in a controlled environ-

Figure 2. Median time vs. readability

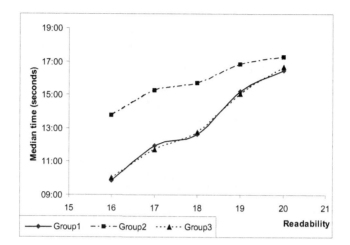

ment (i.e., a usability lab) where they had to answer eight multiple-choice questions while reading a passage. The passage remained open until they finished answering those eight questions, although they were allowed to give up at anytime or to leave any questions unanswered.

They were informed that they were allowed to take a break between passages (the transitional screens between passages clearly stated that they were allowed to take a break as long as they wished). After they finished the main session, they were interviewed on the colour scheme, the topics they just read, and the problems of using computers and the Internet in general.

Results

Figures 2 and 3 show the reading speeds and accuracy of the three groups. Because there are only five participants per group, only the medians are displayed.

The postsession interviews revealed that the main problems for students with dyslexia are related to spelling, understanding how computer applications work, and understanding words/sentences. They felt that the spell checker integrated in Microsoft Word had provided them with tremendous help. The students without dyslexia stated that the main problems they had with computers are related to finding information on the Internet, working with computer applications in which the newer version is incompatible with the older version, and reading long passages online (they prefer to print the passages and read them on paper).

Figure 3. Accuracy vs. readability

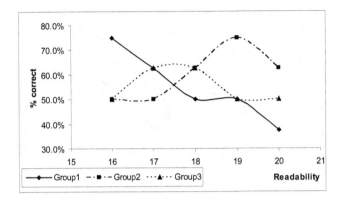

When asked about their most effective colour scheme, each student with dyslexia provided a slightly different answer. Some said that they did not have any problem with black and white as long as the paragraphs were short and the page had plenty of white spaces. Some preferred "any dark coloured text" on baby pink background, dark blue on cream, and black on "any light coloured background." Not surprisingly, all the students without dyslexia preferred black and white. The students without dyslexia who were given the passages in dyslexia—friendly colours stated that they felt very dizzy reading the passages on coloured screen, and they had to use their fingers to follow the sentences because of that. Some suggested that this might be the main cause that their reading speeds were lower than those of the other groups.

Discussions and Conclusion

Even though the students with dyslexia have lower medians in age and computer experience, these are not expected to be the cause of performance differences.

It is expected that because the technological aids were aimed at helping people with dyslexia, the students with dyslexia would use these aids quite often. This is the pattern of use observed in this study with one exception: the tinted overlay. However, it should be noted that students with dyslexia are normally only advised to consider tinted overlays if they have difficulties with the mechanics of reading. If the text can be read easily and is "fixed" on the page, then tinted overlays are rarely suggested. In addition, with Web pages, it is easy to change the colour scheme and the alignment; therefore, tinted overlays are not usually needed.

The pattern of use between students with and without dyslexia is expected to be different, and they do differ in some aids, for example, spell checkers and grammar checkers, address books, and screen-reader software. However, in most aids, the pattern of use is not very different, indicating that these aids are useful for students, whether they have dyslexia or not.

There are several interesting findings from the speed and accuracy charts. Firstly, the reading speeds of participants with and without dyslexia are very similar when they were presented with passages displayed in their optimal colour schemes. However, when the students without dyslexia were presented with the colour scheme that is dyslexia-friendly, their reading speeds are consistently slower than the speeds of the other groups. The speed differences are larger for articles with lower complexity.

In terms of accuracy, however, students with dyslexia noticeably had fewer correct answers as the articles increased in complexity, while the accuracy of students without dyslexia do not seem to be affected by the complexity of the articles.

There are some design implications of this study for designers of online information in general, and Web pages in particular. First and foremost, it is extremely important to ensure that the online material be kept as simple as possible, especially when accuracy is at stake, as this study shows that even though readers with dyslexia can still read as fast as those without dyslexia, their accuracy suffers as the articles get more complex. Secondly, each reader has a colour scheme where they would be most effective in their comprehension. Ensuring that the Web pages are designed with flexible colour scheme will help readers with dyslexia.

There are some limitations of this study. Very few participants were involved; therefore, the results are most likely still too early to generalise. This study also only involved university students; a more heterogeneous sample would be more informative to designers of Web pages in general. And finally, the experiment was performed on a series of simulated Web pages; it would be more meaningful to test it on Web sites that students with dyslexia would normally access.

References

Bradford, J. *Designing Web pages for dyslexic readers*. Retrieved April 19, 2006, from http://www.dyslexia-parent.com/mag35.html

The British Dyslexia Association. *Dyslexia style guide*. Retrieved April 19, 2006, from http://81.89.134.99/main/information/extras/x09frend.asp

Drewe, R. (2004). *Adult dyslexia*. Retrieved April 19, 2006, from http://www.dyslexia-inst.org.uk/articles/adult_dyslexia.htm

Dyslexia Services of University of Southampton. (2005). *Dyslexia and other specific learning difficulties: A guide for academic staff.* Retrieved April 19, 2006, from http://www.dyslexia.soton.ac.uk/newtutors%20guide.doc

ETS. (2003). *GRE reading comprehension.* Retrieved April 19, 2006, from http://www.gre.org/practice_test/takerc.html

ETS. *GRE for test takers.* Retrieved April 19, 2006, from http://www.gre.org/gendir.html

Hudson, K. (2005). *Designing accessible Web sites.* Retrieved April 19, 2006, from http://www.oit.umass.edu/academic/acco_resources/accessibility.html

The International Dyslexia Association (IDA). (2004). *Testing for dyslexia.* Retrieved April 19, 2006, from http://www.interdys.org/servlet/compose?section_id=5&page_id=63

Long, A. (2002). *Calculating reading level.* Retrieved April 19, 2006, from http://www.tameri.com/edit/levels.html

Singleton, C. H. (Chair). (1999). *Dyslexia in higher education: Policy, provision and practice.* Report of the National Working Party on Dyslexia in Higher Education.

TechDis. (2003). *A dyslexic perspective on e-content accessibility.* Retrieved April 19, 2006, from http://www.techdis.ac.uk/seven/papers/dyslexia.html

Townend, J. (2004). *Principles of assessment.* Retrieved April 19, 2006, from http://www.dyslexia-inst.org.uk/articles/prin_ass.htm

Chapter XII

Implementing Accessible Online Learning for Blind and Visually Impaired Students:
A Pilot Study

Hugh O'Neill, Central Remedial Clinic, Ireland

Inmaculada Arnedillo-Sánchez, Centre for Research in IT in Education (CRITE), University of Dublin, Ireland

Brendan Tangney, Centre for Research in IT in Education (CRITE), University of Dublin, Ireland

Abstract

This chapter presents a framework for the design of accessible online learning environments for blind and visually impaired students in terms of accessibility and the design process. The conjunction of the Web content Accessibility Guidelines Version 1 and the Principles of Universal Design for Learning (Centre for Applied Special Technology) into the instructional design process forms the basis of our approach. The first cycle of this iterative study implements objectivist instructional design theory to teach blind and visually impaired students how to write Web pages in HTML. For future iterations, we argue for the implementation of objectivist instructional design theories to provide clarity of structure beneficial for blind and visually impaired learners, together with constructivist notions such as a client-centred design approach and mechanisms for interaction to promote collaborative construction of knowledge.

Introduction

Accessibility is mainly concerned with designing in such ways as to make items, services, learning materials, and others, available to people with disabilities. Clark defines the concept as "making allowances for characteristics a person cannot readily change" (Clark, 2003, p. 37). A particular area of concern within this sphere is accessibility on the World Wide Web (WWW) for blind and visually impaired (BVI) students. A number of guidelines for the creation of accessible online material, such as the Web Content Access Guidelines (WCAG 1.0) and the Principles of Universal Design for Learning (Centre for Applied Special Technology), aim at guaranteeing accessibility for all. The previous are good attempts to safeguard the rights of disabled users; nonetheless, it is feasible to adhere to one of these guidelines and still create inaccessible online learning for BVI students.

Our work presents an approach to the development of accessible online learning environments for BVI learners through the combination of instructional design theory and universal design principles. Given the proposition that hypertext markup language (HTML) is a universal language to write Web pages (Berners-Lee, 1999), and that the WWW is an increasingly universal medium of communication, arguably for a predominantly sighted audience, the authors propose to arm BVI students with the skills to communicate with sighted people. Thus, core to our approach is to teach BVI students to create Web sites that are not only aimed or created for a BVI audience, but rather for the widest possible audience, including sighted people. While this approach may present difficulties for the students, inherent to their condition (i.e., some might not have a two dimensional concept of table), it will potentially contribute to overcoming communication barriers within the context of HTML- and WWW-mediated communication.

The structure of this chapter is as follows: the literature review briefly establishes some characteristics of BVI students in relation to accessing and engaging in online learning. It also outlines key features of HTML, the language used to write Web pages, within the context of our work. This is followed by an introduction to premises of online accessibility through exploring existing guidelines such as the WCAG 1.0, and the Principles of Universal Design for Learning (Centre for Applied

Special Technology). Leading from this, an examination of the extent to which the application of the previous actually results in accessible Web pages is presented. The review finally provides an analysis of two instructional design approaches, objectivist and constructivist, in order to establish pros and cons in terms of learning for BVI students. The following section highlights the design of the learning environment, taking into account the principles distilled from the literature. A brief explanation of the implementation and research methodology serves as a preamble to a short account of the data collection tools. Findings are discussed in relation to the strengths and weaknesses of our approach. The difficulties of BVI learners to grasp visual concepts such as tables, layout, and stylesheets, and to create an accessible Web site for sighted users are also examined.

Literature Review

With the absence of sight, the main obstacles faced by BVI students when engaged in learning are information availability and means of studying, editing, and archiving material (Ghesquire & Laurijssen, 1999). These difficulties are greatly determined by the reliance of these students on auditory and/or tactile learning methods (Ghesquire & Laurijssen, 1999). Thus, priority learning skills for BVI students, such as Braille reading and writing, handwriting, notetaking, listening, keyboard, and computer skills (The American Federation for the Blind) heavily depend on auditory and/or tactile input and output mechanisms that enable learners to engage with the learning materials, peers, tutors, and tools. To this end, computers and assistive technology such as screenreaders (which read out text on the screen) can help overcome some of the barriers reported in the literature. However, the real challenge remains access to information. Within the context of our framework, accessibility is facilitated by taking advantage of listening, keyboard, and computer skills that allow all information to be received and sent through auditory (screenreader) and/or tactile (keyboard) means.

Evans (2004) suggests that once information is available digitally, access becomes easier. In this respect, the emergence of the Internet as one of the largest repositories of digital information should contribute to ease of access for BVI users. Furthermore, the founding principle of universality of the Internet realised through HTML, a universal language to write Web pages (Berners-Lee, 1999), points to the medium as an optimal tool to facilitate BVI students' learning. Additional advantages of HTML rest on the fact that any computer with a browser can read a document written in it, and the possibility to link pages through hypertext.

In terms of learning, hypertext can transform the reading process from passive and predetermined to active and exploratory (Kirschenbaum, 2000). While this may add to the experience of sighted learners, who can decide in the blink of an eye where to go next, Bruce and Hwang (2001) note that multiple links on Web pages are fatiguing for students with visual disabilities. This fatigue is caused by "listening overload," since screenreaders will read out everything that goes before the link learners want. This highlights that what users experience depends on the equipment used to browse the Internet, and that, although there is a universal language to write Web pages, not all browsers view them the same (Castro, 2003). Consequently, *how* pages are written is of paramount importance in designing online learning for BVI learners.

In embracing Clark's definition of accessibility, we view "enabling" design as the practice of "making allowances for characteristics a person cannot readily change" (Clark, 2003, p. 37). The WCAG 1.0 and the Principles of Universal Design for Learning (Centre for Applied Special Technology) are examples of different approaches to "making allowances."

In relation to BVI users, the WCAG 1.0 guidelines advise on technical requirements in four main areas: visual information; layout; recommended HTML markup; and multimedia. While informative for Web designers, these guidelines are primarily technical in focus, covering the HTML mark-up that should be used to create accessible Web sites. Thus, the overly technical nature of the advice may lead to confused interpretation of the requirements. In addition, they can also be discouraging for designers using visually based HTML editors such as Dreamweaver or FrontPage. Most importantly, they do not provide overall principles for accessibility, with the potential danger of designers following the guidelines and still creating inaccessible Web sites. Instead of providing a technical checklist of requirements, the Principles of Universal Design for Learning (Centre for Applied Special Technology), offers designers three broad guiding principles to be followed when designing and creating Web sites. These are the provision of multiple representations of content; the provision of multiple options for expression and control; and the provision of multiple options for engagement and motivation. While the WCAG 1.0 guidelines ensure technical accessibility, we argue for the conjunction of these with the Principles of Universal Design for Learning (Centre for Applied Special Technology) in order to ensure actual accessibility.

So far in our review we have established some characteristics of our target learners: BVI students; explored the nature of the content to be learned: HTML; and outlined existing mechanisms to create accessible online material: WCAG 1.0 and the Principles of Universal Design for Learning (Centre for Applied Special Technology). The following section will discuss objectivist and constructivist instructional design approaches. These will be analysed in light of online learning for BVI students in order to establish a suitable theory to implement within this context.

Gagne's instructional design theory (1985) adheres to the objectivist school of thought, which views instruction as a transfer of knowledge from instructor or technologies to learners. This transmission involves the analysis, representation, and resequencing of content and tasks in order to assist the process (Jonassen, 1999). In contrast, the constructivist school supports that knowledge is individually constructed and socially co-constructed by learners based on their interpretations of experiences in the world (Jonassen, 1999). Although the latter provides a more student-centred approach, Fosnot notes (1996) that it does not lend itself to a "pat set of instructional techniques."

Gagne's is a comprehensive attempt to examine the main areas of human capabilities such as verbal information, intellectual skills, cognitive strategies, and motor skills and attitudes (Gagne, 1985). Our work is set within the realm of intellectual skills that are subdivided into internal (inherent to the student) and external (put in place by instructor and learning environment) conditions of learning (Gagne, 1985). In objectivist instructional design the designer devises the learning experiences, while in constructivist, students are encouraged to partake in the process (Willis, 2000) to further enrich their learning. A further breakdown of the external conditions for learning leads to four main areas: stimulation and recall of subordinate skills; informing learners of the objectives; guidance of students through new learning; and provision of occasions for the performance of the new skills (Gagne, 1985). While here explored through Gagne's proposition, the previous are recognised principles discussed by others. For instance, Giguere and Minotti (2003) note the importance of clearly defined objectives and expectations and Merrill (2002) underlines the significance of activation (use of prior experience to complete a task) and application (use of knowledge gained to solve a problem).

To provide a more comprehensive framework for instruction and ensure that the external conditions are met in order for learning to occur, Gagne developed the nine events of instruction. These are gaining attention; informing learners of the objectives; stimulating recall of prior learning; presenting the stimulus (displaying the content); providing guidance; eliciting performance; providing feedback; assessing performance; and enhancing retention and transfer (Gagne, 1985, p. 246). Although objectivist in nature, parallels can be drawn between these events and constructivist notions. Thus, alluding to capturing attention, Schank, Berman, and Macpherson (1999) suggest that students need an opportunity to pursue new knowledge in the service of achieving "intrinsically motivating goals." Giguere and Minotti (2003) advise of the importance of informing adult learners of the objectives of the lesson. Reflection (Kolb, 1984) indicates a recall of prior learning or experiences. Stimulus, in constructivist methodologies, is often promoted by providing context and activities that are authentic in that they have a direct application in the real world (Herrington, 2000). Scaffolding, which can be reduced as the student progresses (Schutt, 2003), is, in fact, a form of guidance. And processes, rather than outcomes performance, are common in constructivism, which regards "incorrect" performance as an opportunity for learning to occur (Schank et al., 1999). Corresponding ideas within constructivism exist for the remaining events; nevertheless, turning our attention to differences seems, at this stage, a more fruitful exercise.

Two tenets of constructivism and constructivist instructional design are worth mentioning: the social nature of learning (Vygotsky, 1978) and the client-centred design (Willis, 2000). The notion of learners individually constructing and socially reconstructing knowledge based on their interpretations of experiences in the world (Jonassen, 1999), highlights the need to design with collaborative construction of knowledge in mind (Herrington, 2000; Nelson, 1999). Furthermore, it points to the benefits of adopting a more client-centred (Willis, 2000) or participatory design process in which the users' knowledge reverts on their own learning environment.

In conclusion, to design accessible online learning environments for BVI learners, we propose the conjunction of the WCAG 1.0 guidelines and the Principles of Universal Design for Learning (Centre for Applied Special Technology) to ensure the creation of truly accessible Web sites. Furthermore, we argue for the implementation of a modified version of Gagne's instructional design theory (Gagne, 1985). This should encompass Gagne's clarity of structure, beneficial for BVI learners, a more client-centred design approach (Willis, 2000), and mechanisms for interaction that would facilitate collaborative construction of knowledge (Herrington, 2000; Nelson, 1999).

Design of the Learning Environment

Throughout the design of our environment, the WCAG 1.0 guidelines are implemented in association with the Principles of Universal Design for Learning (Centre for Applied Special Technology) and Gagne's Instructional Design Theory. However, due to the overly technical nature of the first, the description of the design elements presented here will focus on the remaining components that integrate our approach: the multiple representation of content; the multiple means of expression and control; the multiple means of engagement and motivation; and the events of instruction (Gagne, 1985).

To achieve multiple representation of the content, our course provides rich-text transcripts as well as audio files of each lesson. Although the inclusion of audio files may seem redundant, taking into consideration that blind (and some visually impaired) learners use screenreaders, our design attempts to address the difficulties BVI students face with notetaking (Ghesquire & Laurijssen, 1999). In terms of multiple means of expression and control, one of our major design considerations was to provide alternatives to navigating the site with a mouse due to its visual nature. To tackle this design issue, keyboard control is implemented and, for instance, the course is accessible by a screenreader using a keyboard. In addition, the navigation system is accessible by mouse as well a s keyboard, and faster navigation is possible through the implementation of a tiered navigation system adapted from http://www.

Figure 1. Site navigation

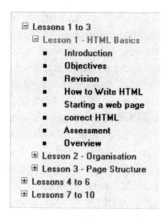

Figure 2. Navigation at end of HTML page

gazingus.org (Figure 1). Finally, the navigation is located at the end of the HTML page (Figure 2), in order to tackle the fatigue BVI learners face (Bruce & Hwang, 2001) when experiencing what we regard as "listening overload."

A variety of strategies and design considerations are put in place in order to realise multiple means of engagement and motivation. The actual content of the course is HTML, a practical skill that allows students to create their own Web pages, as well as to gain insights into accessibility online. Furthermore, our approach is aimed at providing BVI students with the skills to build Web sites that are accessible to both BVI and sighted people, and not only to a minority, often isolated, BVI audience. In order to combat this isolation, skills pertinent to sighted viewers, such as page layout, tables, or insertion of images, are covered in the course to enable BVI students to communicate with the widest possible audience. In addition, the fact that the medium of delivery is the Internet, and that the course is written in HTML, sets the entire experience in the actual context for which the learning is intended. An additional attempt to engage and motivate learners is made by integrating mechanisms and occasions for collaborative construction of knowledge (Herrington, 2000; Nelson, 1999). Thus, the learners are supported and scaffolded by mentors who provide assistance, when required, through e-mail. Mentors also provide learners with timely, personal feedback on the work submitted. Moreover, consideration is given to the presentation of the material with increasing difficulty as the learner progresses through the course. This is done to provide measured challenges and help maintain the motivation among the participants. Finally, a clear purpose for learning is established through implementing Gagne's instructional design theory, as discussed next.

The nine events of instruction form the basis of the structure of the course, and they are executed as follows. Gaining attention is attempted through providing an introduction to each lesson to draw the participants in; informing learners of the objectives is achieved by clearly outlining these at the beginning of each instructional unit; stimulating recall of prior learning is addressed by providing a brief summary of what participants need to know from previous units in each section; presenting the stimulus is implemented through the presentation of the actual lesson; provision of guidance is inbuilt throughout the course and also offered by mentors available when assistance is needed; eliciting performance is facilitated through the provision of exercises and activities and the "requirement" to submit the work for correction; provision of feedback is realised through the intervention of mentors and through online and e-mail input and output mechanisms; assessing performance is also implemented through the participation of mentors, but most importantly through the immediate feedback students get from the work completed. Thus, students also had the option of testing their HTML through the use of an interactive form. This displayed the HTML that they wrote within a live Web page, using php scripting and a MySQL database; enhancing retention and transfer is attempted by revisiting the topics covered at the end of a lesson and at different stages throughout the course. In addition, the exercises provided are also aimed at reinforcing what has been learnt.

A final design consideration worth mentioning is the fact that our course adheres to the principle of HTML universality in that it is written with HTML that is accessible and consistently read and understood by different browsers (Figures 3 and 4).

Figure 3. Course viewed in an Internet Explorer browser

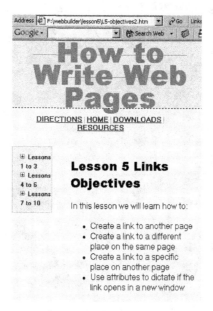

The students are also taught to implement this universality as part of the course by creating pages that can be universally understood. As a result, the visual layout of the page is included as part of the course, even though some of the concepts (such as the concept of tables) are sometimes alien to blind people.

Implementation and Methodology

The participants required for this study were BVI computer users interested in learning how to create Web pages in HTML. Geographically, we limited our research to the UK and Ireland, and this meant a further reduction of the potential pool of volunteers to draw from. In the UK, out of a population of 58.6 million, only 1.8% are BVI (European Blind Union http://www.euroblind.org/fichiersGB/STAT.htm). Likewise in Ireland, only 0.47% of its 3.6 million population falls into this category (European Blind Union http://www.euroblind.org/fichiersGB/STAT.htm). Furthermore, in 2003, 67.7% English BVI people were over 75 years of age (United Kingdom Department of Health http://www.dh.gov.uk/assetRoot/04/07/23/38/04072338.pdf), which further reduces their likelihood of being computer users. Ultimately, four

Figure 4. Course viewed in a text only Lynx browser

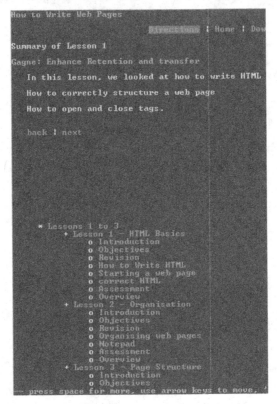

sources were used to gain access to participants. These were The Blind Computer Association of Britain (BCAB) mailing list; The Irish Visually Impaired Computer users (VICS) mailing list; personal contacts by the researchers; and a call for participants through the blind interest radio programme, Audioscope. Twenty people expressed initial interest in our programme; of those, only eight participated in the course. Out of the eight participants, five were from the BCAB mailing list, two from VICs, and one the sole respondent from the Audioscope interview. Of those who started the course, four completed it, one withdrew due to health problems, two due to personal reasons, and the remaining one due to technical difficulties not related to our environment. The relatively small sample size in this case is consistent with research into instructional design for BVI people. For example, Van Reusen (1994) based his work on educational theory, and provided anecdotal evidence of the experience of a single student. Similarly, Gouzman and Kouzlin (2000) focus on

Figure 5. Level of participation

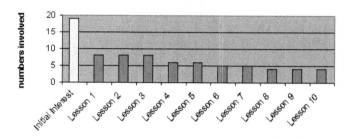

their theoretical argument and omit information on the size of their student group. Our reliance on volunteers may have influenced the sample size. However, all participants in our study provided varying degrees of useful data for the research. The participation level is charted in Figure 5.

In terms of the participants' prior knowledge in the field, five people had programming experience, and the remaining three were computer users. In relation to the equipment they used, seven accessed the learning environment through Internet Explorer, while one used Lynx, a text-only browser, in combination with an MS-DOS machine. Six participants were blind and two were visually impaired; the four who completed the course were blind.

The course was self-pacing, consisting of 10 lessons, with an increasing level of complexity, and were divided as follows: Lesson 1 – 3 Basic HTML and Web sites; Lesson 4 – 6 Links, HTML elements and images; Lesson 7 – 10 Tables, templates, forms, stylesheets. Exercises and activities, to be completed by the learners and sent to the mentor, were inbuilt throughout the course, while communication with the participants was carried out through e-mail. Once the programme was completed, the participants were asked to create a Web site to demonstrate the skills they had acquired.

This piece of research is an iterative study, whereby the results and findings are used to inform the future design and implementation of the course. This is a common approach in the user-centred design adopted for this work. This design process consists of five major activities (Figure 6): planning of the user-centred process; understanding and specification of the context of use; specification of users and organisational requirements; production of the design solutions; and evaluation of the design solutions against the user requirements. The previous process is repeated until the design meets the needs of the users involved. Our study is the first cycle of this process (Maguire, 1998).

Figure 6. User-centred design activities

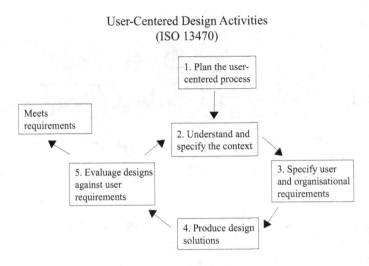

In the case of our learning environment, the planning and identification of the users' needs is done through examining the needs of BVI learners. The context of use is the Internet. The users are our volunteers, and there are no specific organisational requirements. Our design solution is the actual course, and our evaluation of the design solutions is undertaken by delivering the course in its first iteration.

This research was carried out using qualitative research methods and, as a consequence, qualitative data was favoured over quantitative. The overarching aims of our investigation required insights into the learning process that figures cannot often provide. In this regard, Bryman (2001) suggests that the researcher, in the case of a quantitative piece of research, tends to be distant and give the results from the point of view of the researcher. Instead, in a piece of qualitative research, the perspective tends to be closer to the participants, and the results produced from the perspective of the participants (Bryman, 2001). Our client-centred focus required this kind of approach. In addition, quantitative research is generally "fixed" or "static" (Bryman, 2001; Robson, 2003) while qualitative has a more "flexible" (Robson, 2003) nature. This flexibility allows the researcher to respond to findings as they occur, favouring the process over the product (Bryman, 2001). Furthermore, due to our small sample, qualitative data would have been meaningless. The data collection tools used, and main data sets analysed, include prequestionnaires, interviews with the learners, the students' work, and e-mail correspondence. The prequestionnaires were used to establish the initial technical ability of the participants and the software used to access the course. The HTML created by the learners, during and after the course, as well as the e-mail correspondence between learners and mentor, were analysed to learn about our design and the learners' experience. Interviews with the participants who completed the course were conducted to verify findings through triangulation.

Findings and Discussion

In general, the level of participation in the course was low, with only four students of the initial eight who started completing it in its entirety. All participants reported lack of time as one of the main barriers to partaking in the experience. However, it is worth noting that all four students who completed the course had programming experience. Out of the remaining four who did not complete the course, one had programming experience while the others were computer users. Although none of these reported difficulties with the course as a reason for not persevering, the fact that only participants with programming experience completed the course may indicate that, against our initial belief, prior knowledge is required to successfully complete the programme. Alternatively, this result may indicate that those who could not complete the course due to time considerations may have found it took longer than expected due to the difficulty of the material. Further investigation into this issue is required, and possible ways forward may be the selection of a different target group with prior knowledge, or the re-examination of the difficulty of the material.

Overall, it is reasonable to suggest that the course achieved its objective of teaching HTML to those students who completed the course. This statement is supported by the exercises completed by the students and returned to the mentor, and by the actual Web sites that the participants built. Furthermore, an analysis of the correspondence between learners and mentor and the exercises and activities completed show gradual progression in each of the participants in terms of understanding, application, and mastering of the HTML concepts dealt with. During the implementation of the course, all issues that arose we recorded for latter analysis, in order to establish where the difficulties with the programme and our approach lay. The analysis of the episodes logged yielded conceptual areas of interest such as weaknesses in our design, suggestions for additional or modified design solutions, the difficulty on the side of the environment to transmit visual concepts such as tables, layout, and stylesheets and, most interestingly, the difficulty on the side of BVI participants to grasp visual concepts and to create accessible Web sites for sighted users. Other minor difficulties inherent to the learning process, such as the incorrect use of HTML, also took place. The majority of HTML errors occurred in the first six lessons and were eliminated by the end of the course. This demonstrates an improvement in the writing of HTML by the participants, and it is in part attributed to the availability of a mentor who provided advice and feedback when needed.

One of the main shortcomings of the design of our learning environment was the use of our tiered navigation system. This was adopted in order to provide faster navigation, but generated problems for the participant who used Lynx, a text only browser, and an MS–DOS machine. The difficulties faced by this learner were in terms of understanding the menus due to the fact that this browser interpreted the tiered headings in the navigation as links. An additional design problem that arose was in relation to the semantics of HTML and, in particular, with the differences in spelling between British and American English. Both HTML and CSS use American English and, as a result, when the participants typed into their stylesheets "colour" or "centre" the commands were not recognised. Only awareness of this issue on the part of the instructional designer could prevent it from occurring, since the use of the Principles of Universal Design would not account for this.

Suggestions for additions or modified design solutions were mainly arrived at through the recurring issue of time constraints. To this end, one of the most interesting omissions was that of the doctype by one of the participants. When she was asked as to the reason of this omission, the participant informed that it was done "to save time." This suggests that an approach that allows for pages to be built upon, as opposed to recreated each time, may be beneficial. A further occurrence of a time-saving exercise, as shown in the following quote:

As lessons 7-10 got more time consuming, I couldn't find enough time. I decided to work on my practicing homepage in little bursts here and there, and rather than sending you each lesson's result individually, send you the finished site, in which I hope to implement all that I've learned.

While this may seem irrelevant, it translated into a disadvantage for the learner in terms of the learning experience. The fact that all the exercises where sent together at the end of the course meant that the mentor could not address problems as they aroused, and the opportunities for feedback and collaborative knowledge construction were missed. In order to address this potential shortcoming of the course, it would be desirable to inbuild in the environment other mechanisms for interaction and communication, such as a discussion board.

One of the most interesting findings of our research is the difficulty to transmit very visual concepts, such as tables, layout, and stylesheets, to BVI participants. An additional issue was the creation of inaccessible or difficult to access Web sites for sighted users. The previous items are discussed through a number of examples drawn from the participants' work. Tables proved difficult for the participants, as can be seen be this quote:

I am currently doing lesson 7, Merging table cells. This part of the course is not so intuitively obvious to me and perhaps to blind people in general, as the other bits. I need more time to play with the concept to try to work out what is going on here, but my initial thought is that some more detailed description of the layout is required to explain clearly what 'merging cells' really means..

While the participant was able to carry out the task after receiving further explanations, the idea of tables is very visual and was very challenging. A contributing factor to the difficulties encountered by BVI students when dealing with tables resides on the assistive technology, as noted by a participant:

Because I use a speech output system (window eyes) to read the screen, layout information is more difficult to obtain, particularly from a Web browser.

Thus, the student refers to the fact that screenreaders linearise tables by reading then out row by row and, for instance, the table in Figure 7 would be read out as follows: "Group Name, Subscription, Votes, Paid, Werkgroup Rotterdam, 90 Euros, 1 , yes….." Columns of information are not distinguished, making the concept of a table harder to grasp. The visual appearance of the table is due to the combination of the <td> and <th> tags (Figure 8), which could not be identified by the learner due to the way in which screenreaders deal with tables. Overall, tables proved problematic. They are frequently used for layout purposes, but judging by the problems the users had in implementing them, in future iterations of the course it would be better to teach BVI people how to use stylesheets for layout instead of tables.

Figure 7. Disrupted table

Table showing subscriptions due and paid

	Group name		Subscription	Votes	Paid?
Werkgroep Rotterdam	90 euros	1	Yes		
Open Church Group Norway	270 euros	3	sent not received yet		
Icelandic Group	90 euros				
Latvian group in Riga	Not known				

Figure 8. Use of <td> tags combined with <th> tags

The creation of inaccessible Web pages for sighted users was also a recurrent theme in the participants work. Without sufficient care, pages could be written that could only be accessible to blind people. An example of this is the form page provided (Figure 9), in which the radio button list and the checkbox list appeared blank. In this case, as shown in the accompanying HTML, the participant neglected to type in the text into the main part of the page. However, anyone using a screenreader would hear the words in the "title,", for example, "drums," read out. Unfortunately, the implementation of the Principles of Universal Design do not provide a means for the students to adequately check their work for how it would appear to a sighted person, so proofreading of pages by a sighted person may be necessary.

```
<label>
Which instruments do you require?</br>
<input type="checkbox" name="Instrument" value="Drums" title="Drums"><br />
<input type="checkbox" name="Instrument" value="Guitar" title="Guitar"><br />
<input type="checkbox" name="Instrument" value="Bass" title="Bass"><br />
<input type="checkbox" name="Instrument" value="Keyboard"
title="Keyboard"><br />
```

Figure 9. Inaccessible form to sighted users

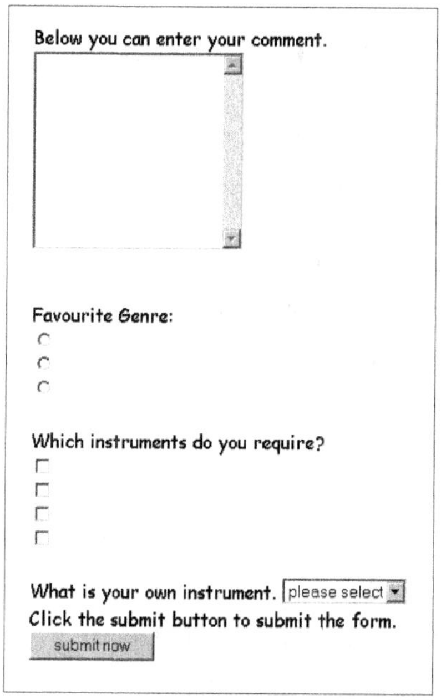

Figure 10. Form page without line breaks

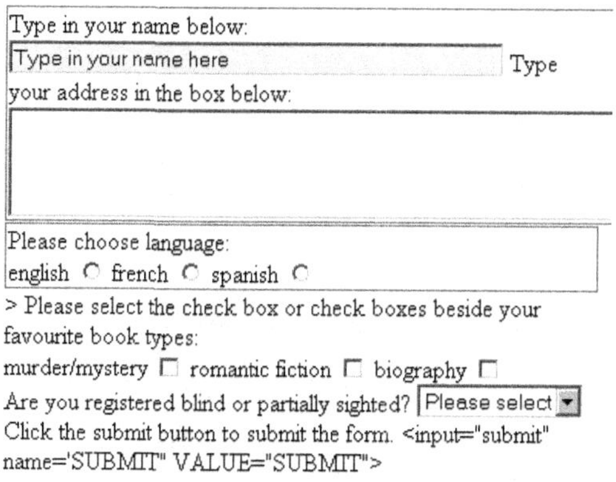

The problems with how things appeared to sighted people are once more illustrated by another form page (Figure 10), where reading becomes difficult due to the lack of line breaks.

As mentioned at the beginning of this section, the work of the students suggests that, overall, the course was successful in teaching the participants HTML. Snapshots of

Figure 11. Web site zoom buttons

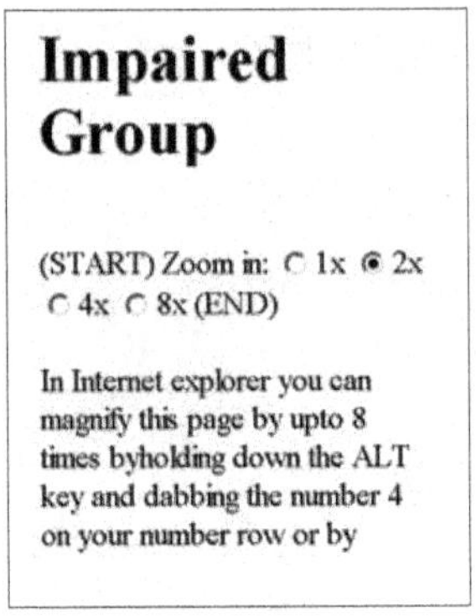

**Impaired
Group**

(START) Zoom in: ○ 1x ◉ 2x
○ 4x ○ 8x (END)

In Internet explorer you can
magnify this page by upto 8
times byholding down the ALT
key and dabbing the number 4
on your number row or by

Figure 12. Contact page with forms

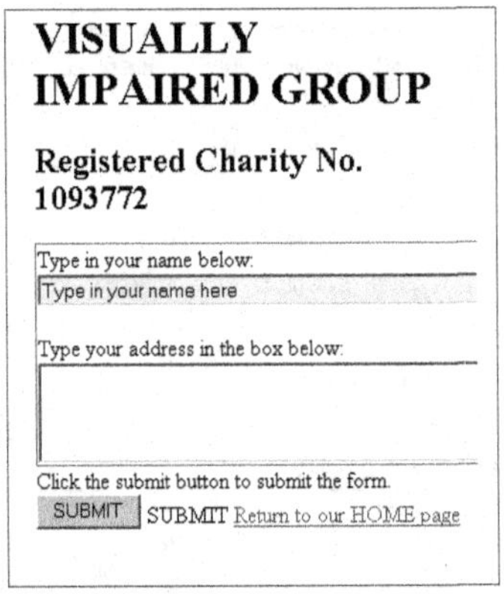

**VISUALLY
IMPAIRED GROUP**

**Registered Charity No.
1093772**

Type in your name below:
Type in your name here

Type your address in the box below:

Click the submit button to submit the form.
SUBMIT   SUBMIT Return to our HOME page

the Web sites created by the learners are provided to illustrate this suggestion. One of the participants created a Web site for his local visually impaired group. Two things stand out about the same: the first is the incorporation of a facility to zoom in on the page (Figure 11); the second is the incorporation of forms in the contact us page (Figure 12).

A further example of the execution of forms (Figure 13) shows a nontrivial level of complexity, accessibility, and mastery of the concepts involved.

Another participant produced a Web site to promote his band, Pascal's Triangle. The layout of the Web site is simple and clear, and it is composed of a large number of pages. One of them (Figure14) includes sample songs, from the students' album, available for download.

Figure 13. Form

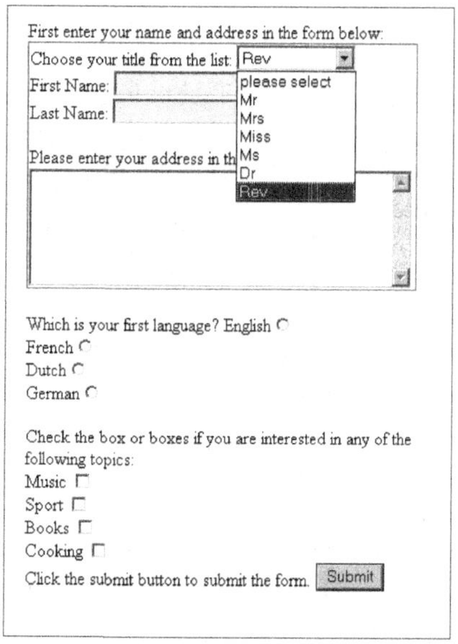

First enter your name and address in the form below:

Choose your title from the list: Rev
please select
Mr
Mrs
Miss
Ms
Dr
Rev

First Name:

Last Name:

Please enter your address in the

Which is your first language? English ○
French ○
Dutch ○
German ○

Check the box or boxes if you are interested in any of the following topics:
Music ☐
Sport ☐
Books ☐
Cooking ☐
Click the submit button to submit the form. Submit

Figure 14. Downloadable music

Conclusion

The combination of the WCAG 1.0 guidelines and the Principles of Universal Design for Learning (Centre for Applied Special Technology) adopted in our approach is a definite move towards achieving actual online accessibility for BVI learners. To this end, a shortcoming in our online learning environment is the tiered navigation system. This was accessible to all the participants, but confusing to the student using the text-only browser. Although multiple means of accessing the content were provided, problems still arose with some of the teaching content. The main difficulties derived from visual concepts, such as table, visual expression, such as page layout, and the ability to check the correct appearance of pages. The previous is intrinsically linked to the absence of sight and the reliance on screenreaders, and proof reading the HTML. A mechanism to aid with "accessibility for sighted" users is much needed, and we urge researchers in the field to pursue this line of research. The inclusion of more opportunities and tools for interaction and communication is also an area for further work. In this regard, the implementation of discussion boards would also provide extra support for the students. Future courses attempting the same content area could also benefit from the elimination of the more repetitive elements of the programme, such as creating HTML documents or inserting doctype statements. A more integrated process, where pages are gradually built up as opposed to recreated every time, is also recommended.

The work presented here is the first cycle of an iterative process with a small sample, but we believe offers an interesting approach to designing online learning for BVI learners. Our investigation suggests that the use of Gagne's instructional theory is suitable for our target learners since it provides a much-needed structure for this cohort. Nonetheless, some of the most successful design elements were those borrowed from constructivism, such as the opportunities for interactions with the mentor and a more user-centred design. These must be further developed.

In terms of practical lessons learnt through our pilot study and recommendations for other designers, the tiered navigation system is recommended to provide general access to the entire course, although additional instructions should be given for those using text-only browsers. Given the difficulties encountered with tables, stylesheets may be a better option to deal with layout matters. Until technology to check "accessibility for sighted" users is available, some proofing of layout by sighted people may be necessary. The clear structure provided by objectivist learning theory should be complemented by giving students the opportunity to comment on the exercises; so discussion forums are recommended as a means of encouraging cooperation and giving feedback on the course.

References

American Federation for the Blind. (n.d.). Retrieved January 10, 2005, from http://www.afb.org/btglogin.asp

Berners-Lee, T. (1999). *Weaving the Web*. London: Texere.

Bruce, S., & Hwang, T. T. (2001). Web-based teacher preparation in visual impairment: Course development, teaching, learning, and quality assurance. *Journal of Visual Impairment and Blindness, 95*(10), 609-613.

Bryman, A. (2001). *Social research methods*. New York: Oxford University Press.

Castro, E. (2003). *HTML for the World Wide Web*. Berkeley, CA: Peachpit Press.

Centre for Applied Special Technology. (n.d.). *Principles of Universal Design for Learning*. Retrieved March 6, 2005, from http://www.cast.org/research/udl/index.html

Clark, J. (2003). *Building accessible Websites*. Indianapolis, IN: New Riders.

European Blind Union. (n.d.). Retrieved February 7, 2005, from http://www.euroblind.org/fichiersGB/STAT.htm

Evans, S. (2004). E-learning: A level playing field? *Proceedings of the 11th ICEVI World Conference*.

Fosnot, C. T. (1996). Constructivism: A psychological theory of learning. In C.T. Fosnot (Ed.), *Constructivism: Theory, perspective & practice*. New York: Teachers College Press.

Gagne, R. M. (1985). *The conditions of learning and theory of instruction*. Japan: CBS College Publishing.

Ghesquire, P., & Laurissen, J. (1999). The significance of auditory study to university students who are blind. *Journal of Visual Impairment and Blindness, 93*(1), 40-45.

Giguere, P., & Minotti, J. (2003). Developing high-quality Web-based training for adult learners. *Educational Technology, 43*(4), 57-58.

Gouzman, R., & Kozulin, A. (2000, Winter). Enhancing cognitive skills in blind learners. *The Educator*. Retrieved February 20, 2005, from http://icevi.org/publications/educator/winter_00/index.htm

Herrington, J., & Oliver, R. (2000). An instructional design framework for authentic learning environments. *Educational Technology Research and Design, 48*(3), 23-48.

Jonassen, D. (1999). Designing constructivist learning environments. In C. M. Reigeluth (Ed.), *Instructional design theories and models: A new paradigm of instructional theory*. Mahwah, NJ: Lawrence Erlbaum Associates.

Kirschenbaum, M. G. (2000). *Hypertext. Unspun – Key concepts for understanding the World Wide Web*. New York: New York University Press.

Kolb, D. A. (1984). *Experiential learning, experience as the source of learning and development*. London: Prentice-Hall.

Maguire, M. C. (1998). *User-centred requirements handbook*. RESPECT consortium. HUSAT Research Institute. Retrieved March 25, 2005, from http://www.idemployee.id.tue.nl/g.w.m.rauterberg/lecturenotes/UserCenteredRequirementsHandbook.pdf

Merrill, D. (2002). First principles of instruction. *Educational Technology Research and Design, 50*(3), 43-59.

Nelson, L. M. (1999). Collaborative problem solving. In C. M. Reigeluth (Ed.), *Instructional design theories and models: A new paradigm of instructional theory*. Mahwah, NJ: Lawrence Erlbaum Associates.

Robson, C. (2003). *Real world research* (2nd ed.). Oxford: Blackwell Publications.

Schank, R. C., Berman, T. R., & Macpherson, K. A. (1999). Learning by doing. In C. M. Reigeluth (Ed.), *Instructional design theories and models: A new paradigm of instructional theory*. Mahwah, NJ: Lawrence Erlbaum Associates.

Schutt, M. (2003). Scaffolding for online learning environments: Instructional design strategies that provide online learner support. *Educational Technology, 43*(6), 28-35.

United Kingdom Department of Health. (n.d.). Retrieved February 17, 2005, from http://www.dh.gov.uk/assetRoot/04/07/23/38/04072338.pdf

Van Reusen, A. K. (1994). Cognitive and metacognitive interventions: Important trends for teachers of students who are visually impaired. *Re:View, 25*(4), 153-163.

Vygotsky, L. S. (1978). *Mind in society*. London: Harvard University Press.

W3C. (n.d.). *Web content access guidelines*. Retrieved February 1, 2005, from http://www.w3.org/TR/WCAG10/

Willis, J. (2000). The maturing of constructivist instructional design: Some basic principles that can guide practice. *Educational Technology, 40*(1), 5-16.

About the Authors

Sri Kurniawan is a lecturer in the School of Informatics at The University of Manchester, UK. Her research interests include human-computer interaction, and usability studies with older persons and people with disabilities. Kurniawan received a PhD in human-computer interaction from Wayne State University, USA. Her publications have appeared in top journals such as the *IEEE Transactions on Neural Systems and Rehabilitation Engineering, International Journal of Human-Computer Studies, IEEE Computer Graphics and Applications*. She has also been invited to give a talk and keynote speeches at various conferences.

Panayiotis Zaphiris is a senior lecturer at the Centre for Human-Computer Interaction Design, School of Informatics of City University, London. Before joining City University, he was a researcher at the Institute of Gerontology at Wayne State University, from where he also earned his PhD in human computer interaction (HCI). His research interests lie in HCI, with an emphasis on inclusive design and social aspects of computing. He is especially interested in HCI issues related to the elderly and people with disabilities. He is also interested in Internet-related research (Web usability, mathematical modelling of browsing behaviour in hierarchical online information systems, online communities, e-learning, Web-based digital libraries, and finally, social network analysis of online human-to-human interactions).

*   *   *

Alison Adam holds a BSc in physics and a PhD in the history of science. She spent several years working in the software industry, building systems used by thousands of users in ICI in Western Europe, before working on an Alvey project in the Department of Systems at the University of Lancaster. She was a lecturer then senior lecturer in the Department of Computation at UMIST from 1986-2000. Her research interests are in computer ethics, and gender and information technology. She joined the ISI as a reader in 2000, and has been head of school since January 2004.

Mauricio Arango (MFA) is a Colombian educator and artist residing in the United States. One of the central questions of his practice is how art can allude to those things that impact the lives of many, but are not registered. In approaching these questions, his work has evolved from issues regarding flow of information and visibility. His work has been shown in the U.S., Scotland, Spain, Australia, Armenia, and Colombia. Currently, he teaches in the Department of Design, Housing, and Apparel at the University of Minnesota and at the Minneapolis College of Art and Design, USA.

Inmaculada Arnedillo-Sánchez, MSc IT Edu (DUB), HdipEd (UCA), BA (UGR), is a lecturer in ICT and Education at Trinity College Dublin, an invited lecturer in a number of international e-learning master programmes, and a researcher in the Centre for Research in IT in Education (http://www.cs.tcd.ie/crite). Ms. Arnedillo's current research interests include mobile learning, enabling technologies, and ICT and social inclusion. At present, she is leading two major research projects: TRUST-E: Teaching and Research in a Ubiquitous Secure Telecommunications Environment, and the Computer Clubhouse in Trinity College in which technology-enhanced learning experiences are implemented. She is the programme chair for the 2006 Mobile Learning Conference.

Jamshid Beheshti has taught at the Graduate School of Library and Information Studies at McGill University (Canada) for 20 years, where he was the director for the past 6 years. Currently, he is the associate dean (administration) of the Faculty of Education. He has also taught at the University of Western Ontario, University of West Indies, and Kuwait University. He is the principal investigator on a funded research project on *A Virtual interface for children's Web portals*. His publications have appeared in the *Journal of the American Society for Information Science and Technology*, *Information Processing & Management*, and other international journals. He has presented numerous papers in Canada, the U.S., Europe, and the Far East.

Stefania Boiano, before becoming a freelance professional Web designer, between 1997 and 2003, worked as a Web project manager for the Web and Education Department at the Science Centre "Città della Scienza" (Naples), at the Science Museum "Leonardo da Vinci" (Milan), and for a Web agency (Milan). Her Web sites have been published in several Web design books. She launched Web Match, an online and offline meeting point for Italian Web Designers. Currently, she is working for the *Nature* magazine Web site.

Ann Borda has held strategic and operational roles in academic and cultural organizations. She recently held the position of head of collections multimedia at the Science Museum in London, where she managed several major Web initiatives such as the award-winning *Ingenious* Web site (http://www.ingenious.org.uk), and was involved in Fathom.com, an innovative e-learning collaboration led by Columbia University. Dr. Borda is presently a research fellow at the Institute for Computing Research, London South Bank University, where she is investigating online gaming and museum e-commerce, among other topics. She concurrently holds the position of programme manager with the Joint Information Systems Committee (JISC) at King's College, London, where she is responsible for the quality delivery of government-funded projects in e-research and Web-based developments across the UK higher education community. Dr. Borda has published in the areas of e-learning, informatics, collaboration technologies, and content delivery.

Jonathan P. Bowen was a professor of computing at London South Bank University, where he is deputy director of the Institute for Computing Research. Previously, he was at the University of Reading, the Oxford University Computing Laboratory, and Imperial College. He has been involved with the field of computing in both industry and academia since 1977. As well as computer science, his interests extend to online museums, and the history of computing. Bowen established the *Virtual Library museums pages* (VLmp, http://vlmp.icom.museum) in 1994, a Web-based directory of museum Web sites worldwide, which has been adopted by the International Council of Museums (ICOM). In 2002, Bowen founded Museophile Limited (http://www.museophile.com), a spinout company from London South Bank University, with the aim to help museums online, especially in the areas of accessibility, discussion forums and collaborative e-commerce. Bowen is a fellow of the Royal Society of Arts and the British Computer Society. He holds an MA degree in engineering science from Oxford University.

Leanne Bowler is a doctoral student and sessional instructor at McGill University's Graduate School of Library and Information Studies, Canada. Her research interests lie in the area of adolescent information behavior, with a focus on the cognitive and affective aspects of information seeking. She has a Master of Library Science and a Master of Education, both from McGill University. Prior to her doctoral studies, she worked as an information professional in a variety of settings including public, school, academic, and hospital libraries, as well as literacy organizations.

Sauman Chu is an associate professor at the Department of Design, Housing, and Apparel, University of Minnesota, USA. She received her PhD from the University of Minnesota in design communication, with an emphasis on educational psychology. Her research focuses on multiculturalism and its influence on design education. Research projects that support this focus include cross-cultural comparisons of visual perception and understanding of symbols, design variables in multilingual printed materials, design of symbols in computer games, and classroom teaching strategies. Her articles have appeared in *Visible Language, Journal of Visual Literacy, Multicultural Education, Journal of Applied Communications,* and *Journal of Family and Consumer Sciences.*

Gerard V. Conroy has recently retired from the position of senior lecturer in the School of Informatics. His research interests included applied artificial intelligence, particularly machine learning and neural networks. He was responsible for developing the post of disability advisor within what was then called UMIST. He has publications in his research areas, but has also published articles in SKILL (the National Bureau for students with disabilities), as well as contributing to national conferences on disability support issues. He is still involved with disability support, and acts as a freelance consultant in the area of academic practice and disability issues.

Aspasia Dellaporta has a background in psychology, and extensive experience in usability and accessibility methods and practices for Web and software interactive systems. Aspasia leads the user experience research and development at Cimex (UK), applying usability and accessibility to the design and development of corporate and e-learning projects with a focus on Web applications. Her interests include Web accessibility, evaluation methods for innovative e-learning applications for children, audio-based e-learning for VI users, and information architecture design. Key projects include BBC jam PE learning resource, BBC jam Science learning resource for blind children, CC4G for Eskills UK, LGiU Web site, Gambling Commission Web site, HMRC accessibility testing. Prior to joining Cimex, she was a Senior Research Assistant at City University, researching Web accessibility and e-learning. She is a member of the Usability Professionals Association (UPA), and she holds an MSc in Human-Computer Interaction with Ergonomics from UCL.

Alistair D. N. Edwards is a senior lecturer in computer science at the University of York, UK. He moved to York in 1989 from the Open University, where he had completed his PhD, and worked as a lecturer. Prior to that, he had worked as a computer officer at the University of Manchester, Institute of Science and Technology. He has a BSc in physics and computer science from the University of Warwick, and an MSc in computer science from the Pennsylvania State University, USA. He is author or editor of 6 books and over 60 refereed publications.

Charles Ess is professor of philosophy and religion and distinguished professor of interdisciplinary studies, Drury University (Springfield, Missouri, USA); and professor II, Programme for Applied Ethics, Norwegian University of Science and Technology (Trondheim). Dr. Ess has received awards for teaching excellence and scholarship, and published in comparative (East-West) philosophy, applied ethics, discourse ethics, history of philosophy, feminist Biblical studies, and computer-mediated communication (CMC). With Fay Sudweeks, Dr. Ess co-chairs the biennial conference "Cultural Attitudes towards Technology and Communication" (CATaC), and has served as a visiting professor, IT-University, Copenhagen (2003), and a Fulbright Senior Scholar, University of Trier (2004).

Xristine Faulkner is a reader in educational development at London South Bank University. She is an associate member of the Institute for Computing Research, and holds a PhD on *The Impact of Usability* from London South Bank University. Her research interests include HCI education, electronic communication, usability, and cognitive ergonomics. She is a member of the BCS British HCI Group.

Giuliano Gaia is a freelance Web consultant specializing in advanced log analysis and online communities, working for cultural institutions and universities. He is the founder of http://www.musei-it.net, the most important online community of museum professionals in Italy. He has been the Webmaster of the Museum of Science and Technology of Milan for 5 years, from 1997 to 2002.

Syariffanor Hisham is a PhD student with the Computer Science Department, University of York, UK. Her research interest is a blend of human-computer interaction, sociology, and psychology, with an emphasis on elderly users and ICT in less developed region. She has an MSc in multimedia technology from UMIST, UK and a Bachelor of Information Technology (BIT) from *Universiti Utara Malaysia*.

David Kreps holds a BA (Hons.) in theatre and arts management, an MA in cultural studies, and a PhD in the sociology of technology. Kreps spent several years as a local government officer, running arts centres, and has been chairman of Kaos Theatre UK since 1997. He has been making Web sites since 1995, and is director of fourquarters IS Ltd (http://www.fourquarters.biz). After several years lecturing part-time, he joined the ISI in January 2004. He has since worked on the creation of the e-government master's programme, delivered from September 2004, and lectures in information society and World Wide Web development.

Andrew Large is CN-Pratt-Grinstad professor of information studies at McGill University, Canada, and the former director of its Graduate School of Library and Information Studies. His major research areas are information-seeking behavior, information retrieval, and HCI, and he has published extensively in these areas. His latest books are *Digital Libraries: Policy and Practice in a Global Environment* (2005), *The Manual of Online Search Strategies*, 3rd edition (2001), and *Information-Seeking in the Online Age* (1999). He is co-editor of the quarterly journal, *Education for Information*, and is on the editorial boards of four other journals.

Sarah McDaid's professional experience includes 8 years as an IT consultant working on high profile local government software projects; head of multimedia training, the Nerve Centre, Derry—a multimedia arts centre; senior lecturer in IT, Camberwell College of Arts, London; lecturer in interactive system design, University of Ulster; Java software developer, Quadriga, London—an interactive television service provider; and freelance Web consultant. Previous research areas include interactive television and plant pathology. Sarah has a BA in history of art, an MSc in computing and design, and is currently undertaking a PhD in HCI at London South Bank University.

Valerie Nesset is currently a doctoral student in the Graduate School of Library and Information Studies (GSLIS), McGill University, Canada, from which she graduated with a Master of Library and Information Studies in spring 2002. Her dissertation research concentrates on the information-seeking behavior of grade-three elementary school students. She is also a sessional lecturer at GSLIS, teaching a first-year required course at the Master's level, and has authored or coauthored several publications.

Hugh O'Neill, MSc IT Edu (DUB), HdipEd (NUI), BA (NUI), is a project coordinator for the Central Remedial Clinic in Dublin, working on two European projects developing technology for people with disabilities: ARTEMIS, a system for remote assessment, and MAPPED, a project developing accessible routing information. He is the coordinator for the Irish Design for All e-Accessibility Network, a network of professionals and academics interested in the area of Design-for-All. His current research interests are enabling technologies and instructional design. He has previously worked in IT for IBM and Perot Systems Information Resource, and as the assistive technology officer in Trinity College Dublin.

Bridget Patel is a producer of children's multimedia who has worked widely in media and education with organizations such as the Public Broadcasting Service (PBS), Educators Resources Information Center (ERIC), and Bolster Education in the U.S., and Espresso Education in the UK. She is a master's candidate in education at the University of Cambridge, UK, and holds a bachelor's degree in psychology and a bachelor's degree in child and family studies from Syracuse University. She has written about sociocultural influences on children's play and early literacy development, and is currently conducting research into digital learning resources, children's digital literacy practices, and the convergence of texts and technology.

Noemi Maria Sadowska, alongside teaching commitments, has spent considerable time undertaking research in design. Increasingly aware of feminist discourse, she chose to use her creative/professional design and research skills to address its implications for the ways in which women are targeted within the Internet publishing industry. These interests have seen Sadowska participate in a number of conferences, and lead her to pursue a PhD that questions whether Web design could potentially offer alternative ways of communicating to female users that resist the gendered status quo. This research work has been recently published as part of *01.AKAD*, Sweden, and it is featured in the *Encyclopedia of Gender and Information Technology*, USA.

Nada Savitch manages the Web site for the Alzheimer's Society, the leading UK care and research charity for people with dementia, their families and carers. Nada joined the Centre for HCI Design at City University, London in October 2003 to investigate issues around usability and accessibility of Web site design for people with dementia and their carers.

Brendan Tangney, BSc (NUI), MSc (DUB), is a senior lecturer with the Department of Computer Science in Trinity College Dublin, and is co-director of the Centre for Research in IT in Education (http://www.cs.tcd.ie/tangney). His current research interests are concerned with the innovative use of ubiquitous technology to enhance the experience of learners. He is coauthor of over 50 peer-reviewed publications in international conferences and journals including *Local Area Networks and Their Applications*, published by Prentice Hall (UK) and Kaibundo (Japan). He has held visiting positions in the Universities of Sydney and Kyoto, and is the program chair for the 2007 Computer Assisted Learning Conference.

Charles Earl Love Yust is an IT professional at the College of Architecture and Landscape Architecture at the University of Minnesota, USA, and teaches Web design at the Minneapolis College of Art and Design. He is a multimedia consultant for nongovernmental and nonprofit arts organizations in the Twin Cities, is enrolled in art and design graduate coursework, and is a freelance Web designer. A number of his projects have been developed in conjunction with the Twin Cities Somali Community, focusing on how digital design can help facilitate cross-cultural consciousness.

Index